THE RAID BOOK
A STORAGE SYSTEM TECHNOLOGY HANDBOOK

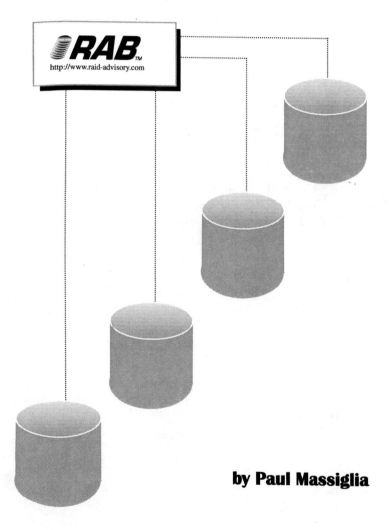

RAB™
http://www.raid-advisory.com

by Paul Massiglia

The RAIDbook

Sixth Edition, Copyright © RAID Advisory Board, 1997

Property of:
Digital Motorworks, Inc.
8601 FM 2222
Bldg. II, 4th Floor
Austin, TX 78730

Table of Contents

Preface to the Sixth Edition xiii

Introduction .... **xv**

Five steps to RAID xv

Part 1: RAID Basics **1**

Chapter 1: An Overview of RAID **3**

The Revolution in Computing 3
The Motivation for RAID 5
Disk Arrays 8
Extending the Disk Array Concept: RAID 12
A Device for Comparing Storage Options 22

Chapter 2: Disk Systems and Disk Arrays **26**

Disk Systems 26
Disk Arrays 33
The *Array Management Function* 40
Other Disk Array Considerations 42

Part 2: RAID Data Protection and Mapping Details **53**

Chapter 3: Disk Array Data Management **55**

Data Mapping in RAID Arrays 67

Chapter 4: Disk Striping and Mirroring **83**

Disk Striping: High I/O Performance at Low Cost 84
RAID Level 1: Disk Mirroring for Enhanced Data Availability 92

Chapter 5: Parity RAID Data Protection **101**

Parallel Access RAID Arrays 101
Parity RAID 102
Parallel Access Parity RAID 107
(RAID Level 3) 107
Independent Access Parity RAID 116
Independent Access RAID With Distributed Parity: RAID Level 5 129

Chapter 6: RAID Level 6 .... **137**

Chapter 7: *RAID* Advisory Board Conformance **143**

RAID Advisory Board Functional Requirements for Striped Arrays.. 143
RAID Advisory Board Functional Requirements for Mirrored Arrays.. 144
RAID Advisory Board Functional Requirements for RAID Level 3 Arrays..................................... 145
RAID Advisory Board Functional Requirements for RAID Level 4 Arrays..................................... 146
RAID Advisory Board Functional Requirements for RAID Level 5 Arrays..................................... 147

Part 3: High-Performance Failure-Tolerant Disk Systems 149

Chapter 8: Hybrid RAID Arrays 151

Combining Striping with Mirroring for High I/O Performance *and* High Data Availability........... 152
Combining Striping With Parity RAID For More Symmetrical Read and Write Performance......... 158

Chapter 9: RAID and Parallel Processing 163

RAID and Parallelism.. 169

Chapter 10: RAID and Cache 181

Parity RAID I/O Performance... 181
Cache and I/O Performance... 185
How Write-Back Cache Can Improve Parity RAID I/O Performance....................................... 187
Conclusion.. 194

Chapter 11: Dynamic Data Mapping... 197

Dynamic Data Mapping Overview 197
Using Disks of Different Capacities in an Array.. 199
Dynamic Data Migration 199
Minimizing The Parity RAID Write Penalty 203
Dynamic Expansion of Storage Capacity... 204
Distribution of Spare Capacity 205

Chapter 12: Distributed RAID Functions 209

Separation of Primitive RAID Operations 209
Reduced Mode Operations 213
Further Optimizations.. 215

Chapter 13: RAID and Functional Redundancy.. 217

RAID and Disk System Availability... 217
Failure Tolerance... 219
Disk System Component Roles in Failure Tolerance 219

Part 4: Appendixes 229

Appendix 1: The *RAID* Advisory Board... 231

Description of the *RAID* Advisory Board 231
RAID Advisory Board Charter 231
RAID Advisory Board Membership... 233

Appendix 2: RAID Reference List... 235

Appendix 3: Glossary of *RAID* Advisory Board Terminology.................. 245

Purpose Of This Glossary... 245
Conventions Used In This Glossary 245

THE GLOSSARY OF *RAID* ADVISORY BOARD TERMINOLOGY 247
APPENDIX 4: *RAB, RAID AND EDAP -*
  UNSCRAMBLING THE ACRONYMS...277
INDEX 293

List of Figures

FIGURE 1: THE "I/O GAP" 5
FIGURE 2: COMMON DISK ARRAY TOPOLOGIES 9
FIGURE 3: TWO COMMON DISK ARRAYS 10
FIGURE 4: A HYBRID DISK ARRAY 12
FIGURE 5: RAID ADVISORY BOARD TRADEMARK 17
FIGURE 6: THE COST, AVAILABILITY, PERFORMANCE (CAP) TRIANGLE 22
FIGURE 7: USING THE CAP TRIANGLE TO POSITION STORAGE TECHNOLOGIES 22
FIGURE 8: SIMPLE DISK SYSTEM MODEL 26
FIGURE 9: A DISK SYSTEM WITH AN INTELLIGENT STORAGE CONTROLLER 28
FIGURE 10: DISK SYSTEM WITH EMBEDDED STORAGE CONTROLLER 30
FIGURE 11: TWO WAYS TO INCREASE A DISK SYSTEM'S CAPABILITY 31
FIGURE 12: THE RAID ADVISORY BOARD'S DISK ARRAY MODEL 34
FIGURE 13: A CONTROLLER-BASED DISK ARRAY 36
FIGURE 14: A HOST-BASED DISK ARRAY 37
FIGURE 15: SOME DISK ARRAY-DISK SYSTEM RELATIONSHIPS 40
FIGURE 16: TIME LINE FOR A LARGE I/O REQUEST 42
FIGURE 17: TIME LINES FOR A LARGE I/O REQUEST 44
FIGURE 18: TIME LINE FOR A SMALL I/O REQUEST SPLIT ACROSS THREE ARRAY MEMBERS 45
FIGURE 19: DATA AVAILABILITY: RAID VS. A FULLY REDUNDANT SYSTEM 49
FIGURE 20: A DISK ARRAY WITH DYNAMIC DATA MAPPING 55
FIGURE 21: TWO-LEVEL DATA MAPPING IN A COMPLEX ARRAY 56
FIGURE 22: EXTENTS OF DISK STORAGE SPACE 59
FIGURE 23: COMBINING EXTENTS INTO DIFFERENT TYPES OF ARRAYS 60
FIGURE 24: ALTERNATE WAYS OF CONFIGURING ARRAYS FROM EXTENTS 61
FIGURE 25: STRIPS AND STRIPES OF STORAGE SPACE 62
FIGURE 26: STRIPES AND STRIPE DEPTH 64
FIGURE 27: PARTITIONS: ARRAYS WITH MULTIPLE VOLUME SETS 67
FIGURE 28: REDUNDANCY GROUPS 69
FIGURE 29: BLOCK NUMBERING IN REDUNDANCY GROUPS 71
FIGURE 30: EXAMPLE: MULTIPLE REDUNDANCY GROUPS ON A SINGLE DISK 72
FIGURE 31: REDUNDANCY GROUP STRIPES 73
FIGURE 32: USER DATA EXTENTS AND VOLUME SETS 75
FIGURE 33: A VOLUME SET WITH DIFFERENT USER DATA EXTENT SIZES 76
FIGURE 34: MULTIPLE PARTITIONS FROM THE SAME REDUNDANCY GROUP 77
FIGURE 35: USING USER DATA EXTENT STRIPE DEPTH TO CONTROL DATA LOCATION 78
FIGURE 36: PARTIAL DISTRIBUTION OF PARITY ACROSS P_EXTENTS 79
FIGURE 37: A COMMON REPRESENTATION OF DISTRIBUTED PARITY RAID ARRAY(BERKELEY RAID
     LEVEL 5) DATA MAPPING 81
FIGURE 38: A CONCEPTUAL REPRESENTATION OF CONCENTRATED PARITY RAID ARRAY(BERKELEY
     RAID LEVEL 3) DATA MAPPING 82
FIGURE 39: A COMMON STRIPED DATA MAPPING 84
FIGURE 40: SCATTER READING TO IMPROVE LARGE I/O REQUEST PERFORMANCE 86

FIGURE 41: CONCURRENT ACCESS POSSIBILITIES IN A STRIPED ARRAY 89
FIGURE 42: COMMON DATA MAPPING FOR A SINGLE-SET MIRRORED ARRAY 93
FIGURE 43: A COMMON DATA MAPPING FOR A MULTI-SET MIRRORED ARRAY.................................. 94
FIGURE 44: USING A PROGRESS INDICATOR TO REBUILD A MIRRORED ARRAY 96
FIGURE 45: READING DATA FROM A MIRRORED ARRAY AFTER AN ARRAY MANAGEMENT FUNCTION
FAILURE 98
FIGURE 46: EXCLUSIVE OR PARITY 102
FIGURE 47: USING EXCLUSIVE OR PARITY TO RECOVER DATA 104
FIGURE 48: PARITY RAID DATA MAPPING AND PROTECTION.. 106
FIGURE 49: STRIPE-ALIGNED WRITE TO A PARITY RAID ARRAY 109
FIGURE 50: GATHER WRITING USING A HARDWARE ASSIST 110
FIGURE 51: REGENERATING DATA IN A REDUCED PARITY RAID ARRAY WITH ALL PARITY LOCATED ON
A SINGLE DISK 110
FIGURE 52: I/O PATH FOR SINGLE-CHANNEL AND MULTIPLE-CHANNEL DISK SYSTEMS 112
FIGURE 53: TWO RAID LEVEL 3 DATA MAPPING EXAMPLES 114
FIGURE 54: DATA MAPPING FOR AN INDEPENDENT ACCESS PARITY RAID ARRAY WITH PARITY ON A
SINGLE DISK... 117
FIGURE 55: SINGLE-BLOCK WRITE TO AN INDEPENDENT ACCESS PARITY RAID ARRAY 119
FIGURE 56: A MULTI-BLOCK WRITE TO AN INDEPENDENT ACCESS PARITY RAID ARRAY 120
FIGURE 57: REGENERATING DATA IN A REDUCED INDEPENDENT ACCESS PARITY RAID ARRAY.......... 122
FIGURE 58: WRITING TO THE FAILED MEMBER IN A REDUCED INDEPENDENT ACCESS PARITY RAID
ARRAY 122
FIGURE 59: WRITING TO A SURVIVING MEMBER IN A REDUCED INDEPENDENT ACCESS PARITY RAID
ARRAY 123
FIGURE 60: TIME SEQUENCE FOR AN INDEPENDENT ACCESS PARITY RAID ARRAY UPDATE 125
FIGURE 61: PARTIAL SURVIVABILITY IN AN INDEPENDENT ACCESS PARITY RAID ARRAY 127
FIGURE 62: TYPICAL DISTRIBUTED PARITY INDEPENDENT ACCESS RAID ARRAY MAPPING 129
FIGURE 63: PARTIAL DISTRIBUTION OF PARITY IN AN INDEPENDENT ACCESS RAID ARRAY 130
FIGURE 64: SINGLE-BLOCK WRITE TO AN INDEPENDENT ACCESS PARITY RAID ARRAY 131
FIGURE 65: MULTI-BLOCK WRITE TO AN INDEPENDENT ACCESS PARITY RAID ARRAY 132
FIGURE 66: REGENERATING DATA IN A REDUCED INDEPENDENT ACCESS PARITY RAID ARRAY.......... 132
FIGURE 67: WRITING DATA TO A REDUCED INDEPENDENT ACCESS PARITY RAID ARRAY 133
FIGURE 68: INDEPENDENT ACCESS PARITY RAID ARRAY WITH VERY LARGE STRIPES 135
FIGURE 69: RAID LEVEL 6 ARRAY WITH ONE-DIMENSIONAL REDUNDANCY 138
FIGURE 70: RAID LEVEL 6 ARRAY WITH TWO-DIMENSIONAL REDUNDANCY 139
FIGURE 71: REGENERATION IN A RAID LEVEL 6 ARRAY 140
FIGURE 72: TIME LINE FOR WRITING TO A RAID LEVEL 6 ARRAY 141
FIGURE 73: A STRIPED ARRAY OF MIRRORED ARRAYS 151
FIGURE 74: A DATA MAPPING FOR A STRIPED ARRAY OF MIRRORED ARRAYS 153
FIGURE 75: STRIPED MIRRORED ARRAY I/O PERFORMANCE DURING REBUILDING............................. 154
FIGURE 76: PRIMARY AND SECONDARY LOAD BALANCING IN A STRIPED ARRAY WHOSE MEMBERS ARE
MIRRORED ARRAYS 155
FIGURE 77: MIRRORING STRIPED ARRAYS.. 156
FIGURE 78: DATA MAPPING FOR A STRIPED ARRAYS WITH PARITY RAID ARRAYS AS MEMBERS 158
FIGURE 79: BEHAVIOR OF A STRIPED ARRAY OF RAID LEVEL 3 VIRTUAL MEMBERS DURING REBUILDING 160
FIGURE 80: PRIMARY AND SECONDARY LOAD BALANCING IN A STRIPED ARRAY WITH PARITY RAID
MEMBERS 161
FIGURE 81: ATOMIC EVENTS COMPRISING THE EXECUTION OF AN I/O REQUEST 164
FIGURE 82: TWO CONCURRENT I/O REQUESTS 166
FIGURE 83: PROCESSING I/O REQUESTS FAIRLY 168
FIGURE 84: LARGE FILE I/O PARALLELISM IN A STRIPED ARRAY WITH ONE DEVICE CHANNEL 169
FIGURE 85: LARGE FILE I/O PARALLELISM IN A STRIPED ARRAY WITH MULTIPLE DEVICE CHANNELS 170
FIGURE 86: TRANSACTION I/O PARALLELISM IN A STRIPED ARRAY WITH ONE DEVICE CHANNEL......... 171
FIGURE 87: TRANSACTION I/O PARALLELISM IN A STRIPED ARRAY WITH MULTIPLE DEVICE CHANNELS 172

FIGURE 88: TYPICAL STORAGE CONTROLLER ARCHITECTURE 173
FIGURE 89: SINGLE-BLOCK WRITE TO AN INDEPENDENT ACCESS PARITY RAID ARRAY 176
FIGURE 90: LARGE FILE I/O IN A CONTROLLER-BASED DISK SYSTEM 177
FIGURE 91: LARGE FILE I/O IN A CONTROLLER-BASED DISK SYSTEM 178
FIGURE 92: USING A HOST-BASED ARRAY MANAGEMENT FUNCTION TO AGGREGATE THE PERFORMANCE OF MULTIPLE ARRAYS 179
FIGURE 93: WRITING AN ENTIRE STRIPE IN A PARITY RAID ARRAY 182
FIGURE 94: CONCURRENT READ REQUESTS TO A PARITY RAID ARRAY 183
FIGURE 95: UPDATING A PARTIAL STRIPE IN A PARITY RAID ARRAY 184
FIGURE 96: DATA RISK INTERVAL WITH WRITE-BEHIND CACHE 186
FIGURE 97: UPDATING A PARTIAL STRIPE 188
FIGURE 98: THE MINIMAL EFFECT OF WRITE-BACK CACHE ON A LONG STREAM OF WRITES 189
FIGURE 99: STRIPE DEPTH 191
FIGURE 100: DATA ACCUMULATES IN A WRITE-BACK CACHE UNTIL FULL STRIPES ARE AVAILABLE 193
FIGURE 101: COMBINING CONSOLIDATION WITH FULL-STRIPE WRITES 194
FIGURE 102: A DISK ARRAY WITH DYNAMIC DATA MAPPING 198
FIGURE 103: A DISK ARRAY WITH TWO REDUNDANCY GROUPS 199
FIGURE 104: A DISK ARRAY WITH DYNAMIC DATA MAPPING 200
FIGURE 105: CHANGING A DISK ARRAY'S DYNAMIC DATA MAP 201
FIGURE 106: AN ARRAY WITH MULTIPLE REDUNDANCY GROUPS 201
FIGURE 107: MOVING DATA WITHIN A DISK SYSTEM 202
FIGURE 108: DATA ACCUMULATES IN A WRITE-BACK CACHE UNTIL FULL STRIPES ARE AVAILABLE 203
FIGURE 109: FULL-STRIPE WRITES WITH DYNAMIC DATA MAPPING 204
FIGURE 110: CHANGING A DISK ARRAY'S DYNAMIC DATA MAP 205
FIGURE 111: CHANGING A DISK ARRAY'S DYNAMIC DATA MAP 206
FIGURE 112: CHANGING A DISK ARRAY'S DYNAMIC DATA MAP 207
FIGURE 113: DISTRIBUTING SPARE CAPACITY ACROSS MULTIPLE DISKS 207
FIGURE 114: SINGLE-STRIP WRITE TO AN INDEPENDENT ACCESS PARITY RAID ARRAY 210
FIGURE 115: SINGLE-STRIP WRITE TO A PARITY RAID ARRAY EQUIPPED WITH EXCLUSIVE OR-CAPABLE DISKS 212
FIGURE 116: REGENERATING DATA IN A CONVENTIONAL INDEPENDENT ACCESS PARITY RAID ARRAY 213
FIGURE 117: REGENERATING DATA IN A PARITY RAID ARRAY EQUIPPED WITH EXCLUSIVE OR-CAPABLE DISKS 214
FIGURE 118: WRITING DATA TO THE FAILED MEMBER OF A PARITY RAID EQUIPPED WITH EXCLUSIVE OR-CAPABLE DISKS 214
FIGURE 119: WRITING DATA TO A SURVIVING MEMBER OF A PARITY RAID EQUIPPED WITH EXCLUSIVE OR-CAPABLE DISKS 215
FIGURE 120: PHYSICAL COMPONENTS OF A DISK SYSTEM 218
FIGURE 121: REDUNDANT POWER DISTRIBUTION SYSTEM AND POWER SUPPLIES 220
FIGURE 122: REDUNDANT CONTROLLERS CONNECTED TO THE SAME STORAGE DEVICES 221
FIGURE 123: REDIRECTION OF AN I/O STREAM TO THE SURVIVING CONTROLLER OF A REDUNDANT PAIR 222
FIGURE 124: A COMMON FAILURE-TOLERANT DEVICE CHANNEL CONFIGURATION 225
FIGURE 125: TWO FAILURE-TOLERANT HOST I/O BUS IMPLEMENTATION OPTIONS 226
FIGURE 126: FAILURE-TOLERANCE WITH A SINGLE HOST I/O BUS CONNECTION 227

List of Tables

TABLE 1: SUMMARY COMPARISON OF RAID TECHNOLOGIES 16
TABLE 2: SUMMARY OF RAID ARRAY APPLICATION SUITABILITY 20

Preface to the Sixth Edition

The RAIDbook is in its sixth edition. The book's evolution continues to reflect developments in disk arrays and storage systems, and the *RAID* Advisory Board's continuing drive toward a common understanding of storage system concepts. This edition continues the shift of emphasis from RAID data protection to a more holistic view of failure-tolerant disk systems. The reader is cautioned that technology described in this book may be covered by patents. The *RAID* Advisory Board makes no representations as to ownership of any technology described herein.

The *RAID* Advisory Board is an association of suppliers and consumers of RAID-related products, as well as other organizations with an interest in RAID technology. The goal of the *RAID* Advisory Board continues to be to foster the development of RAID technology and RAID-related products. Member organizations pay a fee to belong to the *RAID* Advisory Board, as well as devoting the time and cost of their individual representatives' participation. Appendix 1 describes the RAID Advisory Board's activities, and gives references for other sources of RAID-related information.

As with previous editions, terms that the *RAID* Advisory Board regards as important to standardize are defined in insets like the one below near their first occurrence in the text. These definitions are also consolidated in the glossary beginning on page 247. Identical material is contained in *The Glossary of RAID Advisory Board Terminology*, published separately by the *RAID* Advisory Board.

RAID Advisory Board Definition

RAID (1.) An acronym for *Redundant Array of Independent Disks*, a family of techniques for managing multiple disks to provide desirable cost, data availability, and performance characteristics to host environments. (2.) A Redundant Array of Independent Disks (q.v.).

RAID-related product Any computer system storage product that implements RAID technology as described in RAID Advisory Board publications in some significant way. RAID-related products may include disk controllers, disk systems, disks, software, and test equipment.

Introduction

This introduction, based on a paper by Joe Molina, Chairman of the *RAID* Advisory Board, is a brief, non-technical introduction to the major RAID data protection and mapping models and describes how they combine with other capabilities to produce cost-effective, resilient, high-performing disk systems.

Five steps to RAID

Redundant Arrays of Independent Disks, or RAID, is a rapidly maturing storage technology which has revolutionized the way on-line data is stored. Spanning the entire computing spectrum from desktop to supercomputers, RAID technology offers significant improvements in data availability, along with significantly greater performance than today's magnetic disks. This paper provides a simple explanation of RAID data protection, including the seven basic "RAID Levels," as they are defined by the RAID Advisory Board.

Disk Arrays

Some disk systems organize multiple disks into *disk arrays*, managed by a common *Array Management Function*, and presented to a host environment as one or more *virtual disks*. Disk arrays are the framework to which RAID functionality is added in five steps to produce cost-effective, highly available, high-performance disk systems.

The First Step: Data Redundancy

The first step to RAID divides the available storage capacity of a disk array into space for user data and *check data*. The check data may be a copy of the data ("mirrored", or it may be an error correcting code derived from user data. Each check data item must be stored on a different disk from the user data it protects.

The Second Step: Regeneration

The second step to RAID is to add algorithms for *regeneration* of user data to a disk system's *Array Management Function*. Regeneration uses check data and, in some cases, related user data, to recreate user data from a failed disk on demand. Regeneration also allows application updates to a failed disk by generating and writing any check data implied by application write requests.

The Third Step: Rebuilding

The third step to RAID is to equip a disk system's *Array Management Function* with *reconstruction,* or *rebuilding* capability. Rebuilding is the process by which all user data and check data from a failed disk are transparently regenerated and written to a *replacement disk.* Rebuilding restores redundancy after a failure, thereby protecting against further failures.

The Fourth Step: Functional Redundancy

The fourth step to RAID is to add *functional redundancy* to a disk system. A disk array with check data and the capability to regenerate and rebuild only protects against disk failures. To ensure that data is reliably available to users, *every* functional component of the disk system must be protected against failure. This is usually done by adding redundant components to the system.

The ability to *"hot-swap,"* or replace failed components without downtime, is an important adjunct to functional redundancy. Without hot-swapping capability, the advantages of functional redundancy are diminished. Full functional redundancy can be costly, however. For this reason, vendors typically offer RAID-capable disk systems with varying degrees of functional redundancy.

The first three steps to RAID provide highly resilient on-line data storage. If a disk in a RAID array fails, the array continues to function without data loss. If a disk system offers full functional redundancy, then data is remains available, no matter what system component fails. If the system offers hot-swap capability, serviceability and up-time are further improved, because disks and other components can be replaced while the system continues to function.

Performance

In addition to data protection, RAID arrays can provide substantial performance improvements over individually managed disks. The multiple disks intrinsic to RAID arrays may be configured to match application needs.

➡ For applications requiring high transaction rates, *independent access* RAID algorithms balance multiple concurrent accesses to data items across different disks.

➡ For applications requiring high data transfer rates, *parallel access* RAID algorithms operate some or all of an array's disks in unison. This multiplies the application's data transfer rate by the number of active disks.

The Fifth Step to RAID

A disk system that implements the first four steps to RAID (data redundancy, regeneration, rebuilding, and functional redundancy) may be characterized as a RAID system. Practically speaking, however, a fifth step is necessary. All RAID systems have an intrinsic *write bottleneck* stemming from the requirement to generate and write check data each time user data is written. Because of the write bottleneck, RAID technology by itself is not a practical storage solution.

Minimizing the RAID write bottleneck is the fifth step to RAID. Various techniques are used to improve RAID array write performance, including cache, write-assist-disks, parallel processors and innovative data mapping techniques. Eliminating the write bottleneck makes high-performance, resilient on-line storage solutions out of basic RAID technology.

Backup—Still A System Management Essential

Since they protect data against loss due to component failure, it would be natural to assume that RAID systems eliminate the need for backup. This is emphatically not the case. Backup is a necessity whether or not RAID is used for on-line storage. A natural disaster could destroy disk systems, redundant data and all. More important, the most common cause of lost data—human error—can not be eliminated by RAID technology. It is often said that RAID will store wrong data just as reliably as right data. Only proper backup and data vaulting will allow data recreation when the loss is due to human error. Backup remains a necessary complement to RAID.

The Berkeley Papers

The acronym "RAID," for *Redundant Arrays Of Inexpensive Disks*, first appeared in 1988 in a paper written by David Patterson, Garth Gibson and Randy Katz of the University of California at Berkeley **[Patterson88]**. The *RAID* Advisory Board has since voted to substitute "independent" for "inexpensive," since the former term more accurately reflects the situation today.

A series of papers written by the original three authors and others defined and categorized several data protection and mapping models for disk arrays. Some of the models described in these papers, such as mirroring, were known at the time, others were new. The word *level*, used by the authors to differentiate the models from each other, may suggest that a higher numbered RAID model is uniformly superior to a lower numbered one. This is not the case.

RAID Level 0 (Disk Striping)

"RAID" Level 0 is a performance-oriented striped data mapping technique. Uniformly sized blocks of storage are assigned in regular sequence to all of an array's disks.

"RAID" Level 0 provides high I/O performance at low inherent cost (No additional disks are required). The reliability of "RAID" Level 0, however, is less than that of its member disks due to its lack of redundancy. Despite the name, "RAID" Level 0 is not actually RAID, unless it is combined with other techniques to provide data and functional redundancy, regeneration and rebuilding.

RAID Level 1

RAID Level 1, also called *mirroring*, has been used longer than any other form of RAID. It remains popular because of simplicity and a high level of data availability. A mirrored array consists of two or more disks. Each disk in a mirrored array holds an identical image of user data. A RAID Level 1 array may use parallel access for high data transfer rate when reading; more commonly, RAID Level 1 array members operate independently to provide high I/O transaction rates. Raid Level 1 provides very good data reliability and improves performance for read-intensive applications, but at a relatively high inherent cost.

RAID level 2

RAID level 2 is one of two inherently parallel mapping and protection techniques defined in the Berkeley paper [Patterson88]. It has not been widely deployed in industry, largely because it requires special disk features. Since disk production volumes determine cost, it is more economical to use standard disks for RAID systems.

RAID Level 3

RAID Level 3 adds redundant information in the form of *parity* to a parallel access striped array, permitting regeneration and rebuilding in the event of a disk failure. One strip[1] of parity protects corresponding strips of data on the remaining disks. Raid Level 3 provides high data transfer rate and high data availability, at an inherently lower cost than mirroring. Its transaction performance is poor, however, because all RAID Level 3 array member disks operate in lockstep.

RAID Level 4

Like RAID Level 3, RAID Level 4 uses parity concentrated on a single disk to protect data. Unlike RAID Level 3, however, a RAID Level 4 array's member disks are independently accessible. Its performance is therefore more suited to transaction I/O than large file transfers. Raid Level 4 is seldom implemented without accompanying technology, such as write-back cache, because the dedicated parity disk represents an inherent write bottleneck.

RAID Level 5

By distributing parity across some or all of an array's member disks, RAID Level 5 reduces (but does not eliminate) the write bottleneck inherent in RAID Level 4. As with RAID Level 4, the result is *asymmetrical performance*,—with reads substantially outperforming writes. To reduce or eliminate this intrinsic asymmetry, RAID level 5 is often augmented with techniques such as caching and parallel multiprocessors.

---

[1] This, and other RAID technical terms are defined in Chapter 3.

RAID Level 6

RAID Level 6 is a further development of RAID Level 5. It protects against simultaneous failure of any two member disks by using two independent forms of check data. Although RAID Level 6 offers ultra-high data reliability, its write penalty is even more severe than that of RAID level 5 because check data must be generated and written twice for each application update. As with RAID Levels 4 and 5, the RAID level 6 write penalty is often mitigated by techniques such as caching.

Conclusion

This paper has explained the five steps to RAID and defined the basic RAID Levels (0 through 6) in order to provide some insight into the roots and evolution of RAID technology. Disk system vendors often embed the term RAID in the names of products which combine RAID with other technologies to produce highly available storage solutions. Examples include *RAID 7* and *AutoRAID*.[2] In no known case, however, have additional data protection techniques been introduced.

The *RAIDbook*, a publication of the *RAID* Advisory Board, contains detailed definitions of the basic RAID Levels, as well as descriptions of product nomenclature used by RAB members to describe specific products. These definitions and descriptions are an important part of the RAB's educational program. The Board expects, however, that the role of RAID Levels in differentiating disk systems will diminish in time. Of greater importance will be the "five steps to RAID" because of the benefits they convey. Data redundancy, regeneration, rebuilding, functional redundancy and minimizing I/O bottlenecks are the essentials for a high-performance, resilient disk system. Disk systems that implement these five steps to RAID provide significant reliability, availability, serviceability and performance enhancements over the technology they replace.

Joe Molina

Chairman RAID Advisory Board

September 23, 1996

---

[2]   AutoRAID is a trademark of Hewlett-Packard Corporation.

Part 1: RAID Basics

Chapter 1: An Overview of RAID

Disk Arrays, RAID, and their Significance in Computer Systems

The Revolution in Computing

The last two decades have witnessed a revolution in information technology. Information handling and processing problems once thought to be well outside the realm of possibility have been solved, and the solutions have become part of daily life. Instant travel reservations, instant credit validation, completely automated factories, up-to-the-minute weather forecasting, and a host of other services all represent formidable computing challenges, yet all have become commonplace.

These computing challenges have been met and mastered in large part because of the phenomenal rate of technological progress in computer system components. Within the last two decades:

➡ Computers have shrunk from unwieldy racks of equipment to small enclosures that can be placed on or beside a desk. While they have been shrinking physically and in cost, computers' performance has been doubling about every three years, so that today's personal computer has 50 times the power of a mainframe of the early 1970s.[3]

➡ Memory density has increased, from racks holding 16 Kbits of memory to chips with 64 Mbits.

---

[3] This and some of the following comparisons are based on a paper given by Mr. Roger Cummings, Chairman, ANSI X3T11 Committee, at The Nikkei Interface Conference, Tokyo, Japan, September 18, 1996.

- Graphics have progressed from fixed-font character cell displays to high-resolution color displays, with advanced features such as hardware assists for three dimensional rendering.
- Networks have proliferated. Where once connecting terminals to a computer was regarded as sophisticated, high-speed campus-wide peer networks of powerful workstations and personal computers are now the norm, with the world-wide Internet growing rapidly. Low-cost local communication speeds have increased from thousands of bits per second to tens of millions of bits per second, with billions of bits per second visible on the horizon.
- The capabilities of these machines' on-line data storage are equally impressive. Ten billion bytes of magnetic storage, that twenty years ago would have required as much space and electrical power as several hundred washing machines, today fits in a package that can easily be held in one's hand.
- The shrinking computer and the high-performance local area network have combined to create *client-server computing*, in which a small number of powerful *servers* provide application, storage, backup, printing, wide-area network access, and other services for a large number of desktop *clients*.

These raw capabilities have led to the development of visionary and imaginative applications that have altered our relationship to computer systems. Today, many aspects of society and our lives rely completely on properly functioning computer systems. Defense systems, air traffic control, financial networks, police and fire dispatching are routinely expected to be absolutely reliable. Even a decade ago, these systems would have been backed up by manual procedures. Today, however, the pace of change is so great, and the reliance on computer systems so absolute, that manual procedures no longer exist for many essential functions. Essential services routinely depend completely on their computer systems functioning properly.

Never in history has so much reliance been placed on such complex technology. Components from many vendors installed at many locations are routinely expected to integrate flawlessly into systems that function reliably throughout their useful lives. Furthermore, they are expected to do this at increasingly competitive cost.

This book describes how on-line disk systems fulfill their role in cost-effective, flawless, high-performance computing, with a focus on one particularly effective technology—Redundant Arrays of Independent Disks, or RAID. RAID technology is sweeping the computer storage industry. Informed estimates place its rate of installation at over 50% of all disk systems today, and most predictions are that it will be ubiquitous by the year 2000. Information technology professionals owe it to themselves to learn the benefits and costs of RAID so they can make informed decisions about deploying it. This book provides the necessary background.

The Motivation for RAID

Computer Systems Become Unbalanced

While improvements in the cost of on-line storage have generally kept pace with those in computers themselves, improvements in input-output (I/O) performance have not. Today's high-performance servers are easily 100 times as powerful as their predecessors of 1985, while today's disks perform at about three or four times the rate of 1985 disks. The result is the so-called "I/O gap" illustrated in Figure 1. The reason for the I/O gap is understandable: disk performance is dominated by mechanical motion, while processing performance is completely electronic. Nonetheless, the gap poses a problem for computer system designers: how to keep from "starving" high-performance computers for data to work on.

Not only is there a widening gap between computing and I/O performance; there are also increasing reliability expectations for data that are far greater than those for the computing components of the system. More and more applications require continuous data availability. Even applications which can tolerate service outage, however, cannot tolerate permanent loss of data.

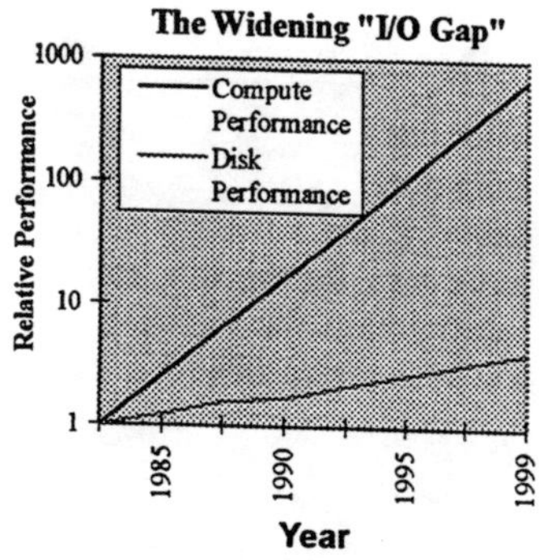

Figure 1: The "I/O Gap"

The storage industry's two biggest challenges in recent years have therefore been:

- to improve system I/O performance at the pace of computing performance increases so that access to data does not become a limiting factor for applications, and,
- to provide uninterrupted access to on-line data at levels of reliability well in excess of the expected lifetimes of the computer systems that process it.

Moreover, these challenges must be met cost-effectively with solutions that are affordable for the majority of applications.

These challenges are doubly difficult because the most cost-effective on-line storage technology, the magnetic disk, has electromechanical components. Disks rotate, and electromechanical *actuators* position heads radially (between disk center and edge) for data transfer to or from circular *tracks*.

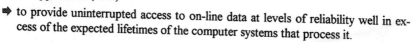

RAID Advisory Board Definition	
disk	A non-volatile, randomly addressable, re-writable data storage device. This definition includes both rotating magnetic and optical disks and *solid-state disks,* or non-volatile electronic storage elements. It does not include specialized devices such as *write-once-read-many (WORM)* optical disks, nor does it include so-called *RAM disks* implemented using software to control a dedicated portion of a host computer's volatile random access memory.
host computer	Any computer system to which disks are attached and accessible for data storage and I/O. Mainframes, servers, workstations and personal computers, as well as multiprocessors and computer complexes such as clusters and sysplexes are all referred to as host computers in RAID Advisory Board publications.

Electromechanical components operate orders of magnitude more slowly, require more power, and create more heat, vibration, and noise than purely electronic devices. Magnetic disks therefore have inherently lower performance and are more failure-prone than, for example, electronic memories. While it is to the credit of designers that magnetic disk Mean Time Between Failure (MTBF[4]) values approaching a million hours have been achieved, and data access times have been reduced to less than a third of what they were a decade ago, the access performance and reliability of data stored on disks remains a concern for many system users.

So the challenge for disk system designers is to start with devices that by themselves can be the limiting factor in system performance and data availability, and use them to build disk systems that make data the most reliable and accessible resource in the computing environment. In the course of doing this, on-line storage must remain affordable and I/O performance is expected to improve!

Solving the System Imbalance Problem

Disk I/O limits system performance for two reasons:

➡ data must be located mechanically by the relatively slow processes of seeking and disk rotation, and,

➡ once located, data is transferred to or from the disk surface in a one-bit wide serial stream.

---

[4] The *Mean Time Between Failures* of a device is the average time from start of use to failure in a large population of identical devices. It is more appropriately used to assess the failure rate in a population of identical devices than the probable lifetime of a single device.

Experienced system and application designers have long known how to make slow disks keep pace with fast computers: use lots of them in parallel. It is not uncommon for a large computer system to be connected to hundreds of disks, not just for the storage capacity they provide, but for the number of parallel I/O streams they permit. Even in smaller departmental and work group systems, multiple disks are becoming the rule.

On the surface, concurrent use of multiple disks is an attractive solution to I/O performance problems. If one disk can perform 100 I/O operations per second, two should be able to perform 200, and so on. In principle, any computer system's appetite for I/O could be satisfied in this way.

Imbalance Persists...

But, as experienced designers also know, computer systems' I/O loads are rarely distributed neatly across a system's disks. It is far more likely for most of a system's I/O requests to be addressed to a small fraction of its storage. One sometimes hears of an "80/20 rule"—80% of the total I/O load is directed at 20% of the I/O resources. Applying this rule to 10 disks, each capable of 100 I/O operations per second:

➡ Two of the disks (20%) together deliver 200 I/O operations per second (all they are capable of). This becomes 80% of the I/O work that can be done.

➡ the remaining eight disks deliver a total of 50 I/O operations per second (the remaining 20% of the I/O load).

This totals 250 I/O operations per second—far fewer than the 1,000 I/O operations per second theoretically available from 10 disks with a perfectly balanced I/O load[5].

Using I/O Resources Effectively

The obvious solution to this sub-optimal use of resources is to *tune* the I/O system, rearranging data items (e.g., files) on the disks until the most frequently accessed items are evenly distributed, or *balanced*, across the I/O resources.

A considerable amount of system management effort today goes into I/O system tuning, with considerable success. But tuning I/O systems this way has limits:

➡ It may be impossible to balance an I/O system perfectly. Suppose that a multi-user application makes 200 requests per second for data in a single file. Using the disk properties from the preceding example, the disk containing that file will receive twice as many I/O requests per second as it can execute. The application's requirement will not be met, nor will the I/O load be balanced.

➡ Even when it *is* possible to balance a system for a particular I/O load, there is no guarantee that the system will remain balanced. In most systems, the I/O load changes with time. Which data are accessed depends on which applications and

---

[5]   There is some evidence from examination of actual systems that suggests that while the 80/20 rule is somewhat extreme, a 55/20 rule (55% of I/O load directed at 20% of the I/O resources) is not unreasonable. Using a 55/20 rule, the ten disks in the example of this section could handle about 360 I/O requests per second, still only 36% of the hardware's potential.

users are active. Even within a single application, as new data are created and old data deleted, the location of the system's active data tends to change.

Thus, while I/O system tuning can be an important (if expensive) step toward optimizing I/O resource utilization, it is neither sufficiently precise nor sufficiently responsive to keep a dynamically changing system operating at peak efficiency. A *disk array* is usually a more effective solution to I/O tuning problems.

Disk Arrays

A disk array is a collection of disks from one or more disk systems whose actions are coordinated by a body of software or firmware known as an *Array Management Function*. The *RAID* Advisory Board distinguishes between the terms *disk array* and *disk system*, as the following definitions illustrate.

RAID Advisory Board Definition	
storage system	A system consisting of one or more storage controllers (q.v.) or I/O bus adapters connected to storage devices such as CDROMs, tape transports, removable media loaders and robots, that provides I/O services to one or more host computers.
disk system	A storage system (q.v.) capable of supporting only disks. The ANSI X3T10 SCSI-3 Controller Command Standard refers to a disk system that uses SCSI-3 as its host attachment as a *SCSI Disk Array* (SDA).
I/O system	A collective term for all of a computer system's or integrated computing environment's storage systems.
disk array	A collection of disks from one or more commonly accessible disk systems, combined with an Array Management *Function* (q.v.). The Array Management Function controls the disks' operation and presents their storage capacity to hosts as one or *more virtual disks*. The ANSI *X3T10 committee refers to* the Array Management Function as a *storage array* conversion layer (SACL). The committee does not have an equivalent *of* the term *disk array* in the sense in which it is used by the *RAID* Advisory Board.
member (disk)	A disk that is in use as a member of a disk array. A disk may be a member of an array at times and used independently at other times.

This definition of the term *disk array* is deliberately flexible. In addition to disk arrays consisting of some or all of the disks in a single disk system, the definition allows arrays whose *Array Management Function* executes in host computers and controls disks in multiple disk systems. Figure 2 illustrates these three disk array topologies.

Figure 2 illustrates an array comprising all of a disk system's disks (Disk Array 1), an array comprising some of a disk system's disks (Disk Array 2), and an array whose members reside in multiple disk systems (Disk Array 3).

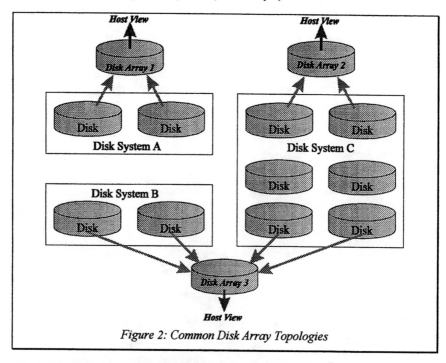

Figure 2: Common Disk Array Topologies

Most disk arrays are contained within a single disk system (as with Disk Array 1 or Disk Array 2 in Figure 2), so the systems are sometimes informally called *disk array systems*, or simply *disk arrays*. The essence of a disk array, however, is not where its member disks reside, but the fact that a single *Array Management Function* manages them and presents them to hosts as *virtual disks* with different cost, availability, and performance characteristics than the underlying members.

RAID Advisory Board Definition
virtual disk   Synonym for volume set (q.v.).

volume set	(An ANSI X3T10 term) A collection of user data extents (q.v.) presented to an operating environment as *a range of* consecutive logical block addresses. A volume set is the disk array object most closely resembling a disk when viewed by the operating environment.

The Role of the *Array Management Function* in Disk Arrays

A disk array's *Array Management Function* may execute either in the disk system or in the host computer(s). Its principal functions are:

➡ mapping the storage space presented to applications to the array member disks in a way that achieves some desired balance of cost, availability, and performance,

➡ presenting the storage to the operating environment as one or more virtual disks by transparently converting I/O requests directed to a virtual disk to I/O operations on the underlying member disks, and,

➡ protecting the data stored by applications from loss or unavailability due to disk failure.

Figure 3 illustrates two common types of disk array:

➡ *a mirrored array*, in which two member disks contain identical user data, and,

➡ *a striped array*, which distributes application data across two or more members disks in a regular pattern.

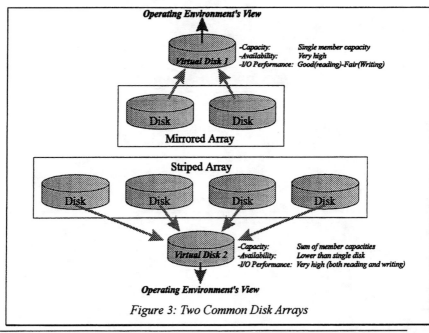

Figure 3: Two Common Disk Arrays

The two models in Figure 3 illustrate disk arrays with different cost, availability, and I/O performance characteristics:

➡️ A mirrored array presents very reliable virtual disks whose usable capacity is equal to that of the smallest of its member disks (making the cost high), and whose I/O performance is usually measurably better than that of a single disk for reads and slightly lower for writes.

➡️ A striped array presents virtual disks whose total usable capacity is approximately the sum of the capacities of its members, and whose read and write performance are both very high. The reliability of a striped array's virtual disks, however, is less than that of the least reliable member disk.

Why Disk Arrays?

System designers use disk arrays to enhance some or all of three important properties of on-line storage:

➡️ Disk arrays with striped data mapping almost always improve *I/O performance* because they tend to balance streams of either sequential or random I/O requests[6] approximately evenly across the member disks. Mirrored arrays can improve read performance because each member can process a separate read request simultaneously, thereby reducing the average read queue length in a busy system.

➡️ RAID disk arrays improve *data availability* by storing check data that allows user data to be reproduced if the disk on which it is stored fails. Mirrored arrays do this by replicating every block of user data on each member disk. Parity RAID arrays use a more elaborate check data technique involving both user data and check data in reproducing data from a failed disk. Striped arrays without some form of RAID do not improve data availability because the failure of any one disk in the array renders all user data inaccessible.

➡️ A disk array that aggregates multiple physical disks into one large virtual disk may simplify *storage management* by treating more storage capacity as a single management entity. A system manager who is managing four-disk arrays, with each presenting a single virtual disk, has one fourth as many directory trees to create, one fourth as many disk space quotas to set, one fourth as many backups to schedule (although, alas, not one fourth as much data to back up!), etc.

The principle of disk arrays is simple—trade abundant resources (disk capacity and the computing capacity required by the *Array Management Function*) to improve desirable qualities (data availability and/or I/O performance). Disk arrays are attractive because in most cases, the extra resources used pay disproportionate benefits.[7]

---

6   This book refers to consecutively issued requests to read or write blocks of data at adjacent ascending disk addresses as *sequential* read or write request streams of consecutively issued I/O requests which to not have this property are called *random* I/O requests, whether or not the addresses of the requested data are actually random.

7   This is not necessarily the case with RAID Levels 4 and 5, described in Chapter 5. Particularly with older disk array systems that use these technologies, the user must carefully consider the I/O workload to which the array will be subjected.

Hybrid Disk Arrays

Some disk arrays combine two or more techniques to achieve a combination of their benefits. One popular example of this is a striped disk array whose members are actually the virtual disks presented by mirrored arrays.

Figure 4 illustrates this using six disks arranged as three mirrored arrays, each presenting a virtual disk with a capacity equal to that of one member. These virtual disks are presented to another *Array Management Function* which uses them to create a striped array. The striped array's virtual disk is presented to the operating environment for application use.

The mirrored arrays in this example are very reliable virtual disks. The striped array balances the I/O load evenly across its members, providing high I/O performance.

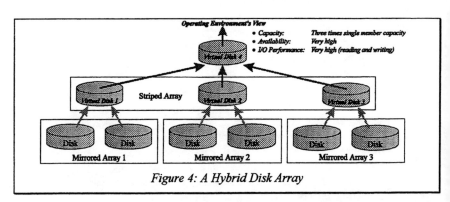

Figure 4: A Hybrid Disk Array

This combination of striping and mirroring therefore offers both high data availability and high I/O performance, albeit at a fairly high cost (in the example of Figure 4, the user must pay for 6 disks, enclosures, and host connections, but has usable storage capacity equal to that of only three disks). Chapter 6 contains further discussion of hybrid disk arrays.

Extending the Disk Array Concept: RAID

The striped and mirrored disk array models discussed above have been very successful in the market. Most major disk system vendors have offered mirroring and striping in their systems for several years.

The Berkeley RAID Levels

The popularity of early mirrored and striped disk arrays, coupled with the growing imbalance between computing and I/O capabilities has prompted researchers to look for other ways of combining disks into arrays with desirable combinations of affordability, data availability and I/O performance. In 1988, David A. Patterson, Garth Gibson, and Randy H. Katz of the University of California at Berkeley published the landmark paper entitled *A Case for Redundant Arrays of Inexpensive Disks* **[Patterson88]**, which outlined five disk array models, or *RAID Levels*. The goal of the paper was to explore whether arrays of the low-cost disks of modest capacity and performance that were being used in the personal computers of the time could effectively substitute for the high-capacity, high performance disks used in the data center systems of the day. The paper introduced mirroring, suggested that its shortcoming was cost, and went on to propose another "level" of RAID that would deal with this shortcoming. That level had its shortcomings as well, so another "level" was introduced, and so on, to a total of five RAID Levels.

Each RAID level was described as:

➡ a mechanism for protecting data against loss or inaccessibility due to disk failure, and,

➡ an algorithm for mapping the data blocks of the virtual disk presented to applications onto physical storage.

In 1989, the same three authors published a further paper entitled *Disk System Architectures for High Performance Computing* **[Katz89b]**, in which a sixth model offering protection against two concurrent disk failures was described. This double protection model became known as RAID Level 6.

RAID Advisory Board Definition

Redundant Array of Independent Disks   A disk array (q.v.) in which part of the physical storage capacity is used to store redundant information about user data stored on the remainder of the storage capacity. The redundant information enables regeneration (q.v.) of user data in the event that one of the array's member disks (q.v.) or the access path to it fails.

Berkeley RAID Levels   A family of disk array data protection and mapping techniques described by Garth Gibson, Randy Katz, and David Patterson in papers written while they were performing research into I/O systems at the University of California at Berkeley [Patterson88, Katz89b]. There are six Berkeley RAID Levels, usually referred to by the names RAID Level 1, etc., through RAID Level 6.

Three of the Berkeley RAID Levels have proven especially important commercially, and are found either singly or in combination in a variety of RAID-related products:

➡ *RAID Level 1*, or disk mirroring. RAID Level 1 offers the highest data reliability[8] of the first five Berkeley RAID Levels. Most RAID Level 1 arrays offer significantly better read performance than an equivalent single disk, and slightly lower

---

[8]   for member disks of a given reliability (MTBF).

write performance. The primary drawback of RAID Level 1 is its inherent cost (the number of components required) compared to other forms of RAID.

➡ **RAID Level 3** stores check data corresponding to user data on several data disks in the form of bit-by-bit *parity*. Strictly speaking, RAID Level 3 mapping distributes the data in each virtual disk block evenly across all array members but one, and writes the parity for the distributed data segments in that one. Many implementations approximate this behavior for smaller data transfers. Most RAID Level 5 implementations use RAID Level 3 write algorithms to optimize performance when full "stripes of data" are written.

RAID Level 3 provides excellent I/O performance for applications which must transfer large amounts of sequentially addressed data quickly. These applications include image and video processing, scientific data collection and reduction, and batch data processing.

RAID Level 5, like RAID Level 3, stores check data corresponding to user data on several data disks in the form of bit-by-bit *parity*. It differs from RAID Level 3, however, in that a RAID Level 5 array's disks may operate independently of each other.

From a practical standpoint a RAID Level 5 array using modern reliable disks offers data reliability approaching that of mirroring,[9] with read performance increases similar to those of striping. There is a substantial inherent performance reduction when data is written, however. Many RAID Level 5 implementations incorporate features specifically designed to mitigate this *write penalty*.

RAID Level 5 is well suited for applications with I/O loads consisting predominantly of concurrent read requests. Transaction processing, office automation, and many file and database serving applications often fall into this category. RAID Level 5 can also perform very well with data transfer-intensive applications, such as image analysis, which make mostly read requests. It is not as well suited for write-intensive applications such as data entry or scientific and engineering data collection.

RAID Levels 3, 4, and 5 are sometimes collectively called *parity RAID* because they all use the same mechanism for protecting data against loss due to disk failure. The parity (modulo-2 count of "1" bits) mechanism is conceptually similar to the longitudinal parity formerly used to protect data stored on magnetic tape.

RAID Advisory Board Definition	
parity RAID	A collective term used to refer to Berkeley RAID Levels (q.v.) 3, 4, and 5.

---

[9] Although numerically, it is substantially less, both are large compared to the typically expected 3-5 year life of disk systems.

In addition to RAID Levels 1, 3, 4, and 5, RAID Level 6,[10] in which two sets of independently computed check data protect the same each bit of user data, has been implemented commercially. RAID Level 6 protects against data loss due to double as well as single disk failures. For large arrays, it provides extremely high data reliability (higher than mirroring) at modest cost, but is complex to implement, and has an even more substantial inherent write penalty than RAID Level 5. RAID Level 6 implementations include additional features for enhancing application write performance.

RAID Level 0

The term *RAID Level 0* is often used to describe disk striping without data protection because of the similarity to striped data mapping as used in parity RAID implementations[11]. Strictly speaking, the absence of redundancy in a striped array, makes the term RAID a misnomer. Because it is in common use, however, the *RAID* Advisory Board endorses the term *RAID Level 0* to refer to disk striping. This book uses the terms disk *striping* and *RAID Level 0* interchangeably.

Disk striping and the six Berkeley RAID Levels are described in detail in Chapter 4 and Chapter 5. Table 1 (page 16) compares the cost, data availability, and I/O performance comparison of these RAID Levels for reference. In Table 1, I/O performance is shown both in terms of *data transfer capacity*, or ability to move data, and *I/O request rate*, or ability to satisfy I/O requests, since these RAID Levels inherently perform differently relative to these two metrics. Each RAID Level's strong point is highlighted.

---

[10] The term *RAID Level 6* has been used to refer to a combination of RAID Levels 0 and 1 (described in Chapter 8). The *RAID* Advisory Board usage of RAID Level 6 conforms to the Berkeley definition **[Katz89b]**.

[11] In fact, the Berkeley researchers recognized striped data mapping as a desirable feature for any RAID Level, including RAID Level 1, rather than a level in its own right.

RAID Level	Common Name	Description	Disks Req'd (Cost)	Data Availability	Large I/O Data Transfer Capacity[12]	Small I/O Request Rate
0	Disk Striping	Data distributed across the disks in the array. No check data.	N	lower than single-disk	very high	very high for both read and write
1	Mirroring	All data replicated on N separate disks. (N is usually 2).	2N, 3N, etc.	higher than RAID Level 2, 3, 4, or 5; lower than RAID Level 6	higher than single disk for read; similar to single disk for write	up to twice that of a single disk for read; similar to single disk for write
2		Data protected by a Hamming code. Check data distributed across m disks, where m is determined by the number of data disks in the array.	N+m	much higher than single disk; higher than RAID 3, 4, or 5	highest of all listed alternatives	approximately twice that of a single disk
3	RAID 3, Parallel Transfer Disks with Parity	Each virtual disk block subdivided and distributed across all data disks. Parity check data stored on a separate parity disk.	N+1	much higher than single disk; comparable to RAID 2, 4, or 5	highest of all listed alternatives	approximately twice that of a single disk
4		Data blocks distributed as with disk striping. Parity check data stored on one disk.	N+1	much higher than single disk; comparable to RAID 2, 3, or 5	similar to disk striping for read; significantly lower than single disk for write	similar to disk striping for read; significantly lower than single disk for write
5	RAID 5, "RAID"	Data blocks distributed as with disk striping; check data is distributed on multiple disks.	N+1	much higher than single disk; comparable to RAID 2, 3, or 4	similar to disk striping for read; lower than single disk for write	similar to disk striping for read; generally lower than single disk for write
6	RAID 6	As RAID Level 5, but with additional independently computed Check data.	N+2	highest of all listed alternatives	similar to disk striping for read; lower than RAID Level 5 for write	similar to disk striping for read; significantly lower than RAID Level 5 for write

Table 1: Summary Comparison of RAID Technologies

When referring to Table 1, it is well to be aware that few if any disk systems implement any Berkeley RAID level in its pure form. Most augment one or more Berkeley RAID data protection and mapping models with additional features designed to enhance I/O performance and data availability. Some of these features are described in Part 3 of this book. Table 1 is best viewed as a rough guideline to potential performance characteristics of a disk array using a particular RAID model under extreme circumstances, and should not be used to draw conclusions about products.

Other Forms of RAID

While RAID Levels 0, 1, 3, 5, and 6 are all useful data protection and mapping models, each has drawbacks when applied by itself. Most failure- disk systems, therefore, use RAID data mapping and protection as kernel technologies enhanced either by:

➧ combining multiple RAID Levels, for example as described on page 12, or,

➧ combining RAID data protection with other features, such as cache, redundant I/O paths, multiprocessing controller architectures, redundant components, hot swap capability, and others.

---

12   The Data Transfer Capacity and I/O Rate columns reflect only the write performance inherently implied by RAID data mapping and protection, and do not account for the performance enhancement features in many implementations.

The goal of such combinations is to improve I/O performance while retaining or improving on the data availability characteristics that accrue from RAID data protection. Part 3 (beginning on page 149) describes disk system features that are often combined with RAID in high-performance, failure tolerant disk systems.

One such combination available in many disk systems is a combination of RAID Levels 0 and 1. This combination, which provides high data reliability and high inherent I/O performance, has been referred to as *RAID 10*, *RAID Level 0+1*, and *RAID Level 0&1*, and possibly by other names as well.

RAID in Product Names

Many vendors incorporate the acronym RAID in product names or descriptions. *RAID 5+*, *RAID 6+*, *RAID 7*, *RAID 10*, *RAID30*, *RAID50*, *RAID-S*, and *AutoRAID* have all been used.[13] Typically, such products either blend multiple Berkeley RAID Levels, or add additional features to a disk system that implements one or more Berkeley RAID Levels.

To date, there has not been industry-wide agreement on definition of data protection and mapping models other than RAID Level 0 and the six Berkeley RAID Levels. This is not to say that other useful data mappings will not be created and standardized. RAID technology continues to

Descriptive Legend

Figure 5: RAID *Advisory Board Trademark*

be the subject of substantial research and development. It is the *RAID* Advisory Board's role to describe precisely and endorse any such models as are developed and become generally accepted in the industry and market.

RAID Advisory Board Designators

The *RAID* Advisory Board has established programs under which vendors may submit RAID-related products to the Board, which determines whether the products conform to certain functionality or failure tolerance criteria. Vendors who do this successfully may be licensed by the *RAID* Advisory Board to display a designator similar to that shown in Figure 5 in their product literature, documentation, or name plates. The "Descriptive Legend" attached to the designator indicates the type of *RAID* Advisory Board scrutiny undergone by the product.

For example, authorized use of a *RAID* Advisory Board *RAID Level Conformance* designator means that a product has been determined to have certain characteristics of the designated RAID Level(s). These are listed in Part 2. Similarly, use of a *RAID* Advisory Board *Compliance* designator indicates that the product has successfully undergone the *RAID* Advisory Board's battery of functional tests.

Authorized use of a *RAID* Advisory Board designator means only that a product or its documentation has been examined by the *RAID* Advisory Board, and found to con-

---

13   AutoRAID is a trademark of Hewlett-Packard Corporation. RAID-S is a trademark of EMC Corporation. Other names listed may also be vendor trademarks.

form to the Board's requirements. No inference should be made about product features not related to use of the designator.

RAID Advisory Board designators, examination and licensing procedures, and rules for display are described in the publication *RABInfo*, available from the RAID Advisory Board.

Inexpensive or Independent?

The original Berkeley paper **[Patterson88]** generated considerable interest in the user community with its title—Redundant Arrays of Inexpensive Disks, in large measure because of its thesis that RAID could offer a substantial decrease in the cost of high-performance storage for large computer systems. The paper proposed the use of arrays of the small, low-performance, inexpensive disks made for personal computers as substitutes for the Single Large Expensive Disks (SLEDs) commonly used with the data center systems at that time. A combination of extra inexpensive disks and RAID data protection and mapping would allow these arrays to surpass the performance and data reliability and availability of the larger units at lower cost.

Had storage technology remained static for the last ten years, this would have been the case. While RAID was gaining acceptance, however, storage technology was in rapid transition. Today the SLED is essentially a thing of the past. RAID array member disks are no longer inexpensive relative to conventionally managed disks; they are the same. The cost of RAID today must be compared to that of equivalent capacity in a disk system without RAID capability.

RAID arrays are therefore no longer inexpensive compared to on-line storage without RAID, but the independence of array member disks still creates significant data reliability and performance advantages. By common consent, therefore, the industry has transmuted the RAID acronym to mean Redundant Arrays of *Independent* Disks. The *RAID* Advisory Board follows this usage.

Another Way Of Looking At RAID[14]

The Berkeley RAID data protection and mapping models may be classified according to whether they require data to be updated using:

➡ *parallel access*, in that they require all member disks to participate concurrently in every I/O operation directed at the array, or,

➡ *independent access*, in that their member disks may operate independently of each other, executing multiple unrelated application I/O requests concurrently.

RAID Level 2 and 3 arrays are inherently parallel access, because the data protection model assumes that all member disks write in unison. Strictly speaking, parallel access arrays require member disk rotational synchronization. Some implementations, however, approximate strictly parallel access behavior, allowing the use of disks that are not synchronized,.

---

[14] The concepts in this section were originally proposed by *RAID* Advisory Board member firm Formation, Inc., whose contribution is gratefully acknowledged.

RAID Level 4 and 5 arrays are inherently independent access. In principle, it is possible for every member of an independent access array to be engaged in satisfying a separate application write request at one instant.

In principle, RAID Level 1 (mirrored) arrays may implement either parallel access or independent access. In practice most mirrored arrays feature independent access.

Classification of RAID data protection models according to the update parallelism they allow or require gives rise to names that are perhaps more descriptive of the technologies' actual characteristics than the level numbers used by the Berkeley researchers, particularly in disk systems which use RAID in combination with other performance enhancing technologies.

RAID Advisory Board Definition

mirrored array   Common term for a disk array that implements RAID Level 1, or mirroring (q.v.) to protecting data against loss due to disk or channel failure.

mirroring   A form of RAID in which *the Array Management Function* maintains two or more identical copies of data on separate disks. Also known as RAID Level 1 and disk shadowing.

parallel access array   A disk array in which the data access model assumes that all member disks operate in unison, and that all member disks participate in the execution of every application I/O request. A parallel access array is inherently capable of executing one I/O request at any instant. True parallel access arrays require physical disk synchronization; much more commonly, arrays approximate true parallel access behavior. *cf.* **independent access array**

Independent access array   A disk array whose data mapping is such that different member disks can execute multiple application I/O requests concurrently. *cf.* **parallel access array**

An independent access parity RAID array with parity concentrated on a single disk is said to use RAID Level 4 data update algorithms. Conversely, an independent access parity RAID array with parity distributed across some of all of its disks is said to use RAID Level 5 data update algorithms.

In general, parallel access arrays are most suitable for applications requiring high data transfer capacity, while independent access arrays are more suitable for applications requiring high I/O request rates. This characterization is less clear-cut in RAID array systems that include some or all of the performance enhancing features discussed in Part 3. Chapter 5 describes how most arrays adapt their behavior between parallel and independent access, depending on instantaneous I/O load requirements, further blurring distinctions among RAID Levels.

For a RAID system user, classification by update access mode is likely to be of more practical value than a classification by Berkeley RAID Level, because it relates to an array's suitability for use in certain classes of applications. Table 2 on page 20 summarizes RAID array applications.

Array Type	Application Suitability	Examples
Parallel Access	High data transfer rate requirements	Video and imaging
		Data mining
		Batch processing of large sequential files
		Seismic or telemetric data collection
Independent Access	high read access rate requirements	Interactive transaction processing
		Multi-user file services (e.g. office environments).

Table 2: Summary of RAID Array Application Suitability

Why Is RAID Important?

System managers who provide information services to their organizations, as well as managers who make information technology purchase and configuration decisions should be aware of the new richness of on-line storage alternatives offered by RAID. parity RAID, for example, offers data reliability comparable to that of disk mirroring (from a practical standpoint) at significantly lower inherent cost,[15] particularly when high capacity is required. There may be performance tradeoffs, however. Awareness of RAID and its relationship to other storage technology options can help managers make important decisions about on-line storage alternatives.

Users of networked personal computers should be concerned about the quality of the data storage services provided by their data servers. Low-cost RAID technology, both in the form of host software and RAID disk systems, is readily available in the server market. The material in this book can help make the personal computer user aware of the significance of the storage alternatives available for his server. Moreover, the first RAID systems for the desktop have already appeared on the market. As disk size and cost continue to decline, widespread use of RAID on the desktop is only a matter of time.

---

[15] The *inherent* cost of a product is the aggregate cost of components contained in it. This book uses inherent cost as a way of normalizing the cost of various RAID alternatives. Vendors may set prices on some basis other than inherent cost.

The purpose of this book is to provide the background to help prospective purchasers with storage decisions, particularly with respect to RAID capable systems. Only three years ago, RAID was viewed as an add-on "extra" most suitable for larger disk systems and mission-critical applications. In 1995, according to one analyst, more than half the disk systems shipped were RAID-capable. It appears that within a very few years the average disk will be part of a RAID array; in other words, non-arrayed disks will be the exception rather than the rule.

A Device for Comparing Storage Options

Figure 6 illustrates a simple device for visually indicating the properties of a storage technology—the *cost-availability-performance (CAP) triangle*. The CAP triangle is useful for comparing the inherent properties of different RAID Levels.

The CAP triangle encapsulates the three main properties used to evaluate disk systems in a single graphic. Purchasers generally seek an optimal balance among:

➡ low cost per MByte,

➡ high I/O performance[16], and,

➡ high data reliability.

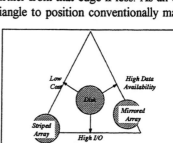

Low Cost

High Data Availability

Disk

High I/O Performance

Figure 6: The Cost, Availability, Performance (CAP) Triangle

Of course, the optimal balance of these properties is different for each user, and even for each application. The challenge for disk system purchasers is to determine the correct balance of cost, availability, and performance each time they make a purchase.

The CAP triangle represents a three dimensional continuum of affordability (low cost), availability, and I/O performance in two dimensions. Each edge of the triangle represents an extremely high value for one of the three properties. Every on-line storage technology may be characterized by a point within this continuum—closer to an edge if it possesses a property to a greater degree; further from that edge if less. As an example, Figure 7 illustrates the use of a CAP triangle to position conventionally managed disks, a striped array, and a mirrored array relative to each other.

In Figure 7, conventionally managed disks are arbitrarily positioned at the center of the triangle. As the most common on-line storage technology in use today, this technology arguably represents a norm for cost, availability, and performance. Of course, different disk types have different properties, but to a first approximation, compared to arrays and other alternatives, it is fair to regard all conventional disks as a single class of storage.

Low Cost

High Data Availability

Disk

Mirrored Array

Striped Array

High I/O Performance

Figure 7: Using the CAP Triangle to Position Storage Technologies

The striped array is positioned close to the low cost and high I/O performance edges, because it is a low cost means of achieving high I/O performance. It is far from the

---

16 I/O performance may mean either data transfer performance or I/O request performance depending on the context. For evaluation purposes, it is usually necessary to distinguish between the two, since both application demands and array capabilities are sometimes tunable to favor one performance requirement over others. As a device for concisely summarizing storage technology characteristics, however, the CAP triangle does not attempt to do so.

high availability edge, however, because its overall data reliability is less than that of a single disk.

The mirrored array, on the other hand, offers considerably greater data reliability than a comparable single disk, so it is closer to the high availability edge of the triangle. Moreover, since mirrored disks typically outperform individual disks, the mirrored array is closer to the high I/O performance edge as well (although not as close as the striped array). The cost of mirroring, however, is relatively high—two or more times the cost of equivalent conventional disk capacity—so the mirrored array is far from the affordability edge.

The CAP triangle is used in the Part 2 chapter introductions to position various technology alternatives relative to each other in terms of affordability, availability, and I/O performance. The triangle has been used only to compare RAID data protection and mapping models, and not actual disk array products, which usually combine RAID technology with other features that enhance data availability or I/O performance.

Where To Go From Here?

Chapter 2 contains an overview of the disk system and array characteristics related to RAID. It provides useful background for Part 2. Chapter 3 discusses algorithmic data mapping for disk arrays. It includes a discussion of the ANSI X3T10 SCSI-3 Controller Command Standard's SCSI Disk Array data protection and mapping model.

Part 2 of this book, starting with Chapter 4, provides more detailed descriptions of the Berkeley RAID Levels.

Part 3 of this book, starting with Chapter 9, describes how RAID is integrated with other technologies to produce highly available, high-performance disk systems.

Appendix 1 describes the RAID Advisory Board and its other publications and services.

Appendix 2 contains a reference list of RAID-related publications.

Appendix 3 is a glossary of RAID- and storage-related terms as they are used by the RAID Advisory Board in this book and its publications. Other organizations and publications may apply alternative definitions and connotations to these terms.

Chapter 2: Disk Systems and Disk Arrays

Common Aspects of Disk Systems and Arrays

This chapter discusses common characteristics of disk systems and disk arrays as a foundation for the more detailed RAID model descriptions in the chapters that follow[17].

Disk Systems

RAID Advisory Board definitions related to disk systems given in Chapter 1 are repeated here for convenience.

RAID Advisory Board Definition	
storage system	A system consisting of one or more storage controllers (q.v.) or I/O bus adapters connected to storage devices such as CDROMs, tape transports, removable media loaders and robots, that provides I/O services to one or more host computers.
disk system	A storage system (q.v.) capable of supporting only disks. The ANSI X3T10 SCSI-3 Controller Command Standard refers to a disk system that uses SCSI-3 as its host attachment as a *SCSI Disk Array* (SDA).

---

[17] This chapter and the two that follow are based on material supplied to the *RAID* Advisory Board by member company Array Technology Corporation. Their contribution is gratefully acknowledged.

I/O system	A collective term for all of a computer system's or integrated computing environment's storage systems.

Simple Disk Systems

Figure 8 illustrates a simple disk system model that satisfies this definition. An *I/O bus adapter* residing in a host computer connects to one or more disks via an I/O bus.

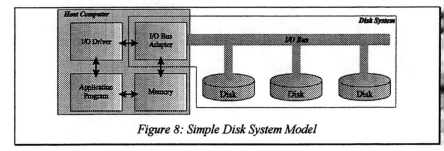

Figure 8: Simple Disk System Model

In this model, the host:

➡ executes applications,

➡ uses I/O driver software to communicate application requests to the I/O bus adapter and disk system responses to the application,

➡ contains the main memory that is the destination for data read from disks and the source for data written to them.

The I/O bus adapter:

➡ provides an interface between the I/O bus and the host computer's memory bus,

➡ accepts commands from the I/O driver, converts them into the I/O bus protocol, and relays them to the disks to which they are addressed,

➡ arbitrates among the disks' and its own attempts to use the bus,

➡ processes disks' responses itself or converts them to data structures in host memory for host processing,

➡ moves data between host memory and the disks via I/O bus.

The I/O bus:

➡ is the vehicle for moving host commands, disk responses, and data between the I/O bus adapter and the disks.

The disks:

➡ provide block-addressable[18] random read/write access to data storage,

---

[18] Descriptions and explanations in this book are predicated on a model of a disk as a linear address space of blocks of a fixed size. While this *fixed block architecture* is almost universal in computer systems today, other disk architectures, notably the *count-key-data* (CKD) variable track capacity architecture found in large data center systems, do exist.

➡ provide data conversion, buffering, device control, and first-level error recovery as necessary.

RAID Advisory Board Definition	
protocol	A set of rules for using a signaling channel so that information conveyed on the channel can be correctly interpreted by all parties to the communication. Protocols include such aspects of communication as data item ordering, message formats, message and response sequencing rules, block data transmission conventions, and so forth.

In the model illustrated in Figure 8, which represents the disk systems commonly found in personal computers, workstations, and small servers, the disks are highly capable storage elements, able to execute complete I/O commands autonomously. This is characteristic of virtually all modern disks, and is assumed throughout this book. Some older disk designs rely on shared control logic to perform many of their low-level functions. Host-based array implementations can make some disk array and RAID advantages possible for these older disks.

The most common I/O bus in use today is the Small Computer System Interface (SCSI). While the model illustrated in Figure 8 is representative of small SCSI-based disk systems, it is not intended to be SCSI-specific, but representative of any of the small disk systems in use today (e.g., IDE-based systems).

As discussed in Chapter 1, the growing mismatch between host computer and disk performance capabilities makes increasingly less likely that a single disk can satisfy the I/O needs of even relatively small server systems. More and more workstations and small server systems are being equipped with multiple disks using the architecture illustrated in Figure 8. In larger systems, however, the I/O driver, I/O bus adapter, I/O bus, or a combination of them are likely to become an *I/O bottleneck*, since their capabilities must be shared among all of the system's disks.

RAID Advisory Board Definition	
I/O bottleneck	Any resource in the I/O path (e.g., a device driver, an I/O adapter, an I/O bus, an intelligent controller, or a disk) whose performance limits the performance of a storage system or I/O system as a whole.

In larger systems, multiple I/O adapters can usually be added to the host computer, but performance, configuration limits, disk addressing limits, operating system support limits, and other considerations may make this impractical or undesirable.

Intelligent Disk Controllers

Larger, more sophisticated disk systems typically interpose *intelligent disk controllers* between the host's I/O adapter and the disks. Intelligent controllers, in a configuration such as that illustrated in Figure 9, have several benefits:

➡ They facilitate the connection of larger numbers of disks and other storage devices to host computers.

➡ They represent additional processing resources for I/O-specific tasks, so that RAID and similar features do not affect application computing capability.

➡ They can be enclosed, powered, and cooled separately from their host computers, providing greater failure-tolerance than the configuration illustrated in Figure 8.

In Figure 9, the host computer's I/O bus connects to an intelligent disk controller rather than directly to disks. The controller in turn connects to disk I/O buses, commonly called *channels* or *ports*, using its own disk I/O bus adapters.

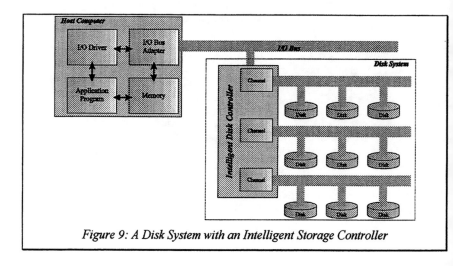

Figure 9: A Disk System with an Intelligent Storage Controller

Channels are functionally identical to the I/O bus illustrated in Figure 8. They may require extensive assistance from a processor, or may contain sufficient internal intelligence to accept a sequence of pre-programmed responses called a *script*. Executing scripts allows a channel to function autonomously (i.e., without assistance from the host or from the disk controller's *policy processor*) for relatively long periods of time.

Larger intelligent disk controllers incorporate multiple channels. In the simplest case, a controller accepts host I/O requests addressed to disks and relays them to the channels to which the addressed disks are connected. The role of the controller is typically threefold:

➡ It increases host disk connectivity (i.e., it allows the host to connect to more disks than its I/O buses alone would accommodate).

➡ It increases I/O performance potential by making available more I/O resources (disks and channels) across which the host computer's I/O load can be spread.

➡ It assists in scheduling and processing I/O requests, thereby minimizing the impact of a heavy I/O load on host computer application processing capacity.

Embedded Disk Controllers

The original intelligent controller-based disk systems were physically large, often housed in separate enclosures from their host computers. In recent years miniaturization has made possible *embedded* intelligent controllers that attach one or more channels directly to a host memory or internal I/O bus. Many embedded controllers connect to the Peripheral Component Interface (PCI) bus, for example. Since they mount in the host computer enclosure, embedded controllers cost substantially less than free-standing ones. Direct attachment to an internal host bus usually means that their data transfer performance is quite high. Today, embedded controllers are not capable of connecting storage devices to multiple host computers, so the system level availability

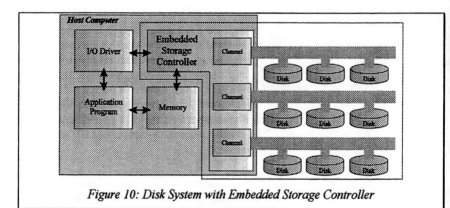

Figure 10: Disk System with Embedded Storage Controller

they provide is lower than that of independent controller-based disk systems.

Embedded disk controllers typically include two or three SCSI device channels, although five-channel controllers exist. With today's disk capacities, this makes them practical for applications requiring up to about 100 Gbytes. Embedded controllers are often found in departmental network operating system (NOS) servers, where cost and data reliability, rather than continuous availability, are the major concerns.

How Intelligent Controllers Increase
Disk System Capabilities

Each of an intelligent disk controller's channels is both an independent path for data and commands and a way to attach more storage capacity to the host. The way in which adding disks to a disk system with a multi-channel controller affects its I/O performance potential depends on how the disks are configured:

➡ Disks can be added to a single channel. For I/O loads consisting primarily of small random I/O requests, this can increase the disk system's I/O request processing capacity. To a limited extent, it can increase the disk system's data transfer capacity, but in data transfer-intensive applications, a single disk channel is usually the first I/O bottleneck encountered.

➡ Disks can be distributed across channels. This can cost more (if the additional channels are extra-cost options), but because each channel is an independent data transfer path, it usually results in greater data transfer capacity as well as increased I/O request processing capacity. Because more channels also increase the potential disk connectivity, this option also increases the system's disk capacity.

Figure 11 summarizes graphically the primary, secondary, and tertiary benefits of adding disks to a channel compared to adding channels.

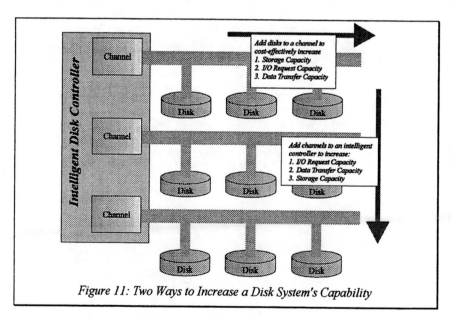

Figure 11: Two Ways to Increase a Disk System's Capability

I/O Load Balance: The Key to
Maximum I/O Performance

Using Figure 11 as an example, if one assumes that:

➡ each of the disks can execute 100 I/O requests per second, and,

➡ each channel can accommodate 7 disks,

➡ the controller includes 6 channels,

then in principle, the system should be capable of handling 2,100 I/O requests per second. This is a substantial I/O capacity for small to medium-size computer system. Several factors may constrain this capacity significantly, however:

➡ To execute this number of requests, the host I/O adapter and the host I/O bus must be capable of transferring the amount of data they imply. Using the parameters above, for example, if each I/O request called for 16 Kbytes of data to be transferred, the host I/O bus would require an available data transfer capacity of almost 70 Mbytes per second (16,384 x 4,200 = 68,812,800). This is well beyond the capability of all but the most advanced host I/O buses today.

➡ Similarly, the data transfer capacity of each channel must be adequate for the demands made on it. Using the same parameters, each channel would require a data transfer capacity of over 11 Mbytes/second (16,384 x 700 = 11,468,800). This is beyond the capability of SCSI-2 with an 8-bit data transfer path. It is within the capability of a 16-bit SCSI-2 bus, however.

➡ The processing resources in the I/O path must be capable of delivering and handling this I/O load. First, the host computer must be capable of interpreting and relaying this many requests. In this example, if processing an I/O request required 500 microseconds of computing, the 2,100 requests would totally saturate the host computer without considering any application work. Similarly, both the host I/O adapter and the controller's policy processor must be able to receive and relay the same number of requests.

➡ More important than any of these, to reach maximum I/O capacity the host's I/O demands must be evenly distributed across all of its disks. If 90% of a host's I/O requests are directed at data on a single disk (admittedly, an extreme imbalance), then that disk's capacity to satisfy I/O requests represents 90% of the I/O that the system will deliver. The system in this example would only deliver about 111 I/O requests per second (100 ÷ 90% = 111.1...), or about 1.8 Mbytes per second with this imbalance.

I/O Load Balancing

I/O load can be evenly balanced, or distributed across resources, but this can be difficult to achieve. What is needed is a means of balancing that is independent of I/O load, or nearly so, in order that all of a disk system's resources be utilized most of the time. I/O load balancing is one of the most important aspects of system tuning. It can be done:

➡ *manually* (i.e., by human action), or,

➡ *automatically* (i.e., by some means that does not require human intervention).

Manual I/O load balancing is a common system management technique. An I/O activity monitor records I/O activity while the system is executing the application for whose I/O load it is to be tuned. A system manager or database administrator then analyzes

I/O activity reports generated from monitored data to determine whether I/O imbalance exists. The analyst looks primarily for:

➡ problems: heavily loaded, or *saturated* disks and channels, and,

➡ opportunities: lightly loaded disks and channels.

If he finds both, I/O load balancing may be possible. The analyst must determine which data objects (files or database storage areas) are the heavily accessed ones,[19] and move some of these to the I/O system's lightly loaded resources. If future I/O loads remain similar to the one analyzed, this balancing should improve performance by diverting part of the load from saturated disks to lightly loaded ones.

While manual load balancing is intuitively attractive, and indeed, is in common use, it has some important limitations:

➡ It may require application changes as files are moved from disk to disk. Applications are sometimes structured to require that the data they process be located on specific disks. If this is the case, moving the data requires informing applications that data is now in different locations. This can be both time-consuming and error-prone, especially if several applications make use of the same data.

➡ It may not be possible. The procedure described above is predicated on the assumption that heavy I/O loads on individual disks can be traced to application accesses to multiple files on those disks. If accesses to a single file are the cause of a heavy I/O load on a single disk, it may not be possible to reduce this by moving other files elsewhere.

➡ It uses the past to predict the future. A disk system or I/O system balanced using this procedure will perform well as long as its I/O load approximates the I/O load during the performance data gathering period. More realistically, data reference patterns shift as individual application programs start and finish. The I/O load moves from disk to disk, and past behavior ceases to be a valid predictor of future behavior.

A better I/O load balancing mechanism would be one that:

➡ was application-independent,

➡ could increase performance for individual files with heavy I/O demands, and,

➡ worked in spite of changes in the I/O load presented to the disk system.

These requirements for universal I/O load balancing have led in part to the development of *disk arrays*.

Disk Arrays

The *RAID* Advisory Board's definition of the term *disk array* given in Chapter 1 is repeated here for convenience.

---

[19] Some monitors report I/O activity by file directly; others require the analyst to determine how disk activity relates to file activity by other means.

RAID Advisory Board Definition	
disk array	A collection of disks from one or more commonly accessible disk systems, combined with an *Array Management Function* (q.v.). The Array Management Function controls the disks' operation and presents their storage capacity to hosts as one or *more virtual disks*. The ANSI *X3T10 committee refers to* the Array Management Function as a *storage array* conversion layer (SACL). The committee does not have an equivalent *of* the term *disk array* in the sense in which it is used by the *RAID* Advisory Board.

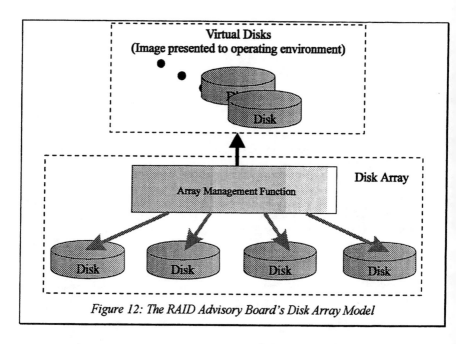

Figure 12: The RAID Advisory Board's Disk Array Model

Figure 12 illustrates the *RAID* Advisory Board's disk array model.

A disk array consists of one or more *member disks* managed by a common *Array Management Function*. The *Array Management Function* presents the disks to an *operating environment* as one or more *virtual disks*. One of its chief functions is to *map* (translate) between virtual disk data addresses used by the operating environment and applications and physical member disk data addresses. The *Array Management Function* may execute either in a storage controller or in a host.

```
┌─────────────────────────────────────────────────────────────────────┐
│                 RAID Advisory Board Definition                        │
│                                                                       │
│  operating environment   The hosting environment within which a storage │
│                    system operates. The operating environment includes │
│                    the computer(s) to which the storage system is attached, │
│                    I/O buses and adapters, host operating system instances, │
│                    and any required software. For host-based disk arrays │
│                    (q.v.), the operating environment includes I/O driver │
│                    software for the array and possibly also for the member │
│                    disks, but does not include Array Management Func-  │
│                    tion, which is more properly regarded as part of the ar- │
│                    ray itself.                                        │
│                                                                       │
│  member (disk)     A disk that is in use as a member of a disk array. A disk │
│                    may be a member of an array at times and used inde-  │
│                    pendently at other times.                          │
└─────────────────────────────────────────────────────────────────────┘
```

Implementing Disk Arrays

An array's member disks may be specially adapted for use in the array,[20] or they may be general purpose disks, as is commonly the case with striped and mirrored arrays. When special-purpose disks are used, the *Array Management Function* usually executes within the disk system's intelligent controller.

```
┌─────────────────────────────────────────────────────────────────────┐
│                 RAID Advisory Board Definition                        │
│                                                                       │
│  controller-based array   A disk array whose Array Management Func-   │
│                    tion executes in the disk system's controller or host I/O │
│                    bus adapter. The member disks of a controller-based ar- │
│                    ray are necessarily part of the same disk system. cf. │
│                    host-based array.                                  │
└─────────────────────────────────────────────────────────────────────┘
```

---

[20] As with some RAID Level 3 implementations which require that disks be rotationally synchronized.

In many cases, all of a disk array's components reside in a single enclosure. This can obscure the distinction between the disk system (the set of disks physically connected to and controlled by an intelligent controller or I/O bus adapter) and the disk array (the

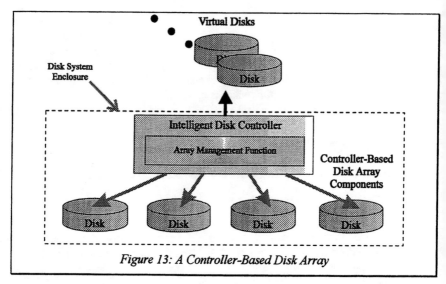

Figure 13: A Controller-Based Disk Array

set of disks managed by the *Array Management Function* as a common unit). Figure 13 illustrates one kind of controller-based disk array.

The key factor defining a controller-based array is that the *Array Management Function* executes in a disk controller (either independently housed or embedded in a host) rather than in a host computer. Controller-based arrays offer certain advantages:

➡ Controller-based arrays can survive the failure of a host, and can therefore continue to service I/O requests in a *clustered* computing environment.

➡ Controller-based disk arrays that use standard buses such as SCSI-2[21] to connect to hosts can be used with many different types of host computer. This makes the array's capabilities available to a wide range of operating environments.

➡ The *Array Management Function's* computing requirements are fulfilled by dedicated processors within the disk system's controller, and therefore do not affect application performance. This can be an important consideration for compute-intensive parity RAID (Levels 3, 4, or 5) algorithms.

➡ Controller-based arrays can more easily accommodate special disk requirements (e.g., rotational synchronization of disks, assisted device error recovery, etc.).

---

[21] Small Computer System Interface; the most widely used disk interface in the industry today. The *2* refers to the second major version of the interface, which was accepted as a standard in late 1994. Work is well underway on SCSI-3.

⇒ It is often easier to integrate a controller-resident *Array Management Function* with other I/O enhancement facilities (e.g., cache) for improved performance or data availability.

It is also possible to implement the *Array Management Function* in one or more host computers rather than in a controller.

RAID Advisory Board Definition
host-based array   A disk array whose *Array Management Function* executes in host computer(s) rather than in a disk system. The member disks of a host-based array may be *part* **of different** disk systems. *cf.* **controller-based array.**

Figure 14 illustrates a host-based disk array[22].

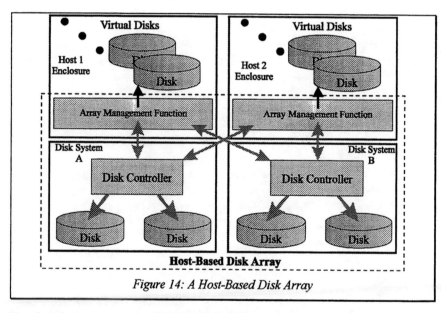

Figure 14: A Host-Based Disk Array

Host-based arrays are made up of conventional disk system components. The example illustrated in Figure 14 highlights two key differences between host-based and controller- or disk system-based disk arrays:

⇒ disks belonging to different disk systems may be members of the same host-based array.

---

[22] A complex multi-host system topology is deliberately illustrated to highlight the differences between host-based and disk system-based arrays. Most host-based array system topologies are considerably simpler.

➡️ the *Array Management Function* for a host-based array may be *distributed* in a multi-host configuration. This can be an important system and data availability consideration (the failure of one processor executing the *Array Management Function* does not make data stored in the array inaccessible), as well as a performance one for parity RAID (the RAID-related processing load may be distributed in proportion to processors' requirement for array I/O).

Neither of these is normally a feature of controller-based arrays.

Host-based arrays' advantages make them suitable for many applications:

➡️ Their inherent cost is negligible.

➡️ Since their member disks may be attached to multiple disk systems, host-based arrays may offer higher data availability[23] and I/O performance than controller-based arrays.

➡️ Host-based arrays can extend the useful life of installed disk systems that would not otherwise be array-capable. By installing a host-based *Array Management Function* for use with existing disk systems, users may realize many of the benefits of a disk array technology without the cost of a major storage upgrade.

➡️ Host-based arrays often permit more configuration options; (e.g., variable array sizes, arrays of different disk types, etc.). Moreover they can usually be reconfigured to meet changing requirements by operating system commands rather than by hardware actions (e.g., re-cabling or physical device removal and replacement), which may require service calls and/or hardware purchases.

The advantages of controller-based arrays are essentially the disadvantages of host-based arrays:

➡️ The *Array Management Function* uses the host computing resource. While this overhead should be negligible for RAID Levels 0 and 1, it is not for parity RAID (RAID Levels 3, 4, and 5). RAID-related computing load can be a major consideration for compute-intensive applications, and even for lightly loaded applications that are sensitive to I/O response time.

➡️ Array functions such as error recovery can be constrained because the interface to disks and host computers generally does not allow a host-based *Array Management Function* to exercise low-level control over array members.

➡️ It can be more difficult to effectively integrate host-based array functionality with related capabilities (e.g., write-back cache) in a general-purpose operating system context than in the dedicated context of an array controller.

Storage purchasers must sometimes choose between host-based and controller-based array alternatives, and should therefore appreciate these inherent differences between the two. Combining host-based and controller-based arrays is sometimes technically possible. For example:

---

[23] Including *disaster tolerance* (survival of a site failure) if the hosts can be distributed over a wide area.

➡ A host-based striped array whose members are controller-based mirrored arrays or parity RAID arrays can outperform a single disk system.

➡ In a multi-host cluster environment with widely separated hosts, a host-based mirrored array whose members are controller-based mirrored or parity RAID arrays can provide long-distance disaster tolerance with local failure protection at each site.

Disk Array Topologies

The *RAID* Advisory Board defines disk arrays in terms of data mapping (between virtual disk block addresses and member disk block addresses) only, and specifically excludes characteristics such as disk system or controller affinity, and hardware and interface type. In consequence of this definition:

➡ a single disk system can contain multiple disk arrays, or,

➡ disks attached to multiple disk systems can be members of a single (host-based) array.[24]

Figure 15 illustrates these cases. Array 1 and Array 2 are controller-based arrays whose member disks are attached to disk system α. Array 3 is a single host-based array whose member disks are attached to disk systems β and γ.

Many controller-based disk arrays are actually marketed as features of disk systems. Disk systems that include RAID capability are often simply called *disk arrays*, *RAID arrays*, or *RAID systems* by their vendors. The purchaser must understand what disk *array* capabilities are offered by a disk *system* product.

---

[24] The ANSI X3T10 SCSI-3 Controller Command Specification's definition allows even greater flexibility—arrays may have members that are themselves arrays. This feature has not appeared in products as yet, and the *RAID* Advisory Board has yet to define terminology for describing it.

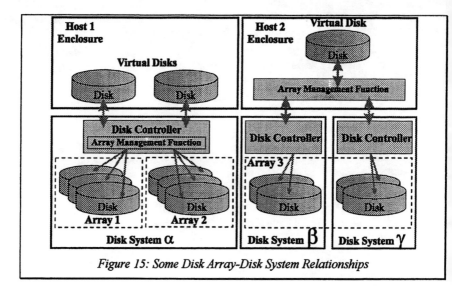

Figure 15: Some Disk Array-Disk System Relationships

The *Array Management Function*

The Host's View of a Disk Array

The purpose of disk arrays is to combine the capabilities of hardware components to produce a desirable net effect—either high data availability, high I/O performance, or a combination of the two. Ideally, the *Array Management Function* should make the array's virtual disks functionally identical to physical disks from an application standpoint.[25] All application I/O operations that are meaningful for a physical disk should have the same meaning when performed on the virtual disk presented by a disk array. The *Array Management Function* masks the internal complexity of the array from the operating environment by:

➡ *mapping*, or translating virtual disk block addresses to member disk block addresses so that I/O operations are properly targeted to physical disks,[26]

➡ *implementing I/O algorithms*, or translating each virtual disk I/O into one or more member disk I/O requests and controlling their execution so that disk-like behavior is achieved[27], and,

---

[25] Functional identity at the application level is specified because there are obvious exceptions at the management level. For example, formatting is either not meaningful for virtual disks, or has a different meaning than physical disk formatting.

[26] Most disks implement a further level of abstraction, and provide their host environments with a *logical* block interface. This is usually done to isolate hosts from media defects and disks' mechanisms for handling them internally. This book treats disk logical addresses as if they were physical addresses.

[27] Two fundamental properties of a disk that must be duplicated by disk arrays are: (a.) the data on any consecutively numbered sequence of blocks on the disk can be read or written in a single operation (up to some fairly large maximum limit); and, (b.) in the event of a failure while a write is in progress, the block being written is either completely written, not written at all, or subsequently reported as unreadable.

➡ *handling errors* so that disk-like behavior is presented to the host environment while the array's performance and data reliability goals are met. For RAID arrays, this includes regenerating data requested from a failed disk.

An array's virtual disks should be usable by higher-level host operating system components as if they were physical disks. In particular,

➡ file systems,

➡ record managers and database managers,

➡ system utility programs (e.g., backup programs, performance monitors, etc.), and,

➡ applications

should all function identically whether the data they operate on is stored on physical disks or the virtual disks of a disk array.

Disk Array Usable Storage Capacity

Every disk array has a *usable storage capacity*, or number of Mbytes available for storing application and operating environment data. Usable storage capacity is the sum of member disks' physical capacities minus any capacity required for check data and administrative overhead, and any unusable capacity.

➡ *Check data* is information derived from user data that protects against data loss due to disk failure. It is normally present only in RAID arrays.

➡ *Administrative overhead* is data used internally by the *Array Management Function* to maintain disk and array integrity. For example, most arrays use a small amount of member disk capacity to record a list of all member disks.

➡ *Unusable capacity* is capacity that cannot be used due to mapping restrictions. For example, in parity RAID arrays that permit different types of physical disks, but require that all member disk storage capacities be identical, part of a larger disk's capacity is unusable.

Some arrays use elaborate data mapping techniques that permit *over-commitment* of virtual disk capacity; that is, they permit total apparent virtual disk capacity to exceed the usable storage capacity available internally. Over-commitment may be achieved by:

➡ not *instantiating*, or assigning physical storage to, virtual disk data addresses until an application actually writes to them, and,

➡ compressing the data stored on member disks.

Disk arrays with these data mapping policies may emulate disks imperfectly. For example, a write request to a virtual disk may fail due to lack of underlying member disk space, even though its target is a valid range of virtual disk addresses. Conditions like this require the hosting environment to be aware that its on-line storage devices are more complex than conventional disks. The combination of economy and availability they achieve, however, generally makes users willing to bear the extra complexity.

Other Disk Array Considerations

Data Mapping and I/O Performance

In independent access arrays which use striped data mapping (described on page 271), the *stripe depth*, or number of consecutively mapped virtual disk blocks, can affect I/O performance strongly. Between them, the virtual disk's stripe depth and the I/O load's average request size roughly determine the average number of virtual disk I/O requests that must be split by the *Array Management Function* and satisfied by executing two or more member operations. *Split I/O requests* may be desirable or not, depending on an application's I/O requirements.

RAID Advisory Board Definition

split I/O request   An I/O request made to a virtual disk whose data mapping is such that the request must be satisfied by executing two or more member I/O requests to different member disks.

stripe depth   Synonym for strip size (q.v.). The number of blocks in a strip. Also, the number of consecutively addressed virtual disk blocks mapped to consecutively addressed blocks on a single member of a disk array. In the ANSI X3T10 SCC disk array model, stripe depth is constant for a p_extent (q.v.), but may vary among the p_extents comprising a virtual disk.

Figure 16 illustrates an I/O request execution time line, which subdivides overall request execution time into parts based on the resources used, and shows a relative execution time for each.

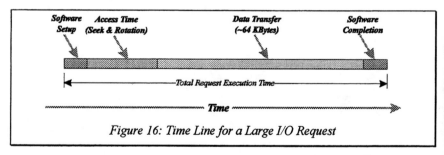

Figure 16: Time Line for a Large I/O Request

According to Figure 16, which is representative of a fairly large I/O request (e.g., 64 Kbytes or more for typical modern disks), I/O request execution time consists of:

⇒ the *software setup* time required to formulate the request in the host and communicate it to the disk system, and for the disk system to interpret it,[28]

⇒ an *access* time during which the target disk is seeking and rotating to a starting point from which the requested data can be transferred,

⇒ a *data transfer* time, during which data is moved between host memory and disk media,[29] and,

⇒ a *software completion* time during which disk system and host software report the completion status of the request to applications.

Based on typical modern disk parameters, Figure 16 qualitatively represents a large I/O request because data transfer time is large compared to software and access times.

Data Transfer-Intensive Application Performance

For application requests which specify large amounts of data (64 Kbytes or more), a significant portion of I/O request execution time consists of data transfer. If such *large requests* are made to a virtual disk whose stripe depth is small compared to the request size, then most application I/O requests to the virtual disk will result in split I/O requests.

RAID Advisory Board Definition	
large I/O request	An I/O request that specifies the transfer of a large amount of data. 'Large' obviously depends on the context, but typically refers to requests for 64 Kbytes or more of *cf.* **small I/O request**
small I/O request	An I/O, read, or write request that specifies the transfer of a relatively small amount of data. 'Small' usually depends on the context, but most often refers to 8 Kbytes or fewer. *cf.* **large I/O request**

Figure 17 compares execution timelines for an I/O request for data stored on a virtual disk in a 3-member independent access array with striped data mapping and a request for the same amount of data stored on a single disk.

---

[28] In disk systems with both intelligent controllers and intelligent disks, software overhead occurs in each. The distinction is not important for this discussion, however, and is not indicated in the figure.

[29] Disk data transfers include inter-sector time, track switching time, and inter-cylinder seek time. For the purposes of this discussion, these are considered part of the data transfer time.

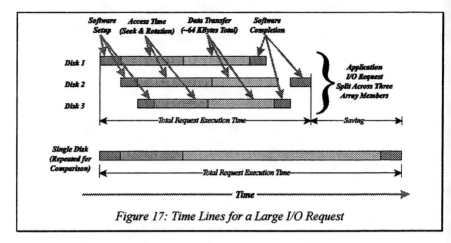

Figure 17: Time Lines for a Large I/O Request

Figure 17 is predicated on the following assumptions:

➡ The requested data is mapped evenly across the 3 member disks, indicated by the three data transfer segments being the same size. This is a somewhat idealized situation, used more to emphasize the point than to represent probable reality.

➡ Some software optimization is possible, indicated by a slight shortening of the individual request software setup and completion times compared to the single disk example repeated at the bottom of Figure 17.

➡ The *Array Management Function* uses a single processing resource, indicated by the sequential nature of the software set up and completion times (i.e., only one setup or completion occurring at any instant).

➡ The disks are not synchronized, indicated by varying access time from disk to disk.

➡ The disks are attached to separate channels, with no other I/O in progress on those channels, indicated by the absence of idle time (to wait for the channel resource).

In this example disk array data transfer time is shortened to a third of the single-disk value because the three member disks concurrently satisfy parts of the application request. Total execution time is substantially shorter than the single disk case, because data transfer time is large compared to access time.

I/O-intensive applications whose I/O loads are characterized by large I/O requests are called *data transfer-intensive* applications. In addition to their I/O requests being large, they are most often *sequential* (consecutive requests for adjacently located data), often because they are processing large files from beginning to end. For these I/O loads, split I/O requests are clearly advantageous. For data transfer-intensive applications that use disk arrays, the ideal I/O request size is an integer multiple of the virtual disk's stripe size, since that allows all member disks to contribute equally to satisfying each application I/O request.

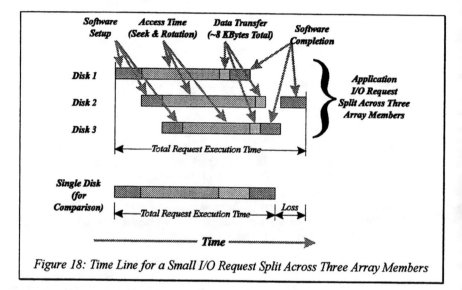

Figure 18: Time Line for a Small I/O Request Split Across Three Array Members

I/O Request-Intensive Application Performance

Another, more frequently encountered type of I/O-intensive application is the *transaction application*, which makes large numbers of small I/O requests. When a transaction application's I/O load is directed at a disk array, the effect of splitting I/O requests, illustrated in Figure 18, is quite different.

Figure 18 illustrates a small I/O request split across three members of a disk array. The same request serviced by a single disk is shown for comparison. For small I/O requests, data transfer time is a small part of total request execution time, so as Figure 18 illustrates, the increased software and access time add more than the time saved by parallel data transfer. For small I/O requests, not splitting across disks is advantageous.

These examples suggest that the ideal stripe depth for a striped disk array depends on the I/O load characteristics of the applications whose data it contains:

➡ For data transfer-intensive applications such as video, image processing, data capture and analysis, batch file processing, etc., the stripe depth should ideally force to most I/O requests' data transfers split as evenly as possible across all array members.

➡ For I/O request-intensive applications such as transaction processing, general purpose file services, office automation, etc., the stripe depth should ideally be set so that most I/O requests' data transfers do *not* split across multiple array members. This is difficult to guarantee because in theory, applications can request data transfers starting at any virtual disk address. A stripe depth of 10 to 20 times the application's average I/O request size usually eliminates 90-95% of split I/O requests, however.

Not all disk arrays permit the user to specify stripe depth, and not all disk array I/O loads can be neatly characterized as data transfer-intensive or request-intensive. For those that do meet these criteria, however, it can be advantageous to match an array's stripe depth to the expected application requirements.

Error Detection and Error Correction

All of the Berkeley RAID Levels protect against data loss due to one or more disk or media failures by recording redundant check data from which user data stored on a failed disk can be regenerated. RAID array check data is not used to detect errors, but to correct them once they are detected by conventional disk and I/O mechanisms. RAID Level 2 is an exception to this, and partly because it does not effectively use mechanisms that exist in any conventional disk to detect errors, is less cost-effective than other RAID Levels, and has not been widely implemented.

If check data is used only to correct errors (rather than to detect them as well), it can provide greater correction capability per bit of check data than if it must be used for both. With parity RAID (RAID Level 3, 4, or 5), the error location is known (e.g., from a disk or I/O failure indicator), before regeneration algorithms are invoked. Parity is therefore used only to correct an error in a known location. It is the combination of the block parity used in parity RAID and member disks' internal error detection mechanisms that provides the unique error correction power of RAID.

RAID and Defective Block Substitution

Disks may fail completely and become entirely unusable, or they may develop minor media defects that leave the disk as a whole usable, but cause data loss over a small media area. Disk error correction codes protect against such defects to a large extent, but the defects can become so severe as to render a block unreadable.

Many disks and disk systems protect against this by reserving *replacement block space* on their media. When a media defect is discovered, they substitute a block from this space for the defective one and transparently map all subsequent application requests to the substitute block. While it is extremely helpful in extending a disk's useful life, defective block substitution often cannot recover the data lost when the block is first discovered to be defective.

When the disk is part of a RAID array, however, data from a defective block can always be regenerated from redundant information stored on other array members. Defective block substitution mechanisms can therefore always be supplied with correct data to store in a replacement block.

Data Reliability and Data Availability[30]

RAID arrays enhance both data *reliability* and data *availability*.

RAID Advisory Board Definition	
data reliability	Expressed as *Mean Time to Data Loss (MTDL—q.v.)*. The length of the expected continuous span of time over which data stored by a population of identical disk systems can be correctly retrieved.
data availability	Expressed as *Mean Time to (Loss of) Data Availability (MTDA—q.v.)*. The length of expected continuous span of time over which applications can access correct data stored by a population of identical disk systems in a timely manner.

Because they increase the number of components in a disk system (e.g., extra disks, cables, controller channels), RAID arrays actually decrease a disk system's mean time between component failures. Because the additional components enable continued operation, however, RAID arrays more than compensate for higher component failure rate by greatly increasing the expected continuous span of time over which a disk system can be expected to do its job of storing and retrieving data.

The net effect of a RAID array is to allow a disk system to continue to operate after one or more of the disks in it have failed. Parity RAID arrays and mirrored arrays protect against single disk failures in this way. RAID Level 6 and three-member mirrored arrays protect against any two disk failures.

RAID also provides for the restoration of data protection if a functional disk can be substituted for the failed one. Restoration of data protection is called rebuilding, and is effected by regenerating (from user data and check data stored on the array's surviving members) the user data and check data that map to the failed disk (which includes any modifications made during the outage interval), and writing it to the substitute disk. The rebuilding of a high-capacity member disk's contents can take from tens of minutes to hours, and depends on:

➡ the complexity of the RAID data protection technique,

➡ the array's I/O channel data transfer capacities and degree of parallelism, and,

---

30 This section is based on material supplied by former *RAID* Advisory Board member Dynatek, whose contribution is gratefully acknowledged.

➡ the application I/O load on the array during rebuilding.

For mirrored arrays, all data from one member must be read from a surviving member and written to the replacement disk. Thus, rebuilding a mirrored array member requires that twice the capacity of a member be transferred.

For parity RAID arrays, all user data and check data from all surviving members must be read, and user data and check data for the replacement disk must be regenerated and written. Thus, rebuilding a parity RAID array member disk requires that an amount of data equal to the full capacity of a member disk times the number of members be transferred. Rebuilding obviously takes longer for parity RAID arrays with more members, although the increase in rebuild time can be less than linear for a disk system with a high degree of parallelism (Chapter 9). RAID array rebuild time is of interest because while rebuilding is occurring, an additional disk failure can cause data loss or unavailability.

When a disk fails, data may or may not be destroyed. If a failure that causes loss of data availability (a.) is repairable, and (b.) does not affect the storage media (e.g., a disk logic module failure), then it does not cause data loss.[31] Thus, MTDL and MTDA are separate measures of data protection.

RAID, with the obvious exception of RAID Level 0, increases data reliability by protecting data against loss due to disk failure. It also protects against loss of data availability due to disk-related failures. If a disk or a path to a disk in a RAID array fails, the data stored on that disk can be regenerated from redundant information stored on other disks, and applications can continue to read and write it (albeit at reduced I/O performance in some cases).

Other system components, however, including:

➡ controller channels,

➡ controllers,

➡ disk system cooling devices and power supplies,

➡ host I/O buses and interfaces,

➡ hosts computers, operating systems, and,

➡ application software,

may fail, causing loss of access to data until the failure is corrected. The technology to provide continued data access in the event of any of these failures exists, and often involves combining RAID with other failure-tolerance techniques such as:

➡ multiple paths from disk to controller,

➡ multiple controllers with common disk connections,

➡ multiple fans and power supplies,

➡ multiple paths from each disk controllers to hosts, and,

---

[31] RAID array disk failures that do not affect availability must all be regarded as causing loss of the copy of data stored on the failed disk, because even if it is retrievable, it is almost guaranteed to be out-of-date.

➡ "cluster" operating system technology which recognizes disk system, host, and application failures and adjusts to them.

A RAID *Array Management Function* provides continued data availability if the failure is in a disk component. If the failure is elsewhere, some other system mechanism must compensate. Figure 19 illustrates the difference between the data availability provided by RAID alone and that provided by a completely failure-tolerant system, using a mirrored array as an example.

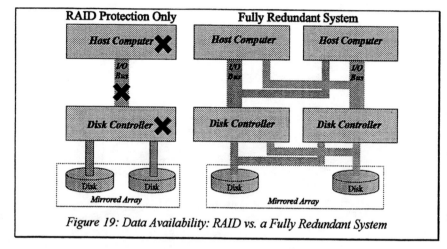

Figure 19: Data Availability: RAID vs. a Fully Redundant System

The system on the left in Figure 19 uses a mirrored array to protect against disk failures. A failure of either member disk leaves data available, but failure of any one of the system components marked with the symbol ✖ results in inaccessible data. Repair or replacement of the failed component is required before access can be restored.

The system on the right side of Figure 19 also uses a mirrored array to protect data against disk failures. In addition, however, it includes:

➡ dual paths from disk to controller,

➡ dual controllers,

➡ dual paths from each controller to each host,

➡ dual host computers.

In this system, any component can fail without affecting data availability (assuming that appropriate operating system and application mechanisms to recognize failures and take advantage of the redundant components and paths are present).

Both mirroring and parity RAID protect against data availability loss due to the failure of one array member. Neither of them, however, provides complete failure tolerance by themselves; they must be combined with other mechanisms such as redundant controllers that support *failover*, multi-host clustered system topology, and application failover for protection against failure of any system component.

RAID Advisory Board Definition

failover	The automatic substitution (q.v.) of a functionally equivalent system component for a failed one. The term failover is most often applied to intelligent controllers connected to the same storage devices and host computers. If one of the controllers fails, failover occurs, and the survivor takes over its I/O load.

Replacement of Failed Components

The process of replacing a failed component in a failure-tolerant disk system may or may not affect data availability. The *RAID* Advisory Board distinguishes among four different types of component replacement according to how they affect data availability.

RAID Advisory Board Definition

cold swap	The substitution of a replacement unit (RU—q.v.) in a storage system for a defective one, where power must be removed from the storage system in order to perform the substitution. A cold swap is a physical substitution as well as a functional one. *cf.* **automatic swap, hot swap, warm swap**
warm swap	The substitution of a replacement unit (RU—q.v.) in a disk system for a defective one, where in order to perform the substitution, the system must be stopped (caused to cease performing its function), but power need not be removed. Warm swaps are manual (performed by humans—cf. **auto-swap, cold swap, hot-swap.**
hot swap	The substitution of a replacement unit (RU—q.v.) in a storage system for a defective unit, where the substitution can be performed while the system is performing its normal function. Hot swaps are manual operations typically performed by humans—cf. **automatic swap, cold swap, warm swap.**

automatic swap	The functional substitution of a replacement unit (RU—q.v.) in a disk system for a defective one, where the substitution is performed by the disk system itself while it continues to perform its normal function (possibly at a reduced rate of performance). Automatic swaps are functional rather than physical substitutions, and do not require human intervention *cf.* **cold swap, hot swap, warm swap**

Disk array components that must be cold swapped clearly disrupt array data availability. Warm swapping also disrupts data availability, however, in some cases, the duration of service interruption may be only a second or two, which is negligible for many applications. In some RAID array designs, components can be hot swapped with no loss of data availability (since the array continues to run in reduced mode while the component swap takes place).

A still higher level of data availability can be provided by RAID arrays which are capable of automatically swapping in a pre-designated spare component to restore full RAID data protection, with no loss of availability.

Automatic swapping differs from cold, warm, and hot swapping in that it refers to functional rather than physical replacement. Swapping a disk into an operating but reduced array (e.g., to logically remove a failed array member and replace it with a spare) is a logical operation. It differs from the ability to physically swap a failed component disk for a replacement. For example, in a disk array system that only supports cold (physical) swapping of disks, a pre-designated spare disk might be automatically (logically) swapped into an array if required, but the failed disk cannot be replaced (physically) until the disk system is shut down.

Part 2: RAID Data Protection and Mapping Details

Chapter 3: Disk Array Data Management

Disk Array Data Protection and Mapping

A key role of the *Array Management Function* is to mask a disk array's internal complexity from applications by converting between virtual disk block addresses and physical block addresses on the underlying member disks. This translation is referred

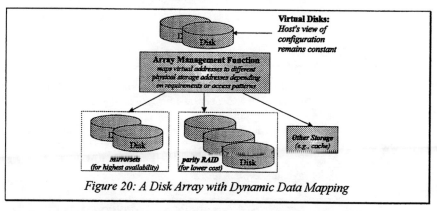

Figure 20: A Disk Array with Dynamic Data Mapping

to as *mapping* between virtual disk data addresses and member disk addresses.

Parity RAID, as defined by the Berkeley researchers, incorporates a geometrically regular mapping algorithm that makes it easy to locate the member disk address(es) corresponding to any given virtual disk address with minimal computation. Other mapping techniques are possible, however, including:

➡ *Tabular* mapping, in which an address correspondence table, usually in RAM, contains the mapping between virtual disk addresses and member disk addresses.

➡ *Dynamic* mapping, usually tabular, that can change the member address(es) to which a given virtual disk data address corresponds depending on changing requirements or usage patterns.

➡ *Non-linear* mapping, in which the member addresses corresponding to a given virtual disk data address may vary according to the data pattern stored. Non-linear mapping is usually a result of data compression.

Using combinations of these mapping techniques, some *complex arrays* (page 41) are able to map between two different disk architectures as illustrated in Figure 21.

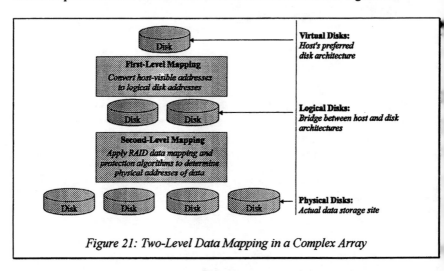

Figure 21: Two-Level Data Mapping in a Complex Array

In the example of Figure 21, the host's architectural view of disks differs from the architecture of the disks used to implement the array. The first-level mapping reconciles this difference by converting host-visible virtual data addresses into logical data addresses which are used by the second-level mapping function to locate data by applying geometric RAID mapping algorithms. This type of mapping is used in disk array systems that use fixed block architecture disks but present their host environments with virtual disks in count-key-data format.

RAID Advisory Board Definition

fixed-block architecture A model of disks in which storage space is organized as linear, dense address spaces of blocks of a fixed size. Abbreviated FBA. FBA is the disk model on which SCSI (q.v.) is predicated. *cf.* **count-key-data.**

---

count-key-data	A disk data organization model in which the disk is assumed to consist of a fixed number of tracks, each having a maximum data capacity. Multiple records of varying length may be written on each track of a count-key-data disk, and the usable capacity of each track depends on the number of records written to it. Count-key-data architecture, also known as CKD architecture, derives its name from the record format, which consists of a field containing the number of bytes of data, an optional key field by which particular records can be easily recognized, and the data itself. *cf.* **fixed-block architecture**

This chapter describes a data mapping model for the simpler geometric arrays in which virtual disk to member data address mapping is algorithmic. In this model:

➡ each virtual disk block is mapped to a constant number of member disk blocks (2 or more for mirroring; one for parity RAID),

➡ sets of consecutive virtual disk block addresses are mapped to consecutive member disk block addresses,

➡ consecutive sets of consecutive virtual disk block addresses are mapped to member disks in some cyclic fashion, and,

➡ check data for any given virtual disk data address is always found at the same member disk location.

While recognizing that tabular, dynamic, and non-linear mapping techniques exist, the *RAID* Advisory Board, began in 1992 to formally define an architecture for describing simple algorithmic data protection and mapping techniques with the characteristics enumerated above. The *RAID* Advisory Board felt that a common architecture for simple RAID arrays was important because these arrays comprised the vast majority of actual and planned implementations at the time. A common architecture adopted by a meaningful number of disk array vendors would enable common drivers and management software, promoting market acceptance of RAID technology. This chapter describes the work begun by the *RAID* Advisory Board, and later adopted by the ANSI X3T10 SCSI Controller Commands (SCC) Committee, and carried forward to draft standardization.

The ANSI X3T10 Disk Array Model

Thus far, this book has described disk arrays as consisting of collections of (physical) disks. The disk array data mapping architecture defined by the ANSI X3T10 SCC Committee is more general, however. It allows disks to be subdivided into one or more *extents* of consecutively addressed physical disk blocks, and for arrays to be formed from those extents. This additional level of flexibility provides several potential implementation benefits described throughout this chapter and the ones that follow.

To introduce the discussion of data mapping, the definitions of the terms *disk array* and *virtual disk*, or volume set are repeated from Chapter 2 (page 26).

RAID Advisory Board Definition	
disk array	A collection of disks from one or more commonly accessible disk systems, combined with an *Array Management Function* (q.v.). The *Array Management Function* controls the disks' operation and presents their storage capacity to hosts as one or more virtual disks. The ANSI X3T10 committee refers to the *Array Management Function* as a *storage array conversion layer* (SACL). The committee does not have an equivalent of the term *disk array* in the sense in which it is used by the *RAID* Advisory Board.
volume set	(An ANSI X3T10 term) A collection of user data extents (q.v.) presented to an operating environment as *a* range of *consecutive logical block* addresses. A volume set is the disk array object most closely resembling a disk when viewed by the operating environment.
virtual disk	Synonym for volume set (q.v.).

In an effort to foster adoption of the ANSI terminology, this book uses the more precise term *volume set* and the more intuitive and popular term *virtual disk* interchangeably, choosing the appropriate one for the context.

Member Disk Extents

The foundation of the ANSI X3T10 SCC data mapping model is the concept of *extents* of storage space.

RAID Advisory Board Definition	
extent	A set of consecutively addressed member disk blocks that is part of a single virtual disk-to-member disk mapping. A single member disk may have multiple extents of (possibly) different sizes, and may have multiple (possibly) non-adjacent extents that are part of the same virtual disk-to-member disk mapping. Extents are sometimes called *logical disks* (q.v.).

The purpose of extents is to subdivide the linear block address spaces of member disks for later steps in the mapping process. Figure 22 illustrates the concept of extents using the block address spaces of four disks[32].

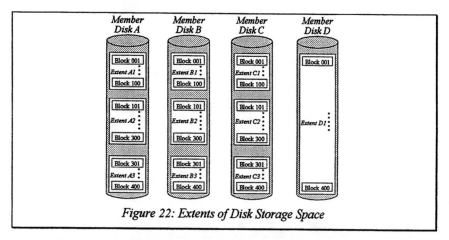

Figure 22: Extents of Disk Storage Space

In Figure 22, each of the labeled extents may be used either independently of or in conjunction with the others to construct a disk array. The extents defined on a disk need not all be of equal capacity. For example, in Figure 22, Extents A2, B2, and C2 each contain 200 blocks, whereas Extents A1, B1, C1, A3, B3, and C3 contain 100 blocks each. Extent D1 occupies the entire capacity of Member Disk D.

Within broad limits, extents may be used arbitrarily in constructing arrays. The dotted lines in Figure 23 illustrate some array possibilities:

➡ Extents A1 and B1 are combined into a mirrored array with 100 blocks of usable storage capacity.

➡ Extents A2, B2, and C2 are combined into a striped array with 600 blocks of usable storage capacity.

➡ Extents A3, B3, and C3 are combined into a parity RAID array with 200 blocks of usable storage capacity (after further mapping operations described below).

➡ Extent C1 is reserved for use as a replacement in case a failure that incapacitates any of Extents A1, B1, A3, B3, or C3. Extent C1 might also be used as a virtual disk by itself.

---

[32] Throughout this and later discussions of data mapping in this book, artificially small disks, extents, and other mapping entities are used to simplify the drawings and descriptions. The principles described pertain equally at realistic disk capacities.

➡ Extent D1 is used directly by the operating environment as a virtual disk.

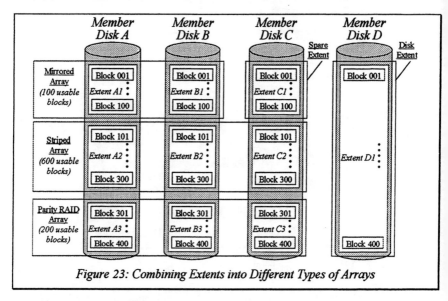

Figure 23: Combining Extents into Different Types of Arrays

The key properties common to all of these extents are:

➡ An extent consists of a fixed number of blocks located on a single member disk.

➡ An extent has a starting member disk physical block address.

➡ The physical addresses of the member disk blocks comprising an extent run consecutively from the starting block address.

These properties do not restrict how extents may be combined into higher-level mapping entities (e.g., virtual disks). For example, in principle:

➡ Multiple (consecutive or non-consecutive) extents located on the same member disk may be part of the same virtual disk.

➡ Extents of different sizes may be part of the same virtual disk.

Figure 24 illustrates these two configurations.

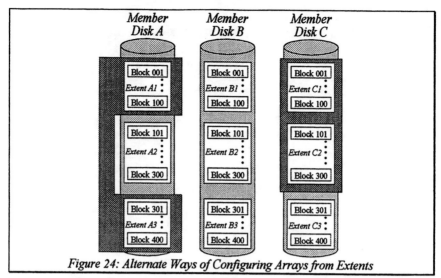

Figure 24: Alternate Ways of Configuring Arrays from Extents

In Figure 24, non-contiguous Extents A1 and A3 have been combined into an array of 200 blocks (assuming no space is reserved for check data). Extents C1 and C2 have been combined to make a 300-block virtual disk. These examples illustrate the generality of the ANSI X3T10 SCC disk array architecture model. This generality is present in the model because it allows flexibility in reallocating storage capacity to compensate for component failures and changing operational requirements.

Extents are normally used by a disk array's *Array Management Function*; they are not normally exposed to the operating environment. In user-configurable disk systems, they may be visible to the system manager during array configuration; otherwise they are completely transparent.

Extent Subdivisions: Strips and Stripes

Extents provide the basis for creating virtual disks by combining parts of member disks' block address spaces. The next step in data mapping is to establish the correspondence between member disk data addresses and virtual disk data addresses. This begins with the conceptual division of each extent into a number of identically sized *strips* of consecutively addressed blocks.

RAID Advisory Board Definition	
strip	A number of consecutively addressed blocks in a single extent (q.v.). The *ANSI* X3T10 SCC disk array architecture requires that all strips in an extent contain the same number of blocks. A disk array's Array Management Function uses strips to map virtual disk block addresses to member disk block addresses. Also known as stripe element.
strip size	The number of blocks in a strip (q.v.). The ANSI X3T10 SCC disk array architecture requires that all strips in an extent be of the same size. Also known as chunk size and stripe depth.

Strips result from dividing an extent into identically sized groups of consecutively addressed blocks. Strips are the basis for the striped data mapping that balances I/O load evenly across physical resources. Figure 25 expands the view of Extents A1, B1, and C1 from Figure 22 to illustrate the strip concept.

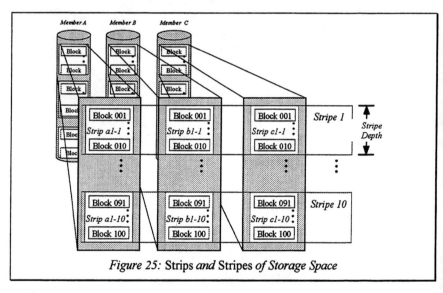

Figure 25: Strips *and* Stripes *of Storage Space*

In Figure 25, Extents A1, B1, and C1 each have a strip size of 10 blocks. Many disk systems allow the system manager to determine stripe size when arrays are configured. Matching strip size to application I/O load characteristics can sometimes have a large effect on I/O performance.

Figure 25 also illustrates the concept of *stripes*, or groups of strips in corresponding positions in each of an array's extents.

The ANSI X3T10 SCC disk array model requires extent stripe depth to be constant. In principle, the model allows different extents of the same virtual disk to have different stripe depths, although this offers no obvious advantage. For independent access arrays, extent stripe depth is an integral number of virtual disk blocks. Parallel access arrays in which stripe depth is a fraction of virtual disk block size have been discussed in the literature, but are seldom implemented for efficiency and simplicity reasons.

Stripe Depth and Virtual Disk Data Addresses

Figure 26 shows how stripe depth affects the mapping of virtual disk addresses to member disk addresses.[33] The stripe depth of the three extents shown in Figure 26 is 10 blocks. Every ten block addresses, the mapping of virtual disk block addresses moves to the next member extent.

The arrows in Figure 26 emphasize the progression of virtual disk addresses. In actual fact, the *Array Management Function* computes the :conversion between

➡ virtual disk addresses specified in application I/O requests, and,

➡ extent addresses to which member I/O requests are directed

using stripe depth and number of extents in the array as parameters. The first step in computing a member extent address from a virtual disk address is to divide the virtual disk address by the array's stripe depth:

virtual disk data address ÷ stripe depth = strip number (quotient) + block within strip (remainder) (a)

---

[33] Configuring virtual disks directly from *p_extents* (see page 263) is an oversimplification of the actual ANSI X3T10 SCC disk array model for tutorial purposes.

The extent on which the addressed block resides can then be computed:

$$member\ extent = [(strip\ number - 1) \div number\ of\ extents\ in\ stripe] + 1 \qquad (b)$$

where [...] denotes integer division with remainder discarded. Finally, the block address within the addressed extent can be computed:

$$member\ extent\ block\ address = member\ extent\ x\ stripe\ depth + block\ within\ strip \qquad (c)$$

These computations are the essence of the *mapping* performed by the *Array Management Function* in striped disk arrays.

Figure 26 illustrates a cyclic mapping in which ranges of virtual disk block addresses are mapped to successive strips of member extent block addresses in the regular repeating sequence A-B-C-A-B-C-etc. This corresponds to formulas (a), (b), and (c) given above. It is only one possible mapping, albeit a natural one. The ANSI X3T10 SCC disk array model specifically does not require this type of cyclic mapping.

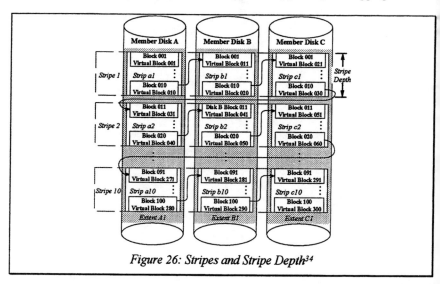

Figure 26: Stripes and Stripe Depth[34]

For independent access arrays, extent stripe depth is an integral number of virtual disk blocks, often chosen to be a multiple or sub-multiple of member disk track capacity.[35] Parallel access arrays in which stripe depth is a fraction of virtual disk block size as small as a bit or a byte have been discussed in the literature, but are seldom implemented for efficiency and simplicity reasons.

---

[34] Throughout this chapter and the following ones, unrealistically small numbers of blocks are used in order to illustrate the concepts without making the drawings overly complex.

[35] This is true for disks with a fixed track capacity. Modern disks are often *banded,* or organized into groups of contiguous cylinders, with each group having a different number of blocks per track, in order to increase storage capacity. For such disks, linking disk array mapping to physical characteristics makes less sense.

The concepts of strips, stripes and stripe depth are generally transparent to application users, but may be of importance to system managers, particularly with independent access arrays, where stripe depth is often adjustable for performance tuning purposes.

I/O Request Mapping

An important task of the *Array Management Function* is conversion of application I/O requests that specify virtual disk block addresses to member I/O requests specifying physical disk block addresses, and issuing these requests to member disks. For example, in the mapping illustrated in Figure 26, an application request to access data in virtual disk blocks 32-34 would be converted into a request to read blocks 12-14 of Member Disk A as follows:

virtual disk data address ÷ stripe depth = strip number (quotient) + block within strip (remainder) (a')

$$32 \div 10 = strip\ number\ 3 + block\ 2\ within\ strip$$

member extent = [(strip number - 1) ÷ number of extents in stripe] + 1 (b')

$$member\ extent = (3-1) \div 3 + 1 = 1$$

*member extent block address = member extent * stripe depth + block within strip* (c')

$$member\ extent\ block\ address = 1 * 10 + 2 = 12$$

Application I/O requests that require access to multiple members are known as a *split I/O requests*. The *Array Management Function* must perform any required splits transparently and route the data from each member to the correct host memory addresses or conversely. Again using Figure 26 as an example, the *Array Management Function* would split an application read request for virtual disk blocks 21-40 into:

➡ a request to read blocks 1-10 from member disk C, and,

➡ a request to read blocks 11-20 from member disk A.

Split I/O requests may be even more complex. An application request to a virtual disk may *wrap around*, and require multiple requests to the same member extent. An application request to read virtual disk blocks 1-40 of the array illustrated in Figure 26 would require:

➡ a request to read blocks 1-10 from member extent A,

➡ a request to read blocks 1-10 from member extent B,

➡ a request to read blocks 1-10 from member extent C,

➡ a request to read blocks 11-20 from member extent A.

Sophisticated *Array Management Functions aggregate* consecutive I/O requests to a member extent into a single request. If aggregation were possible in this example, the member I/O requests would consist of:

➡ a request to read blocks 1-10 from member extent A,

➡ a request to read blocks 1-10 from member extent B,

➡ a request to read blocks 1-20 from member extent C, and deliver them to two distinct ranges of host memory addresses.

Aggregation requires either an intermediate buffer in which data can be staged for delivery or hardware capable of mapping between consecutive I/O bus addresses and non-consecutive host memory addresses.

In the ANSI X3T10 SCC disk array model, stripe depth is constant (all strips in an extent contain the same number of blocks). All arrays which map virtual disk data addresses cyclically to member extent addresses necessarily incorporate the concept of stripes, giving rise to the term *disk striping*, used as a synonym for RAID Level 0.

Arrays with Multiple Virtual Disks: Partitions

The *RAID* Advisory Board's definition of the term *disk array* (page 253) states that an *Array Management Function* maps the block addresses of one or more member disks to block addresses of *one or more* virtual disks. There are several reasons why multiple virtual disks from a single array might be desirable:

➠ Operating system limitations, such as maximum disk size supported, can limit the virtual disk size that can be used effectively.

➠ Management considerations, such as charge back or convenient capacity for disk backups, may influence the optimal disk size for an installation.

➠ Applications may have been designed around commonly available disk sizes. These are typically considerably smaller than disk arrays' virtual disks.

Many *Array Management Functions* can subdivide usable array capacity into multiple virtual disks, or *volume sets*. Each virtual disk consists of all or part of one or more extents. When an array is presented as multiple virtual disks, the virtual disks are sometimes called *partitions*.

RAID Advisory Board Definition	
partition	A virtual disk (q.v.). The term partition is most often used when a redundancy group (q.v.) is presented as more than one virtual disk. Also used in complex arrays with dynamic mapping to denote a collection of redundancy groups that provides storage for a subset of an array's virtual disks.

Figure 27 illustrates disk array partitioning in a striped array. In Figure 27, Array A presents 3 partitions to the operating environment. Each partition has about the same capacity as one member disk,[36] so applications and system management procedures for the partitions can be designed as if they were for physical disks. From a performance standpoint, the partitions should provide the expected benefit of automatic I/O load balancing across physical I/O resources.

---

[36] Some arrays require that a small part of each member's storage capacity be reserved for *metadata*, or descriptive data about the array. In such arrays, the sum of the partitions' capacities is slightly less than the sum of the physical disks' capacities.

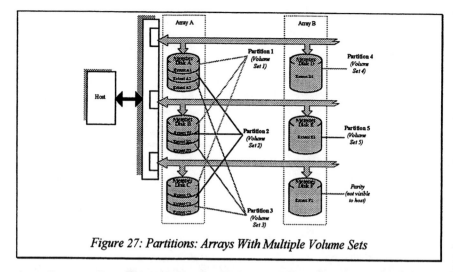

Figure 27: Partitions: Arrays With Multiple Volume Sets

Array B represents a parity RAID array using a stripe depth equal to the full extent size. In this case, extents D1 and E1 are each partitions, presented directly to the host environment as volume sets 4 and 5 respectively. Extent F1 is used to store check data, and is not presented to hosts.

The term *partition* in this context should be distinguished from two other storage-related usages:

➡ operating environment partitions of real or virtual disks that occur in UNIX and other operating system environments, and,

➡ the partitioning of groups of member disks into disjoint pools in complex arrays (see page 41) which map virtual disk addresses to member addresses dynamically.

Data Mapping in RAID Arrays

P_extents

Since RAID arrays hold check data in part of their storage capacity, their data mapping is necessarily more complex than that of non-redundant arrays. As it does with non-redundant disk arrays, the ANSI X3T10 SCC disk array model provides architectural standardization while leaving room for technical innovation.

As with non-redundant disk arrays, the data mapping concept for RAID arrays is based on member disk extents. To distinguish them from other kinds of extent objects in the model, extents of physical storage capacity on member disks are called *physical extents*, or *p_extents*.

RAID Advisory Board Definition	
physical extent	(An ANSI X3T10 term) A number of consecutively addressed physical blocks on an array member disk. Physical extents are created by *Array Management Function* as building blocks from which redundancy groups and volume sets are created. Commonly called p_extent.
p_extent	(An ANSI X3T10 term) Physical extent (q.v.)

A *p_extent* may be part of a single member disk to virtual disk mapping.[37] In principle, a single disk may contain multiple *p_extents* of (possibly) different sizes, and may contain multiple (possibly) non-adjacent *p_extents* that are part of the same higher-level mapping entity.

Redundancy Groups

Conceptually, an *Array Management Function* divides a disk's physical storage capacity into one or more *p_extents*. For purposes of data protection, collections of these *p_extents* are organized as self-contained *redundancy groups*.

RAID Advisory Board Definition	
redundancy group	(An ANSI X3T10 term) A collection of p_extents organized by an *Array Management Function* for the purpose of providing data protection. Within one redundancy group, a single type of data protection is used. All of the user data storage capacity in a redundancy group is protected by check data stored within the group, and no user data capacity external to a redundancy group is protected by check data within it.

---

[37] This book treats the disk blocks comprising a disk's block address space as physical entities (that is, blocks whose media location can be derived from their addresses and knowledge of disk geometry), even though for disks which recover from media defects by re-mapping defective blocks, this is not strictly accurate.

Within a redundancy group, a single form of data protection, either parity RAID, mirroring, RAID Level 6, or some other vendor-unique technique, is employed. Figure 28 illustrates the general concept of redundancy groups.

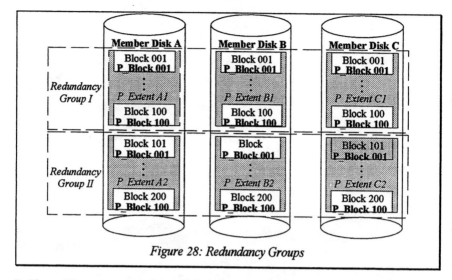

Figure 28: Redundancy Groups

In Figure 28, *p_extents* A1, B1, and C1 comprise a redundancy group, as do *p_extents* A2, B2, and C2. Protection for user data stored within Redundancy Group I is provided exclusively by check data located within Redundancy Group I's *p_extents*, and similarly for Redundancy Group II. As a consequence, the usable capacity of either redundancy group is necessarily less than the 300 physical blocks they each contain.

The blocks in a *p_extent* are considered to be numbered consecutively from a starting value (1 in Figure 28) with *p_extent block numbers*. In Figure 28, *p_extent* block numbers are denoted by the label P_Block. In the ANSI X3T10 SCC disk array model, the sole purpose of *p_extent* block numbers is to help describe the organization of *p_extents* into higher-level constructs. *p_extent* block numbers are *not* the virtual data addresses specified in application I/O requests.

RAID Advisory Board Definition

p_extent block number   (An ANSI X3T10 term) A conceptual position assigned to a block within a p_extent (q.v.). p_extent block numbers are used only to develop higher-level constructs in the *ANSI* X3T10 SCC disk array model, and not for data mapping purposes.

Redundancy Group Storage Capacity

Within a redundancy group, the storage capacity reserved for redundant information may be concentrated in a single *p_extent*, or it may be distributed across some or all of the redundancy group's *p_extents*.

When a *p_extent* is made part of a redundancy group, is is associated with some type of data protection, and therefore has a *usable storage capacity* equal to the total number of blocks it contains minus the number reserved for check data. The usable storage capacity of a *p_extent* that is part of a redundancy group is called its *protected space*. The blocks of protected space in a *p_extent* are considered to be numbered sequentially in the same order as their *p_extent* block numbers. The protected space in a redundancy group *p_extent* is known as a *protected space extent*, or *ps_extent*.

RAID Advisory Board Definition

protected space, protected space extent   (An ANSI X3T10 term) The storage space available for application data in a p_extent (q.v.) that is part of a redundancy group. Also called *ps_extent*.

ps_extent   (An ANSI X3T10 term) Protected space extent (q.v.)

A *ps_extent* occupies the same physical area as the *p_extent* containing it, and contains no more protected space than the number of blocks in the *p_extent* containing it.

Like *p_extent* block numbers, *ps_extent* block addresses are not used for reading and writing data, but for configuration operations. Figure 29 illustrates redundancy group block addressing, and contrasts it with *p_extent* block addressing.

Figure 29 illustrates a parity RAID redundancy group in which parity is distributed across all *p_extents*. Each *p_extent* consists of 6 blocks and its corresponding *ps_extent* has 4 blocks available for storing data. (In Figure 29, each protected space block's *ps_extent* block number is shown below its *p_extent* block number). In configuration operations, these would be referred to as *PS_Blocks 1-4*. Two blocks in each *p_extent* are reserved for storing parity. These are not considered part of the protected space. They have no *ps_extent* block numbers, and are invisible to configuration operations involving redundancy groups.

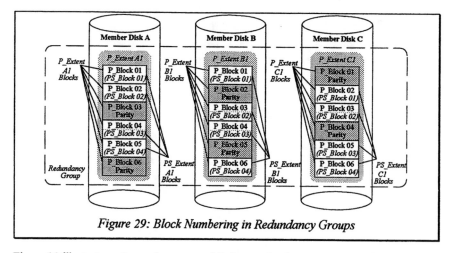

Figure 29: Block Numbering in Redundancy Groups

Figure 30 illustrates a 3-member array with three redundancy groups configured, each employing a different type of RAID protection.

In Figure 30, each of Redundancy Group I's *ps_extents* has 2 blocks of protected space. Because check data is distributed in a rotating pattern (commonly associated with RAID Level 5), the blocks of protected space are in different relative locations in each member *p_extent*.

Redundancy Group II also illustrates parity RAID protection, but with all check data stored in a single *ps_extent*. The *ps_extents* in *p_extents* A2 and B2 are completely available for user data, but all of *p_extent* C2 capacity holds check data.

Redundancy Group III is a 2-way mirrored array. All of the *ps_extent* in *p_extent* A3 is available for user data. All of the *ps_extent* in *p_extent* B3 is reserved for check data (a copy of the contents of the *ps_extent* in *p_extent* A3).

The *p_extent* on Member Disk C labeled *p_extent spare* illustrates an important reason for organizing member disk capacity into *p_extents*. Since its physical capacity is the same as that of the other eight *p_extents* pictured, it can, in principle, substitute for any of them that might become unusable. *p_extents* reserved for this purpose are called *p_extent spares*, or, when the meaning is clear from the context, simply *spares*.

Redundancy Group Stripes

Redundancy groups in which check data blocks are distributed across the redundancy group's *p_extents* in a regular cyclic way are said to contain *redundancy group stripes*.

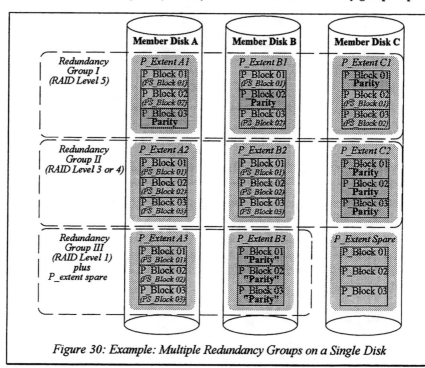

Figure 30: Example: Multiple Redundancy Groups on a Single Disk

RAID Advisory Board Definition
redundancy group stripe (An ANSI X3T10 term) The correspondingly numbered consecutive sequences of p_extent blocks in each of the member p_extents of a redundancy group. The blocks in a redundancy group stripe are either part of the protected space or reserved for check data.
redundancy group stripe depth (An ANSI X3T10 term) The number of consecutively numbered blocks in one p_extent of a redundancy group stripe. The RAID Advisory Board definition requires redundancy group stripe depth to be constant for an entire redundancy group.

Redundancy group stripe depth is the frequency with which check data location rotates among a redundancy group's *p_extents* in a parity RAID array. A parity RAID

---

array with all of its check data located on a single *p_extent* (e.g., Berkeley RAID Level 4) has a single redundancy group stripe whose depth is the size of one of the array's *p_extents*. Figure 31 illustrates redundancy group stripes in a parity RAID array with distributed check data.

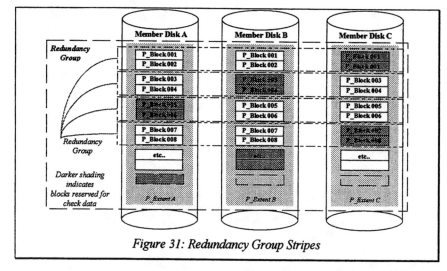

Figure 31: Redundancy Group Stripes

In Figure 31, the shaded areas represent *p_extent* blocks reserved for check data. The redundancy group stripe depth for this example is 2 blocks. In each *p_extent*, 2 blocks of every 6 are reserved for check data. (The *ps_extent* size for the *ps_extents* contained in *p_extents* A, B, and C is therefore 2/3 of the capacity of the *p_extents*.)

In the ANSI X3T10 SCC disk array model, redundancy group stripe depth is used only to declare the frequency with which space reserved for check data rotates among *p_extents*. It need not be the same as the stripe depth defined on page 61, which determines the rotation frequency of virtual disk block addresses, although the two are often the same in practice.

User Extents and Volume Sets

Redundancy groups are defined solely for the purpose of organizing *p_extent* storage capacity for data protection. They are not normally visible to RAID array users, except possibly when an array is configured. A redundancy group's *ps_extents* collectively represent storage capacity available for user data. *ps_extents* may be subdivided into *user data extents*, from which *volume sets*, also known as *partitions*, or *virtual disks*, may be constructed.

RAID Advisory Board Definition	
user data extent	(An ANSI X3T10 term) A collection of consecutively numbered ps_extent blocks. In RAID arrays, collections of user data extents comprise the *volume sets,* or *virtual disks,* presented to the operating environment.
user data extent stripe depth	(An ANSI X3T10 term) The number of consecutive ps_extent blocks in a single user data extent that are mapped to consecutive volume set block addresses. Each user data extent in a volume set may have a unique user data extent stripe depth, which may differ from the redundancy group stripe depth of the ps_extent in which it resides. **partition** A virtual disk (q.v.). The term partition is most often used when a redundancy group (q.v.) is presented as more than one virtual disk. Also used in complex arrays with dynamic mapping to denote a collection of redundancy groups that provides storage for a subset of an array's virtual disks.
virtual disk	Synonym for volume set (q.v.).
volume set	(An ANSI X3T10 term) A collection of user data extents (q.v.) presented to an operating environment as *a range of* consecutive logical block addresses. A volume set is the disk array object most closely resembling a disk when viewed by the operating environment.

Figure 32 illustrates a virtual disk whose user data extent stripe depth differs from its redundancy group stripe depth, and also illustrates the concept of partitions, or multiple virtual disks allocated from a single redundancy group.

In Figure 32, each *ps_extent's* usable storage capacity is 2/3 that of the *p_extent* in which it resides, because two blocks of every six are reserved for check data. A 12-block user data extent has been allocated from each of the *ps_extents* in *p_extents* A1, B1, and C1. These three user data extents are organized as a volume set with a usable capacity of 36 blocks. These user data extents do not encompass all of the usable storage capacity in their respective *ps_extents,* so additional user data extents could be allocated in the same redundancy group, and organized into additional volume sets, or *partitions.* The ability to create multiple partitions within a single redundancy group allows users to define virtual disks whose capacities are convenient for application or system management purposes, but which share a common data protection mechanism.

The user data extent stripe depth illustrated in Figure 32 is 4 blocks. The arrows indicate the resulting progression of virtual disk block addresses. In implementations that allow it to be adjusted by the system administrator, user data extent stripe depth can help optimize an array's characteristic I/O performance for specific types of I/O load.

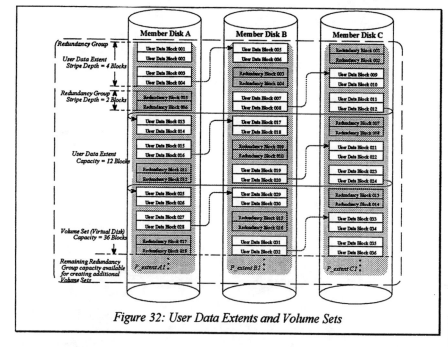

Figure 32: User Data Extents and Volume Sets

Why So Complex?

Defining data mapping in terms of *ps_extents* and user data extents, each with its own stripe depth is somewhat complex, but it provides great flexibility to array designers and, when mapping parameters are adjustable at configuration time, to system managers as well. The model defined in the foregoing sections accommodates a variety of array configurations, including:

➡ volume sets constructed from *p_extents of differing capacities,*

➡ multiple partitions using a common data protection technique from the same set of member disks,

➡ a wide range of volume set data mapping options, allowing I/O performance to be tuned to application requirements,

➡ distribution of check data across some, but not all of an array's members, for expandable arrays with partially distributed check data.

Examples on the following pages illustrate each of these uses of the model.

P_Extents of Different Capacities

Figure 33 illustrates a volume set made up of two small user data extents and one larger one. Striped user data mapping with no check data is illustrated, since data protection in configurations such as this raise complex questions of failure modes.

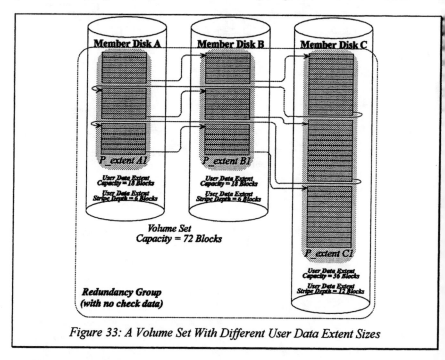

Figure 33: A Volume Set With Different User Data Extent Sizes

In Figure 33, 18-block user data extents from *p_extents* A1 and B1 have been combined with a 36-block user data extent from *p_extent* C1 to produce a 72-block virtual disk. The arrows indicate the progression of virtual disk block addresses. Although few implementations support this generality, it might be useful in arrays designed to take advantage of disks with different storage capacities. Because the performance of such a virtual disk would be very difficult to predict, configurations such as this are probably best suited to applications with light I/O loads.

Multiple Volume Sets With Common
Data Protection

Figure 34 illustrates two volume sets, or *partitions,* whose user data extents are allocated from *ps_extents* in the same redundancy group. Partition I has a usable capacity of 36 blocks, and Partition II has a usable capacity of 48 blocks. Configurations like this are useful when applications, operating environments, or administrative considerations require multiple disks of specific capacities with the same data availability characteristics. In arrays that support this function, identical data protection is afforded all virtual disks (because their user data extents are allocated from the same redundancy

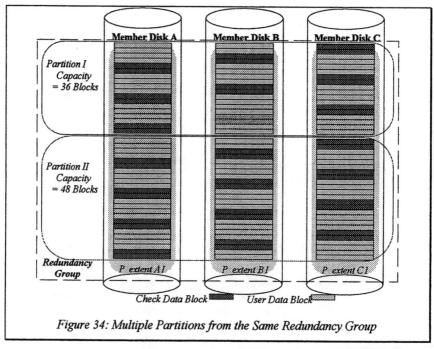

Figure 34: Multiple Partitions from the Same Redundancy Group

group), but virtual disk capacities can be set as required.

Using User Data Extent Stripe
Depth to Influence I/O Performance

Figure 35 illustrates the use of user data extent stripe depth to control how virtual disk data addresses map to user data extent blocks in two different partitions, hence influencing the relative I/O performance characteristics of those partitions.

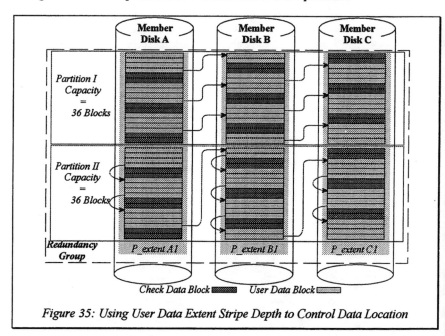

Figure 35: Using User Data Extent Stripe Depth to Control Data Location

In Figure 35, the user data extent stripe depth of Partition I is 4 blocks. Thus, as indicated by the arrows, Partition I blocks 5-8 are located in protected space in *p_extent* B1, blocks 9-12 in protected space in *p_extent* C1, and so forth. This mapping method tends to balance I/O load across an array's physical resources. With this method, however, it can be difficult to add storage capacity to a volume set without completely dismantling and rebuilding it.

Mappings that Allow Addition of
Storage Capacity

In Figure 35, Partition II's user data extent size is the full capacity of the *ps_extent* from which it is allocated (12 blocks). Thus, Partition II blocks 1-12 are allocated from protected space in the second *ps_extent* of *p_extent* A1, blocks 13-24 from protected space in the second *ps_extent* of *p_extent* B1, and blocks 25-36 from protected space in the second *ps_extent* of *p_extent* C1. This mapping method provides less automatic load balancing than that illustrated for Partition I, but, since virtual disk block addresses increase only when moving between successive *ps_extents*, it is theo-

---

retically possible to add capacity to Partition II without removing all user data from it and rebuilding it.

Partial distribution of Check Data

Building on the example of Partition II in Figure 35, Figure 36 illustrates a data mapping in which check data is distributed across some, but not all, of an array's *p_extents*.

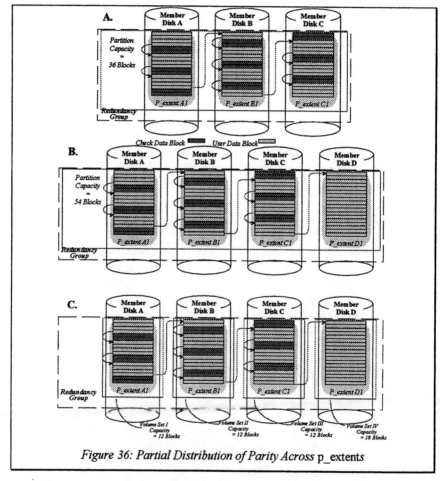

Figure 36: Partial Distribution of Parity Across p_extents

Figure 36 A illustrates a volume set identical to Partition II in Figure 35, with user data block addresses mapping in succession to complete *ps_extents* on each member disk. In Figure 36 B, a member disk (P_extent) has been added to the array. Because of the nature of the mapping, virtual disk data addresses that map to P_extent D1 may simply be appended to the previously existing virtual disk data addresses, effectively enlarging the virtual disk.

To operating environments, partitions represent disks. Most operating environments cannot accommodate the concept of a disk whose capacity can grow (or shrink). For those that can, however, Figure 36 B represents a non-disruptive method for adding protected storage capacity.

Figure 36 C illustrates how storage capacity may be added to most operating environments with little or no disruption. In Figure 36 C, the protected space in each *ps_extent* is allocated to a separate volume set. The original array presents three volume sets to its operating environment. When Member Disk D is added to the array, a fourth volume set is created. None of the original three volume sets is disturbed. Most operating environments can accommodate the addition of disks; at worst, a re-boot of the operating system is required. The key consideration in both Figure 36 B and C is that even though check data may have to be completely re-computed when a disk is added to the array, no movement of user data is required, so disruption to the host environment is minimal.

The array configurations represented in Figure 36 B and C do not naturally balance I/O loads. They forego one advantage of arrays with striped data mapping in favor of the capability to accept additional *p_extents* (e.g., additional member disks) without disrupting access to pre-existing user data.

Subsets of the Model

Today (1996), many disk array implementations do not support the full generality of the ANSI X3T10 SCC disk array model. It is fairly common for disk arrays to require:

⇒ member disks to be of the same type and storage capacity,

⇒ each member disk to consist of a single *p_extent* occupying most or all of its usable capacity,

⇒ each *p_extent* to contain a single *ps_extent* occupying its entire capacity,

⇒ all user data extent capacities to be equal to each other, and equal to the full *ps_extent* size, and,

⇒ redundancy group stripe depth to be equal to user data extent stripe depth.

Examples on the following pages illustrate parity RAID array mappings that result from these restrictions.

Common Distributed Parity RAID
Array Mapping

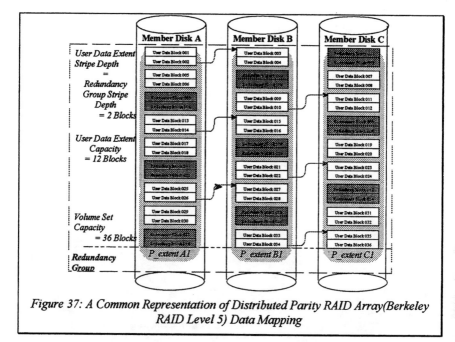

Figure 37: A Common Representation of Distributed Parity RAID Array(Berkeley RAID Level 5) Data Mapping

When the restrictions listed in the preceding section are used in defining a distributed parity RAID array, the result is a familiar array data mapping often illustrated in the literature and reproduced in Figure 37. This mapping is commonly associated with Berkeley RAID Level 5.

In Figure 37, each *p_extent* contains 18 blocks. Check data is distributed evenly throughout the redundancy group, so for a three-disk array, each *ps_extent's* protected space is 2/3 of the capacity of the *p_extent* that contains it, or 12 blocks.

The redundancy group stripe depth and the user data extent stripe depth are both two blocks. As with all data mapping examples in this chapter, the capacities shown are artificially small, both to simplify the drawings and to more clearly illustrate the principles involved. More realistic mappings using today's disks would have *p_extent* capacities in the 2-4 Gbyte (4-8 million block) range. Stripe depths for this type of array are typically 100-300 blocks.

Conceptual Concentrated Parity
RAID Array Mapping

When the restrictions listed in the preceding section are used in defining a parity RAID array whose check data is concentrated in one *p_extent,* and whose stripe depth is small, the result is a familiar array data mapping often illustrated in the literature and reproduced in Figure 38. This type of mapping is commonly associated with Berkeley RAID Level 3.

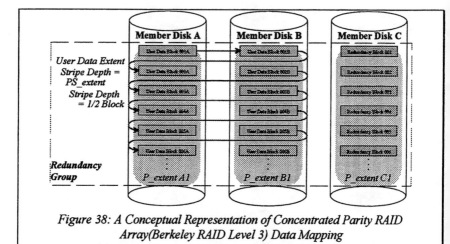

Figure 38: A Conceptual Representation of Concentrated Parity RAID Array(Berkeley RAID Level 3) Data Mapping

In all of the foregoing examples, both redundancy group stripe depth and user data extent stripe depth have been illustrated as multiple virtual disk blocks. Figure 38 illustrates a different application of the model—a stripe depth that is a fraction of the virtual disk block size. In principle, if the disks in this example were rotationally synchronized, the data transfer portion of every I/O request would complete in half the time required for a comparable disk. The difficulties with this approach are:

➡ Many disks are not capable of synchronized operation.

➡ Since the entire array participates in every I/O request, only one request at a time can be executed. This leads to comparatively poor transaction I/O performance.

➡ Most important, smaller physical blocks uses disk capacity inefficiently.

Thus, while this configuration is conceptually attractive, it is not often implemented in its pure form. Most parity RAID implementations use a stripe depth that is a multiple of the virtual disk block size, whether or not check data is distributed.

For simplicity, these restrictions are employed in the more detailed descriptions of the Berkeley RAID Levels in the following chapters.

Chapter 4: Disk Striping and Mirroring

The Origins of RAID

This chapter describes disk *striping* and *mirroring*. Like all the RAID descriptions in this part of the book, this chapter only discusses the implications of data protection and mapping. Other capabilities commonly incorporated in disk systems to improve I/O performance and data availability are discussed in Part 3 (beginning on page 149).

Disk mirroring was certainly the first, and may still be be the most widely implemented, form of RAID data protection. Disk striping is a data mapping technique that is widely used, both with and without RAID data protection, to enhance I/O performance. Both striping and mirroring can be implemented either in:

➡ parallel access arrays in which all member disks participate equally in the execution of every I/O request, or,

➡ independent access arrays in which individual member disks may respond concurrently to different I/O requests.

Independent access implementations of both striping and mirroring are by far the more common.

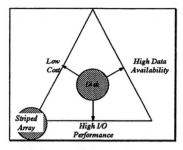

Disk Striping: High I/O Performance at Low Cost

The name *disk striping* is usually used to denote a cyclic mapping of strips of data across an array's member disks. Because it does not protect data against disk, channel, or media failure, a striped disk array is not a RAID array, but a technique for improving I/O performance (compared to that of an equal number of independent disks) for a wide variety of I/O-intensive applications. Since cyclic data mapping is common in parity RAID arrays, the name *RAID Level 0* is widely used to describe disk striping, even though the technique provides no data protection.

Striped Data Mapping

Figure 39 uses a five-member striped array mapped to a single virtual disk to illustrate striped data mapping.

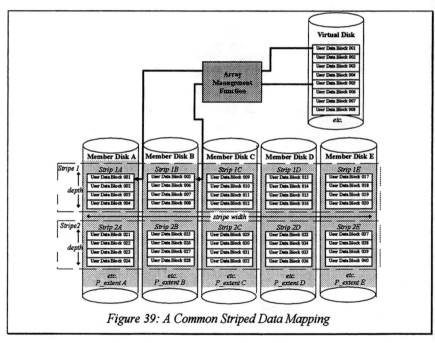

Figure 39: A Common Striped Data Mapping

In the ANSI X3T10 SCC disk array model, the *stripe depth* (number of blocks in a strip) is constant for an entire array. The set of corresponding strips on all array members is collectively called a *stripe*. In Figure 39, strips 1A, 1B, 1C, 1D, and 1E comprise the array's first stripe.

The regularity of the data mapping illustrated in Figure 39 makes it simple to convert application I/O requests to the virtual disk into I/O operations on the underlying member disks. *Array Management Function* overhead is insignificant, so striped arrays can be implemented either in a host or within the disk system. Both are in common use.

Host-based striped arrays are useful in applications that require greater single-stream data transfer capacity than one disk system can provide. Host-based striping can combine the data transfer capacities of multiple disk systems (which may themselves support striped arrays) to support very high single-stream I/O transfer rates.

The *strips* illustrated in Figure 39 are ranges of consecutive block addresses. Strips are not normally part of a host's view of a virtual disk; they are shown in Figure 39 to emphasize the 1:1 correspondence between virtual disk storage capacity as viewed by the host and physical storage capacity within the array.

In the host's view of the virtual disk, all of the data blocks in a stripe are consecutively addressed. By making a single request for the amount of data in a stripe, an application can get all of an array's member disks to work for it simultaneously.

Normal Operation Of Striped Disk Arrays

A striped disk array's *Array Management Function* processes applications' virtual disk read and write requests identically:

1. The application's virtual disk starting block address is converted to a member disk number and a block address on that member as described on Page 63. Since stripe depth is constant, this conversion consists of a division to determine strip number within the array, a second division to determine which member contains the referenced strip, and an addition to determine the starting block number.

2. If the amount of data requested is such that the entire application request can be satisfied from the strip containing the starting block, the *Array Management Function* makes one member I/O request. If the application's request maps to multiple *p_extents* located on different array members, the *Array Management Function* makes one or more requests to each affected member. An optimization for large transfers (discussed below) is possible if the application request maps to multiple adjacent strips on a single member.

3. The *Array Management Function* usually makes all required member I/O requests at the same time (or at least asynchronously with each other). Concurrent member operations are possible, provided that the disk system has adequate hardware resources for request processing and data movement. Concurrent member I/O operations is the main reason that striped arrays complete large I/O requests faster than a single disk whose performance is equivalent to that of one array member.

4. When all member requests are complete, and data has been delivered to the application (or received from it and written to member disks), the *Array Management Function* signals the application that its virtual disk request is complete.

An Important Optimization For
Large I/O Requests

If a computer system or disk system is capable of *scatter reading* and *gather writing*, and the *Array Management Function* takes advantage of this capability, large I/O request performance can be substantially enhanced.

An application I/O request for more than the usable capacity of one stripe necessarily results in transfers from adjacent strips on at least one member disk The array's *Array Management Function* could make two I/O requests to each member disk so affected, with the second executing immediately after the first completed.

If the computer system can *scatter read* and *gather write*, however, all of the requested data that maps to one member disk can be read or written with one member I/O request. *Scatter reading* is the ability to deliver data blocks stored at consecutive disk addresses to non-consecutive memory addresses. *Gather writing* is the ability to deliver blocks of data stored at non-consecutive memory addresses to consecutively addressed disk blocks. Figure 40 illustrates scatter reading used to deliver strips 0 and 4 of a five-strip application request with one request to Member Disk 1.

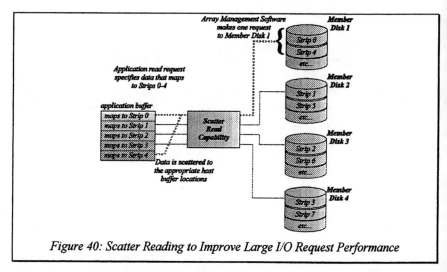

Figure 40: Scatter Reading to Improve Large I/O Request Performance

In Figure 40, an application read request maps to Strips 0-4 of the 4-member array. Strips 0 and 4 are consecutively located on Member Disk 1. Since the array is able to scatter read, it makes a single request for two strips of data to Member Disk 1. The scatter reading facility, which may reside either in the host or in the array's intelligent controller, directs the two strips of the data stream from Member Disk 1 to the appropriate part of the application's buffer.

Gather writing is similar. If Figure 40 represented an application write request, data fetched from host memory or from controller buffers for writing to Member Disk 1 would be *gathered* so that the first strip of the Member Disk 1 write is satisfied from the first part of the host data stream, and the second is satisfied from the last part (which may be non-consecutively located in host memory or controller buffers). Data from intervening strips 1-3 would be written to other member disks in separate member requests.

Failure Protection In Striped Arrays

Improved I/O performance is the only reason to use a striped array without some form of data protection. Striped arrays do not protect against data loss due to member disk failure. A striped array's virtual disk typically contains a single copy of the host operating system's space management structural data. Striped mapping distributes both structural data and user files across the array's members. Failure of a member disk results in "holes" in structural data or files that render them unusable.

From a practical standpoint, failure of one member of a striped array is equivalent to failure of the entire array. If the Mean Time Before Failure (MTBF) of a single disk is λ hours, then the MTBF of a striped array of N such disks is λ/N hours. For example, if a single disk MTBF is 500,000 hours (about 57 years), a striped array of four such disks has an MTBF of a little over 14 years[38].

A striped array is thus unsuitable for valuable data that cannot easily be reproduced, or for data critical to system operation. It is more suitable for data that can be reproduced or is replicated on other media, or data whose unavailability does not prevent the system from carrying out the critical part of its mission. If striped array-type performance and high data reliability are required simultaneously, one solution is to relax the cost constraint and combine striping with mirrored arrays as described in Chapter 8.

Striped Array I/O Performance

Striped arrays provide high performance for most *I/O-intensive* applications. I/O-intensive applications generally make one of two kinds of demands on an I/O system.

➡ *High data transfer rate:* Reading or writing a large amount of data per unit time, usually in a single stream. Applications such as decision support, data warehousing, computer assisted design, image processing, data collection and reduction, and sequential batch file processing require high data transfer rates.

➡ *High throughput* or *I/O request rate:* Executing large numbers of I/O requests per unit time. Generally, the requests are small,[39] and specify a non-sequential assortment of data addresses. Applications such as interactive transaction processing, office automation, and multi-user I/O or file services require high I/O request rates.

Seldom does a single application require both high data transfer rate and high I/O request rate simultaneously.

---

[38] This simplistic analysis ignores the fact that there may be more components in the four member array than just the four disks (e.g., controllers, power and cooling components etc.). MTBF of a real array would be lower than the computation indicates.

[39] As described in Chapter 2, the *size* of an I/O request refers to the amount of data specified to be read or written.

Given an adequate underlying hardware configuration, a striped array can significantly improve either of these types of I/O performance compared to a single disk or independent disks. When used primarily as a parallel access array (i.e., with a small stripe depth compared to average I/O request size) it can improve single-stream data transfer rate. When used primarily as an independent access array (with a large stripe depth compared to average I/O request size), it can improve I/O request rate.

Striped Arrays And High Data Transfer Rate

For an application to realize a high data transfer rate from a striped array, two conditions must be satisfied:

1. There must be adequate data transfer capacity along the entire path between host memory and disks.

2. The application must make adequate data demands to the disk system.

The first requirement not only implies that there must be enough disks in the array for the sum of their full-volume, or, *spiral* data transfer rates to at least equal the application's data transfer rate requirement, but also that there must be sufficient data transfer capacity at each stage between host memory and the disks. This includes disk channels, internal controller buses, host I/O buses, host adapters, and host memory buses.

RAID Advisory Board Definition

full-volume data transfer rate   The average rate at which a single disk transfers a large amount of data (more than one cylinder). The full-volume data transfer rate accounts for any delays (e.g., due to inter-sector gaps, inter-track switching time and seeks between adjacent cylinders) that may occur during the course of a large data transfer.

spiral data transfer rate   The full-volume data transfer rate (q.v.) of a disk.

The second requirement implies that the application must deliver a continuous stream of work to the disk system. A disk's maximum transfer rate occurs when it reads or writes data continuously as it spins (with minor interruptions for track and cylinder switching). For this to occur, there must constantly be an outstanding request for data as it spins past the disk's selected read/write head. This means that:

➡ The application must make requests for relatively large amounts of consecutively located data.

➡ The application must constantly have requests outstanding so that disk revolutions are never "missed" (i.e., elapse without any data being transferred because no request is outstanding). This usually means that the application must *double buffer* its I/O requests, i.e., that it must have at least two requests for consecutively located data outstanding at all times, one being executed by the disk system and one ready for execution as soon as the preceding one is complete.

Ideally, an application using a striped array to achieve a high data transfer rate would match the size of its requests to a multiple of the array's stripe size. If the application fails to do this, then not all array members participate equally in every transfer. This almost guarantees missed revolutions on at least some array members because no I/O request is outstanding when data passes the disk heads.

An application need not match its transfer request sizes to a parallel access array's stripe size as long as it keeps multiple requests outstanding so that when one is finished the next is ready for immediate execution. This assumes that the combination of *Array Management Function* and member disks can make the transition between requests rapidly enough to avoid missing revolutions.

Striped Arrays And High I/O Request Rate

I/O request-intensive applications require a high rate of I/O request execution, but do not usually require that a great deal of data be transferred in each request. Requirements for thousands of small I/O requests per second are not uncommon. As Figure 18 (page 45) illustrates, the execution time for such I/O requests is dominated not by data transfer time, but by motion of the disk heads (seeking) and platters (rotational latency) required to reach the starting point of the desired data.

Independent access striped arrays can provide very high I/O request execution rates for these applications by *balancing* the I/O load across the array's disks. An independent access striped array usually outperforms the same number of independent disks because the striping of virtual disk blocks across all array members tends to balance I/O load. Files stored on a virtual disk are likely to span multiple member disks. Whether the application has a frequently accessed "hot" file, or whether it accesses multiple files, the effect is the same—I/O requests tend to map evenly across member disks.

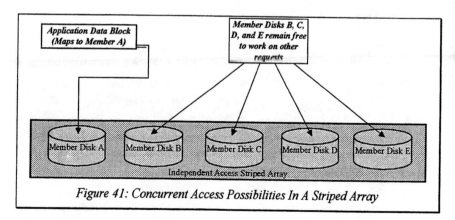

Figure 41: Concurrent Access Possibilities In A Striped Array

Figure 41 illustrates the performance improvement potential of load balancing. While Member Disk A is busy servicing a user request, Member Disks B, C, D, and E remain idle. Assuming a uniform distribution of data addresses, if a second request arrives before the first is complete, there is an 80% probability that the disk to which its data maps will be free to begin servicing it immediately.

Parallel access striped arrays do not perform well in I/O request-intensive applications. Because its member disks operate in unison, a parallel access array only executes one I/O request at a time. With synchronized disks, data transfer time is lower due to concurrent transfer(as discussed on page 45), but for small I/O requests, this is a minor part of total execution time. For small requests, the I/O performance of a parallel access array is only a little better than that of a single disk.

With independent access striped arrays, balancing of I/O request-intensive loads occurs automatically, provided that multiple application I/O requests are outstanding most of the time. An *Array Management Function* can only keep all of the array's hardware resources busy if it has multiple concurrent application I/O requests to process. An independent access striped array performs like a single disk if the application waits until one I/O request is complete before making the next.

Fortunately, most applications with high I/O request rate requirements are structured to make their I/O requests *asynchronously* so that multiple requests tend be outstanding at any instant. This may occur because:

➡ the application itself does its I/O asynchronously (i.e., it is *multi-threaded*),

➡ the application uses a multi-threaded data manager (e.g., a database manager) that makes I/O requests asynchronously on its behalf;

➡ the application consists of multiple processes, each of which makes synchronous I/O requests (resulting in an asynchronous I/O stream), or,

➡ multiple applications operating asynchronously with each other access data stored on the same array.

Where Striped Arrays Do Not Perform Well

Striped arrays without additional supporting performance enhancements are not particularly suitable for:

➡ *applications which read or write small amounts of sequentially located data.* These applications spend most of their I/O time waiting for disks to rotate to the starting location of the requested data, whether or not they use striped arrays for storage. The I/O performance of such applications can sometimes be improved by software tuning (e.g., by raising the operating system *blocking factor* for the application's heavily used files). If this is not possible, application changes (e.g., to make larger I/O requests) are required.

➡ *applications which make synchronous requests for small amounts of non-sequential data.* If these applications cannot be modified to make asynchronous requests, or to use a data management tool that will make asynchronous requests for them, the only way to improve their I/O performance is to move their data to storage devices with higher single-stream performance, such as RAM disks or non-volatile solid state disks.

Applications for Striped Arrays

Compared to RAID arrays, striped disk arrays are not well-suited for on-line storage of "important" data. They can, however, can be useful for storing:

➡ *program image libraries or run-time libraries.* These libraries are normally read-only. They can be backed up on reliable storage devices (e.g., RAID arrays) for security, while a copy on a striped array can provide rapid application access.

➡ *large tables or other read-only data structures.* Like program images, these data can be backed up on reliable storage, while an active copy on a striped array provides rapid application access.

➡ *data collected from external sources at very high transfer rate.* This works best where the data is reproducible by repeating the process which produces it. In some cases, the data acquisition rate and amount of data may be so high that there is no alternative to disk striping.

RAID Level 1: Disk Mirroring for Enhanced Data Availability

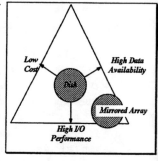

RAID Level 1, or *disk mirroring*, protects against data loss due to disk failure by keeping at least two copies of data written to the virtual disk on separate member disks. Some implementations allow for three or more copies of data. Mirrored disk arrays offer very high data reliability, albeit at a relatively high inherent cost (because all disks and connecting hardware must be duplicated). For many I/O-intensive applications, mirrored arrays can also significantly improve I/O performance compared to individual disks.

A mirrored array may consist of a single set of disks with usable storage capacity equal to that of one member,[40] or it may consist of multiple sets of mirrored disks with striped data mapping and a usable capacity equal to that of the smallest member multiplied by the number of mirrored sets. Vendors sometimes refer to multi-set mirrored arrays by names such as *RAID Level 0&1*, and *RAID 10*, probably to emphasize the combination of mirrored data and striped data mapping.

---

[40] Most arrays use a small part of each member disk's capacity to store descriptive information about the array, so usable array capacity is actually slightly less than the capacity of one member.

Description of Disk Mirroring

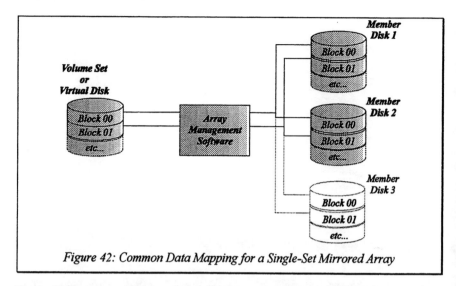

Figure 42: Common Data Mapping for a Single-Set Mirrored Array

Figure 42 illustrates a common virtual disk-to-member disk data mappings for a single-set mirrored array. Mapping to a single virtual disk is illustrated for simplicity.

Each virtual disk block in Figure 42 is mapped to a corresponding block on each of the array members. Thus there is always at least one available copy of data, even if a member disk fails. In single-set mirrored arrays, striped mapping is not advantageous; usually all of each member's available storage capacity is organized as a single *p_extent* with a stripe depth equal to its full size. In multi-set arrays, data striping may be useful, however, as illustrated in Figure 43.

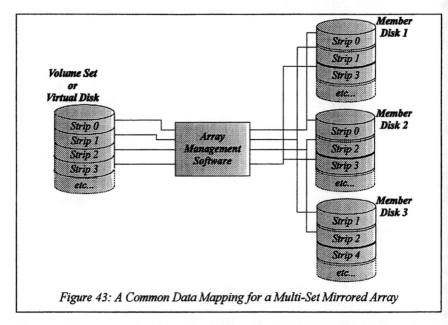

Figure 43: A Common Data Mapping for a Multi-Set Mirrored Array

Figure 43 illustrates a 3-member mirrored array in which successive strips are mapped cyclically to pairs of members. For simplicity, mapping to a single virtual disk is shown. Copies of data written to block addresses in virtual disk Strip 0 are stored on member disks 1 and 2. Virtual disk Strip 1 blocks are written to member disks 2 and 3, and so on. Two copies of every virtual disk strip are stored on separate member disks. The resulting virtual disk capacity is 1.5 times the capacity of a member disk.

Multi-set mirrored arrays with striped data mapping balance I/O load in addition to providing mirrored data protection. A request to read strips 0-2 from the array illustrated in Figure 43 could potentially result in concurrent transfers to or from all three members. Strip 0 could be read from Member Disk 1, Strip 1 from Member Disk 3, and Strip 2 from Member Disk 2.

Normal Operation Of Mirrored Arrays

In principle, a mirrored array can be implemented using either parallel access or independent access. In practice, virtually all mirrored arrays are independent access implementations, so this section describes mirrored array operation from that point of view.

Because application write requests require that check data be updated, a mirrored array's *Array Management Function* processes read and write requests differently.

For read requests, the *Array Management Function*:

1. *selects* the member or members to handle the request. Some implementations have a designated master disk to which all application reads are directed, and use the

---

mirror copy only when the master fails. Others attempt to balance I/O load by executing successive requests using alternate members. Still others choose the least busy member, or the member whose read/write head is closest to the requested data.

2. *converts* the virtual disk addresses specified in the application request to member disk block addresses. Single-set mirrored arrays usually map virtual disk addresses directly to *p_extent* equivalents. For multi-set mirrored arrays with striped mapping, more elaborate mapping is required.

3. *schedules* the member read request(s). From this point on, virtual disk requests that map to a single member disk are equivalent to read request to independent disks. Read requests that map to multiple member disks require the *Array Management Function* to coordinate member request execution so that completion is not reported to the application until data from all members has been delivered.

4. *reports* completion of the virtual disk request to the application.

When an application makes a write request to a mirrored array, all copies of the data must be updated. For a multi-set array, member writes must be scheduled for all members to which data maps. For example, writing data that maps to Strips 0 and 1 of the array illustrated in Figure 43 requires member writes to all three member disks.

For write requests, the *Array Management Function*:

1. *determines* which members must be updated because application data block addresses map to them.

2. *schedules* write requests to all array members to which application data maps. In most implementations, member writes execute concurrently, so the average elapsed time for writing to a mirrored array's virtual disk is only slightly greater than the time for writing to a single disk.

3. *reports* completion of the virtual disk request to the application. For proper data integrity, this should be done only when *all* member writes are complete, and all copies of data on member disks are identical.

Even though the average execution time for a write request to a mirrored array is not much greater than that for a single disk, the physical resource requirement is a multiple of that for individual disk writes. This can be an important capacity planning consideration for write-intensive applications which use mirrored arrays for data storage.

The foregoing paragraphs describe the behavior of mirrored arrays consisting only of disks and an *Array Management Function*. Part 3 (starting on page 149) describes the effect of performance enhancements like cache on mirrored array behavior.

Failure Protection in Mirrored Arrays

Mirrored arrays protect against both data loss and loss of access to data in the event of member disk failure. When a mirrored array member disk fails, its *Array Management Function* simply directs all application requests to surviving members. There is normally little performance impact when a mirrored array is *reduced* (operating with a failed disk). In a two-member array, however, there is no further protection against the failure of the surviving disk.

Recovering From Disk Failures

Because of their high inherent cost of, users tend to reserve mirrored arrays for their most valuable data. The value of data stored on a mirrored array usually means that it important to restore full protection after a failure:

➡ as quickly as possible, and,

➡ without interrupting application access to data.

If a replacement disk is available, or can be made available, the *Array Management Function* can *rebuild* surviving member contents on the replacement disk while application I/O to the array's virtual disks continues.

While a mirrored array member is being rebuilt, application updates must be accurately reflected on all members, including the one being rebuilt. One *Array Management Function* strategy is to maintain a progress indicator indicating how far the rebuilding operation has progressed. For application write requests that map to member *p_extent* addresses higher than the progress pointer, the member being rebuilt need not be written. Those that do not must be satisfied by accessing a survivor. Figure 44 illustrates a rebuilding operation using a progress indicator.

Using a progress indicator can reduce overhead during rebuilding, but requires careful synchronization to insure that application writes for

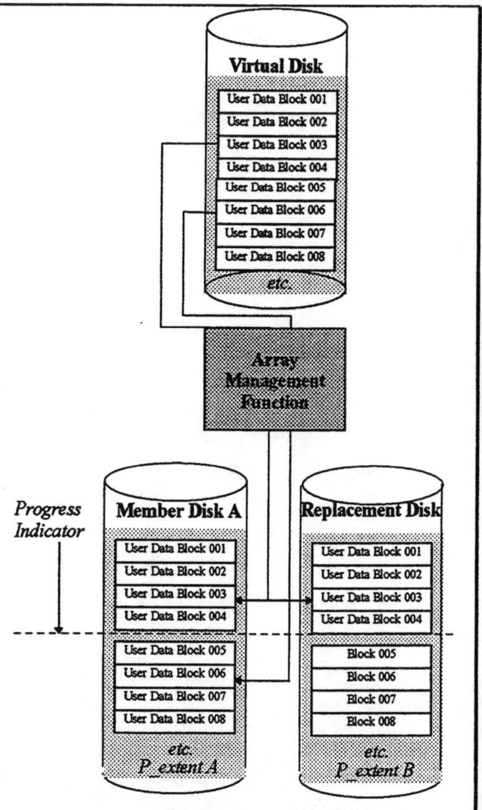

Figure 44: Using A Progress Indicator To Rebuild A Mirrored Array

which the data spans the position of the progress indicator while the progress indicator is changing are handled correctly.

An alternate rebuilding strategy is not to maintain a progress indicator, but to reflect all application writes on all members, including the one being rebuilt. This strategy may result in some needless writes to the member being rebuilt (application writes that map to block addresses greater than the point to which rebuilding has advanced), but it reduces the complexity of the *Array Management Function*.

Similarly, application reads during rebuilding must be directed to array members containing up-to-date data. If a progress indicator is maintained, then reads that map to block addresses below the progress pointer can be directed to any array member. If no progress pointer is maintained, then the member being rebuilt cannot be used for reads until rebuilding is complete.

Data Consistency After A Disk System Failure

A more complex scenario arises when a mirrored array's *Array Management Function* fails, either by itself or as a consequence of an overall disk system failure. For example, in a two-member array, an application I/O request outstanding at the time of *Array Management Function* failure may leave the array in any of four states:

1. neither member disk updated,

2. both member disks updated,

3. member disk A updated; member disk B not updated, or,

4. member disk B updated; member disk A not updated.

After it restarts, the *Array Management Function* must ensure that identical data is stored on all array members. Various strategies are possible to restore an array to a known consistent state.

Without a persistent[41] logging mechanism to record the state of operations in progress, the *Array Management Function* cannot determine whether any update operations were in progress at the instant of failure without reading and comparing all contents of all array members. Furthermore, when a discrepancy is found, the *Array Management Function* cannot distinguish between cases 3 and 4 above. Unless the *Array Management Function* updates array members synchronously in a fixed order (severely degrading responsiveness), there is no way to determine which member's contents are newer when the two do not agree.

The best that can be done in mirrored arrays with no logging mechanism is to make member contents identical so that consistent (new or old) data is delivered for every application read request, no matter which member satisfies it. To do this:

➡ Every block on each member disk must be read and compared with corresponding block(s) on other member disk(s).

➡ If there is a mismatch, the block must be overwritten so that all member disk contents agree.

---

[41] A persistent log is one whose contents can be written prior to and retrieved after an *Array Management Function* failure. It allows *Array Management Function* to determine the state of operations in progress at the time of the failure.

Reconciliation of member contents can take substantial time. The desired objective of presenting consistent data to applications can be achieved immediately after restart, however, by a second *Array Management Function* thread operating in parallel which:

➡ reads every block requested by an application from all members, and writes the data delivered to the application to all members whose contents disagree, or,

➡ reads every block requested by an application from an arbitrarily chosen member and writing it to all member disks but the one from which it was read.

Figure 45 illustrates the latter policy for a two-member array. In Figure 45, whenever an application requests data during a merge operation, it is read from both members. One copy is delivered to the application. If the two copies differ, the data delivered to the application is also written to the second array member. Without knowledge of which data is newer, which member's data is delivered to the host is immaterial.

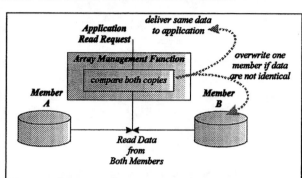

Figure 45: Reading Data From A Mirrored Array After An Array Management Function Failure

In most situations, it is likely that only a few blocks of a mirrored array are being updated at any instant. To minimize the work required to reconcile member contents, some mirrored arrays include a persistent log[42] so that after a restart, the *Array Management Function* can quickly determine which block addresses may be inconsistent (because updates were in progress at the time of failure), and make the data at those addresses consistent across all members.

One simple form of log is a bitmap, with each bit corresponding to a range of block addresses. When the *Array Management Function* begins an update, it first sets the bits that correspond to block addresses that will be modified. When the update completes successfully, the bits are reset. If the *Array Management Function* fails, only blocks that correspond to bits set in the map must be reconciled.

Mirrored Array I/O Performance

For I/O request-intensive applications with a high percentage of reads, the I/O performance increase from distributing reads among members (discussed on page 94) far outweighs the penalty for writes. I/O performance for read-intensive applications can

---

[42] Non-volatile Random Access Memory (*NVRAM*) is sometimes used for this.

approach a multiple of that of a single disk. For applications which predominantly write data, however, the mirrored write penalty can be significant.

Multi-set mirrored arrays can further improve data transfer performance for large I/O requests by striping if requested data maps to multiple members. Single-set mirrored arrays may also improve large read performance if they split each read request so that two or more members participate in its execution. The latter optimization is seldom implemented, however.

For write requests, data must be written to each array member. While member writes can be concurrent, resulting in a minimal increase in elapsed execution time, they do require data transfer resources (disk and channel time). Capacity planning for data transfer-intensive applications with high write percentages must take this into account.

Mirrored arrays require nominal extra processing (compared to a single disk) for generating and tracking member I/O requests. This extra processing is generally negligible, even for host-based arrays.

I/O Performance During Rebuilding

Rebuilding a mirrored array member is I/O intensive. Fundamentally, every block of the member being rebuilt must be read from some surviving member, and written to the replacement disk. While restoring full protection by completing the rebuild operation as quickly as possible is normally desirable, I/O operations occasioned by the rebuild seriously degrade application I/O performance. Some implementations allow the system manager to restrict the resources used in rebuilding in order to limit the effect on application responsiveness. Restricting the speed of rebuilding increases Mean Time To Repair (MTTR), and hence the risk that a second failure will cause loss of data or access to it.

Mirrored Array Applications

Mirrored arrays offer very high data reliability and improved performance for read-intensive applications compared to individual disks of comparable performance. Balancing this is relatively high inherent cost, primarily due to the additional disks and connections required, since each GByte of usable capacity requires two (or more) GBytes of physical storage capacity.

Thus, mirrored arrays are suitable for data for which reliability requirements are paramount, or for data to which high-performance access is required, and for which cost of storage is secondary.

Mirroring is also the only suitable RAID technique for *disaster tolerant* systems, in which copies of data are stored at a long distance from each other, and kept in synchronization using private or public network facilities. The purpose of disaster tolerant systems is to provide continuous data access, even if an entire site should be incapacitated, for example by fire or flood. A complete copy of data at the surviving site is obviously required for disaster tolerance. Widely separated mirrored disk arrays often have mirrored or parity RAID arrays as members so that they provide local failure tolerance as well as disaster tolerance.

A third application for which mirrored storage is uniquely suited is the *cloning* of on-line data by making each of an application's disks into a mirrored array. Cloning is often used to obtain a consistent copy of an application's data for backup purposes with minimal application outage. If each of an application's disks is made into a mirrored array (by a management operation that does not interrupt application service), then as soon as all arrays are consistent (all live data has been copied to the newly added disks), the application can be stopped for an instant to assure data consistency, and the clones separated from the original on-line disks. The clones can then be used as source data for a backup while the application resumes, using the original data.

Mirrored Arrays As System Disks

Because computer systems' *system disks* typically contain so much data and software that is critical to system operation, system managers often want to mirror it to improve overall system availability. It is also common, however, for the system disk to be the disk from which the operating system itself is *bootstrapped* (loaded into memory for execution). Since bootstrapping is a primitive operation, usually built into the host computer's hardware without consideration for RAID, a RAID array used as a system disk must either:

➡ emulate a disk sufficiently closely to be transparent to the bootstrapping process, or,

➡ be integrated with the bootstrapping process so that the latter is aware of any unique characteristics it has.

Transparency to the bootstrapping process is typically possible with controller-based mirrored arrays provided that the arrays can be pre-configured by some external means. Many disk systems include serial interfaces for configuration and management.

Integration with the bootstrapping process, on the other hand, is more likely to be characteristic of host-based mirrored arrays. It is typically found in environments where the mirroring software is supplied by the computer system vendor.

In either case, when one is configuring a system in which *all* storage will be in the form of RAID arrays, it is important to ascertain that the arrays to be used are sufficiently disk-like to be used for bootstrapping the host computers' operating systems.

Chapter 5: Parity RAID Data Protection

Lowering The Cost Of Data Protection

Parallel Access RAID Arrays

Parallel access disk arrays are those which inherently require that all member disks be accessed, and in particular, written, concurrently for every application access to a virtual disk. For this reason, parallel access arrays generally provide very high data transfer rates, but low I/O request rates.

[Patterson88] identified two inherently parallel data protection models, RAID Levels 2 and 3. Striped and mirrored arrays may be implemented using parallel access techniques, but do not inherently require it.

RAID Level 2: A Historical Footnote

As described in [Patterson88], a RAID Level 2 array's user data and check data are interleaved across several disks. The check data described was a *Hamming code*, similar to those often used for error detection and correction in RAM and during data transmission. The Hamming code both detects and corrects errors, so RAID Level 2 does not make full use of the extensive error detection capabilities built into disks. Properties of the Hamming code also restrict possible RAID Level 2 array configurations, particularly the ratio of check data to user data. For these reasons, RAID Level 2 has not been widely implemented.

In view of the lack of RAID Level 2 implementations, the RAID Advisory Board has never defined requirements for arrays using this technology.

Parity RAID

Three of the RAID Levels introduced in **[Patterson88]** have collectively become known as *parity RAID* because they share a common data protection mechanism. RAID Levels 3, 4, and 5 all use the concept of bit-by-bit *parity*, or modulo-2 count of "1"-bits in corresponding positions on each member disk, to protect against data loss and loss of data access due to a single disk, channel, or media failure.

Parity RAID Data Protection

In principle, the term *check data* refers to any kind of redundant information that allows *regeneration* of unreadable data from a combination of readable data and the redundant information itself. RAID Levels 3, 4, and 5 all utilize the Boolean **Exclusive OR** function to compute check data. The function is applied bit-by-bit to corresponding strips in each of an array's user data extents, and the result is written to a corresponding parity strip. Figure 46 illustrates how the **Exclusive OR** function can be applied to data stored in a parity RAID array. In Figure 46, *p_extents* A, B, C, and D contain user data, and *p_extent* E contains the result of a bit-by-bit **Exclusive OR** computation on user data from all four user data *p_extents*.

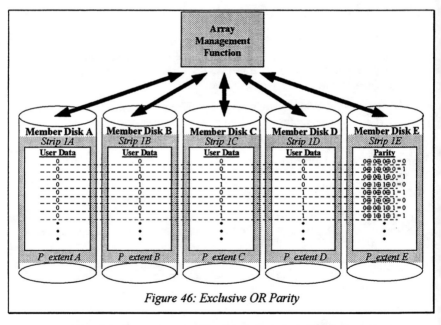

Figure 46: Exclusive OR Parity

Three properties of the **Exclusive OR** function make it desirable as check data:

➡ It is simple to generate, either in software or by an easy-to-implement hardware assist. Simplicity keeps implementation cost low for developers and minimizes I/O performance impact for users.

➡ It is simple to use when user data cannot be read. Again, simplicity keeps implementation cost low and minimizes application I/O performance impact.

➡ It can be applied to an arbitrary number of data extents. Data in a 20 p_extent array would be protected precisely as data in the 5-member array illustrated in Figure 46. This allows the system designer, and in many implementations, the user, to decide between lower cost (more user data protected per unit of parity) and statistically higher data availability (fewer disks protected per unit of parity).

Parity RAID vs. Mirroring

Parity RAID provides the same type of data protection as mirroring—protection against data loss and loss of access to data due to a single disk-related failure. If any block of user data in the array illustrated in Figure 46 cannot be read, either because:

➡ the member disk on which it is stored fails,

➡ the access path to the member disk on which it is stored fails, or,

➡ a media defect develops in the member disk block in which it is stored,

the data from the inaccessible block can be regenerated and delivered to applications.

The primary advantage of parity RAID over mirroring is an inherently lower hardware cost premium than the 100% premium of mirroring. Using Figure 46 as an example, usable storage capacity of 4 disks requires one "extra" disk and associated hardware resources, or a 25% cost premium, to protect against a single disk failure. While each additional data disk in a parity RAID array reduces the array's theoretical Mean Time to Data Loss (MTDL), in principle any number of data disks can be protected by a single parity disk. Parity RAID arrays of 10 or more data disks are used routinely. Parity RAID thus provides significantly enhanced data protection (compared to non-arrayed disks) at a minimal inherent hardware cost premium.

RAID Advisory Board Definition	
MTDL	An abbreviation for *Mean Time until Data Loss;* the average time from startup until a component failure causes a permanent loss of user data in a large population of disk arrays. The concept is similar to that of physical MTBF used to describe physical device characteristics, but takes into account the possibility that RAID redundancy can protect against data loss due to single component failures.

Balanced against the lower inherent cost of larger parity RAID are inherent I/O performance characteristics discussed later in this chapter. Modern disk array systems usually mask these characteristics from applications using technology discussed in Part 3.

Using Parity To Regenerate User Data

When a member read operation in a parity RAID array fails, the unreadable data can be regenerated by computing the **Exclusive OR** of the parity and user data at corresponding *p_extent* addresses on all of the other array members. Figure 47 illustrates this computation.

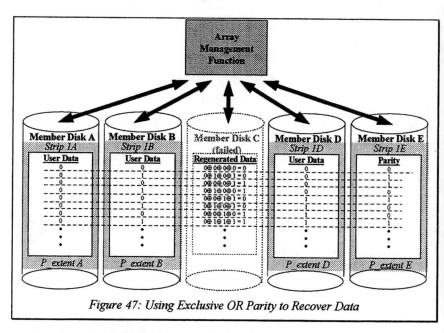

Figure 47: Using Exclusive OR Parity to Recover Data

In Figure 47, Member Disk C has failed. The *Array Management Function* can regenerate any user data stored on Member C, however, by reading the contents of the same locations on Member Disks A, B, D, and E, and computing their bit-by-bit **Exclusive OR.**. Clearly, for this algorithm to succeed, all of the user data strips used to compute a given parity strip must be located on separate disks, otherwise a member disk failure might make two **Exclusive OR** inputs inaccessible, and the computation would be impossible.

Figure 48 expands the example of Figure 47, illustrating strip-by-strip virtual disk-to-member disk user data mapping and check data. For simplicity, mapping to a single virtual disk is shown (i.e., there are no partitions). In this example, check data is located on a single disk (*Member Disk E*); distributed check data is also possible. Check data is computed as the **Exclusive OR** of corresponding strips from each member disk that contains user data.

In Figure 48 the first strip of Member Disk E contains the bit-by-bit *Exclusive OR* of user data strips A, B, C, and D:

$$Parity(A,B,C,D) = User\ Data\ D \oplus User\ Data\ C \oplus User\ Data\ B \oplus User\ Data\ A,$$

where the symbol $\oplus$ denotes the *Exclusive OR* function.

The *Exclusive OR* operation is reversible, i.e., a strip's contribution to the result of an *Exclusive OR* computation is nullified by computing the *Exclusive OR* of the result and the strip's contents. Symbolically:

$$x_C = Parity(A,B,C,D) \oplus User\ Data\ A,$$

$$x_C = User\ Data\ D \oplus User\ Data\ C \oplus User\ Data\ B \oplus (User\ Data\ A \oplus User\ Data\ A).$$

But, the *Exclusive OR* of a binary string with itself is an equal-length string of zeros, therefore,

$$x_C = User\ Data\ D \oplus User\ Data\ C \oplus User\ Data\ B.$$

The computation on partial result x_{rC} can be done twice more using *User Data D* and *User Data B*. The complete computation is:

$$x_C = Parity(A,B,C,D) \oplus User\ Data\ A \oplus User\ Data\ B \oplus User\ Data\ D,$$

in which the contributions of *User Data A, B,* and *D* are successively removed from x_1, finally leaving

$$x_C = User\ Data\ C.$$

In other words, the inaccessible User Data C has been regenerated from check data and surviving user data.

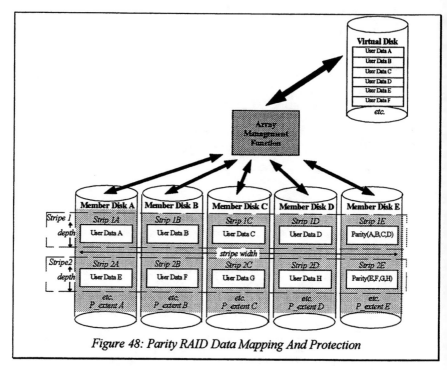

Figure 48: Parity RAID Data Mapping And Protection

Similarly, it is possible to compute:

$x_D = Parity(A,B,C,D) \oplus User\ Data\ A \oplus User\ Data\ B \oplus User\ Data\ C = User\ Data\ D,$

$x_B = Parity(A,B,C,D) \oplus User\ Data\ A \oplus User\ Data\ C \oplus User\ Data\ D = User\ Data\ B,$

and,

$x_B = Parity(A,B,C,D) \oplus User\ Data\ B \oplus User\ Data\ C \oplus User\ Data\ D = User\ Data\ A.$

These computations illustrate the fundamental data protection property of parity RAID:

> **The contents of any strip of data from any disk in the array can be regenerated by computing the `Exclusive OR` function of the contents of the strips at corresponding locations on the array's remaining disks.**

This property is what makes parity RAID work. Because of it, failure of any one member disk leaves a parity RAID array able to satisfy virtual disk read and write requests. RAID Levels 3, 4, and 5 all have distinctive performance characteristics, but all share this common property—they use the `Exclusive OR` function to protect against loss of data and access to it due to disk, channel, and media failures. This protection comes at significantly lower inherent cost than mirrored arrays of equivalent usable capacity.

Differences Among Parity RAID Levels

The differences among the three parity RAID Levels described in **[Patterson88]** lay in stripe depth (larger or smaller than virtual disk block size) and check data location (distributed across array members or concentrated on a single member). Specifically:

➡ RAID Level 3 stripe depth was described as a proper fraction of virtual disk block size. Since the smallest possible I/O request to the virtual disk is for one full block, all data disks in a RAID Level 3 array would transfer an equal fraction of the data for every application I/O request to the virtual disk.

➡ RAID Level 4 and RAID Level 5 stripe depth was described as an integer multiple of virtual disk block size. Thus, it is possible that as few as one member of a RAID Level 4 or RAID Level 5 array would be accessed while executing a virtual disk I/O request.

➡ All RAID Level 4 parity is located on one member disk, whereas RAID Level 5 parity is distributed across member disks. **[Patterson88]** described RAID Level 3 parity as located on one member disk, but this is immaterial to the I/O algorithms.

Today, the sharp distinctions drawn in **[Patterson88]** are no longer representative of most RAID array systems. With few exceptions, today's RAID array systems alternate between parallel and independent access parity RAID update algorithms depending on the I/O load presented to them.

Parallel Access Parity RAID (RAID Level 3)

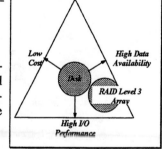

[Patterson88] gave the name *RAID Level 3* to a combination of parity check data and small stripes in a parallel access array (page 18). RAID Level 3 arrays have distinctive performance characteristics stemming from the parallel access property:

➡ excellent read and write performance for applications requiring high single-stream data transfer rates, and,

➡ generally poor performance for I/O request-intensive applications.

Member Disk Synchronization

For truly parallel access, parity RAID array member disks must rotate in *synchronization*, so that member transfers are exactly concurrent. If parity is pre-computed (or computed during member write operations) and written as data is written, member disk synchronization guarantees that parity always remains consistent with user data. Synchronized member disk rotation requires disk and controller capabilities not universally found in these components, however. Many disk array systems do not have these capabilities, and so do not synchronize disk rotation. These systems approximate true parallel access array behavior, even when full stripes of data are written.

If member disk rotation is not synchronized, there may be small intervals of time during which parity strip contents are not consistent with the contents of corresponding user data strips (for example, if a member write to a data strip executes before the corresponding parity strip is written). These intervals are called *write holes*, and are discussed further on page 120. In case an array fails during one of these intervals, there must be a mechanism to detect any data and parity inconsistency and restore it after the array begins to operate again.

Parallel Access Parity RAID: Normal Operation

A virtual disk read or write request specifying a starting block address that corresponds to a stripe boundary as well as an integral number of stripes, may be satisfied using *parallel access* read and write algorithms. A parity RAID array's *Array Management Function* handles stripe-aligned read and write requests differently. For read requests the *Array Management Function*:

1. *converts* the application request's virtual disk block address to a member strip number. The member strip number is the same for every member *p_extent*.

2. *schedules* concurrent read operations for corresponding strips of each member *p_extent* that contains data. (The strip containing parity is not accessed during normal execution of virtual disk read requests.) If scatter reading (page 86) is supported, member reads for consecutive strips can be consolidated.

3. *delivers* data to the destination memory addresses specified in the application's read request. In controller-based arrays, the controller usually provides intermediate buffering. In host-based arrays, intermediate buffering may occur, or data may be delivered directly from disks to the application's destination area.

4. *signals* the application when its request is complete. With synchronized disks, member operations would execute concurrently, and complete at the same time. In any case, the *Array Management Function* must ensure that all data has been delivered before signaling completion of the virtual disk request.

To execute a virtual disk write request, user data supplied by the application must be written, and new parity must be computed and written for each affected stripe. The *Array Management Function*:

1. *acquires* the data to be written from the application. For controller-based arrays, this usually means moving data from the host's memory to a controller buffer. For host-based arrays, data may be moved, or it may be written directly from the application's buffer.

2. *divides* the application's data stream into sequences of consecutive strips to be written to each member *p_extent*.

3. **computes** new parity for each stripe using data supplied by the application, as illustrated in Figure 49. In some implementations, this computation is hardware assisted. Parity may be pre-computed, or may be computed and written as user data is written.

4. **executes** concurrent write operations for corresponding strips on each member disk including the parity disk. If gather writing (page 86) is supported, member writes to consecutive strips may be consolidated.

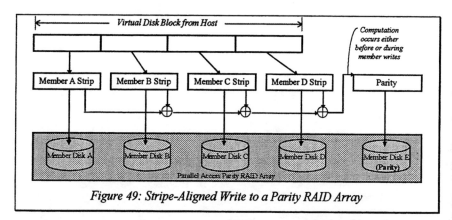

Figure 49: Stripe-Aligned Write to a Parity RAID Array

5. **signals** the application when its request is complete. As with read requests, completion cannot be signaled to the application until all data and parity have been completely written to disk media (unless a write-back cache is present).

Scatter Reading And Gather Writing

A *scatter-read* and *gather-write* hardware assist (described on page 86) can significantly improve I/O performance for multiple stripe read and write requests. With multiple stripe write requests, data that are not contiguous in host memory must be delivered to consecutive member disk locations. For multiple stripe read requests, data stored at consecutive disk locations must be delivered to non-consecutive memory addresses. Both of these are usually accomplished using a mapping facility that maps a consecutive range of I/O bus or channel addresses to multiple non-consecutive host memory address ranges. Figure 50 illustrates gather writing.

Figure 50 represents the first three blocks of an application write request to a 5-member parallel access RAID array with a stripe depth (member block size) of 128 bytes. The three strips of data at host memory addresses 1000, 1512, and 2024 are to be written to consecutive member block addresses on member A, and so forth. A gather write facility in the host maps these non-consecutive blocks of memory to consecutive I/O bus addresses so that each member write operation's succession of data fetch requests actually fetches non-contiguous blocks of data and writes them to consecutive disk addresses. Gather writing using a memory to I/O bus address map is often found in intelligent disk controllers and host I/O adapters.

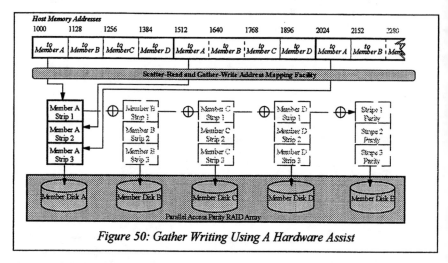

Figure 50: Gather Writing Using A Hardware Assist

For multiple block read requests, a scatter-read facility provides the reverse function—scattering blocks of data fetched from consecutive member disk addresses to non-contiguous blocks of host memory.

Failure Protection In Parity RAID
Arrays With Parity On A Single Disk

A disk or channel failure in a parity RAID array (whether parallel access or independent access) with all parity located on a single disk results in either the parity disk or one of the data disks becoming inaccessible.

If the parity disk fails, the array's ability to read and write application data is not impaired. Application reads are handled exactly as they are when all array members are functioning properly. Application writes are handled as illustrated in Figure 49, except that parity need not be computed, because the parity disk cannot be written.

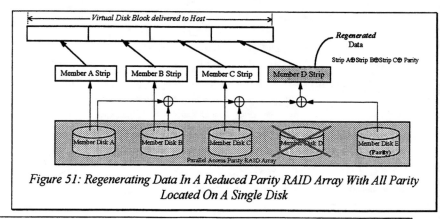

Figure 51: Regenerating Data In A Reduced Parity RAID Array With All Parity Located On A Single Disk

If the failed disk contains data, the *Array Management Function* satisfies application read requests by *regenerating* user data from the surviving member disks, including the parity disk, using the algorithm described on pages 104 *ff*. Figure 51 illustrates regeneration.

In Figure 51, Member Disk D, which contains user data, is inaccessible. The array is said to be *reduced*. Data from Member Disk D can still be delivered to applications, however, by computing the Exclusive OR of the contents of corresponding strips on the surviving member disks, including the parity disk. This computation is often hardware-assisted, and, in principle can be performed as data is being transferred. In such an implementation, reduced operation would not affect performance appreciably. In implementations lacking hardware-assisted Exclusive OR computation, reduced mode read operations would take longer because the *Array Management Function* must regenerate the failed disk's data, which can only be done when all surviving member strip contents have been read into its buffers.

Writes to a parity RAID array reduced by the failure of a member containing data are done as illustrated in Figure 49, except that no data is written to the failed member disk. Parity consistency is maintained, however, so that the missing member's contents can be regenerated on subsequent read requests, and can be rebuilt when a replacement disk is made available.

Restoring Protection After A Failure

When a parity RAID array member fails, data remains available to applications, but there is no protection against further disk, channel, or media failures. To restore protection:

➡ the failed disk must be replaced by a functioning one, and,

➡ the contents of the replacement disk must be made consistent with those of the other array members.

Disk replacement may be either physical or logical. Physical replacement means removal of the failed disk and installation of a working disk in its place. Logical replacement is a management operation which makes an already-installed disk part of the array.

Making a replacement disk's contents of consistent with those of other array members is called *rebuilding*. To rebuild a failed member, *Array Management Function* must:

➡ read corresponding strips from each surviving member disk,

➡ compute the Exclusive OR of corresponding strip contents to regenerate correct strip contents for the replacement member, and,

➡ write the regenerated strip contents to the replacement member.

Rebuilding can require up to several hours in large arrays. Allowing application data access while rebuilding can extend rebuilding time, because application I/O uses resources that would otherwise be available for rebuilding, but it provides the compensating benefit of continuous data availability while protection is restored.

Continuity of data availability in a parity RAID array is affected by the mechanics of failed member replacement. If the array must be shut down before a disk can be replaced (i.e., if the disk must be *warm-* or *cold-swapped*), data availability is lower than if *hot-swap* or *automatic swap* is possible. For maximum data availability, replacement disks should be installable and usable without service interruption (*hot-swapped* or *automatic-swapped*). Many implementations support pre-designation of dedicated *spare* disks which remain idle during normal operation, but which are automatically swapped in as replacements when an array member fails. System administrators must consider RAID array systems' disk replacement requirements when designing failure recovery procedures.

Parallel Access RAID Array Data Transfer Performance

Because every member of a parallel access parity RAID array participates in every I/O operation, the data transfer portion of request execution time is evenly divided among the number of members containing data. This makes parallel access arrays an excellent choice for applications requiring high sequential data transfer rates. For maximum benefit, adequate data transfer capacity must exist along the entire path between member disks and host memory. Figure 52 illustrates two disk systems with equal-storage capacity but different maximum data transfer capacities.

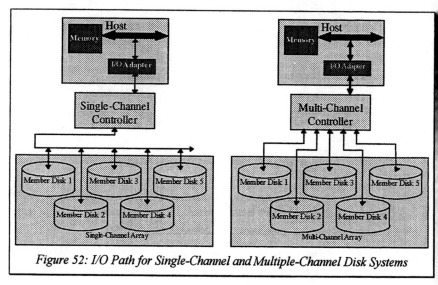

Figure 52: I/O Path for Single-Channel and Multiple-Channel Disk Systems

The array depicted in the left diagram of Figure 52 has all of its member disks attached to a single disk channel. For maximum data transfer capacity, the channel must provide both:

➡ sufficient data transfer capacity to support the sum of the member disks' spiral data transfer rates, and,

---

➡ effective interleaving so that bursts of data from member disks do not interfere with each other and prevent the channel from being used at full capacity.

Moreover, member disks must have internal buffering so that they do not require simultaneous access to the channel. Most modern disks have internal buffering.

Since only one member disk data transfer can occupy the channel at any instant, this type of array cannot be truly synchronized, and hence must include a mechanism for blocking *write holes* (page 120).

The maximum data transfer rate between this array and its host is the maximum that can be sustained by the single disk channel. In this type of array, the single disk channel is likely to be the first I/O performance bottleneck encountered.

The array on the right in Figure 52 is configured with each member disk attached to a separate channel, so no bottleneck occurs at this level as long as member disk and channel capacities are well-matched.

Next in both paths is the controller itself. Whether single- or multiple-channel, the controller must be capable of controlling data transfer operations (allocating buffers, setting up DMA data transfers, etc.) between disks and the host I/O bus at a rate sufficient to support the aggregate of the disks' spiral data transfer rates.

Third, the host I/O bus must be able to transfer data at the rate required by the array's member disks. Moreover, if other peripheral controllers are connected to the host bus, it must be able to interleave their data streams efficiently with that of the disk array.

Fourth, the host I/O bus adapter and memory system must be similarly capable. If the host processor and I/O bus adapter share a single memory port, the port must have sufficient data transfer capacity to satisfy the demands of both.

Any of these system components can become a data transfer bottleneck. Evaluating a parallel access RAID array for a data transfer intensive application requires determining not only that the array itself meets requirements, but also that other system components are capable of supporting its full performance potential.

Parallel Access RAID Array I/O Request Performance

The same property that makes parallel access RAID arrays an excellent choice for data transfer-intensive applications—participation of every member disk in every data transfer—makes them a poor choice for I/O request-intensive applications.

For large I/O requests, seek and rotational latency time is a small part of request execution time (page 44), and the high data transfer rate provides a major performance advantage. I/O request-intensive applications typically specify a small amount of data (e.g., 4-16 Kbytes) in each request, so execution time tends to be dominated by disk seeking and rotational latency. Since its member disks all seek and rotate to corresponding locations for every I/O request, a parallel access array executes one request at a time. The array therefore executes small I/O requests at the speed of a single disk with a high data transfer rate. Independent access arrays, whose members can execute multiple virtual disk requests concurrently, typically perform significantly better in I/O request-intensive applications.

Cache is sometimes used in parallel access RAID array systems to improve I/O request performance. Striped arrays with parallel access RAID arrays as members, sometimes called *RAID 30* arrays, can also improve parallel access RAID I/O request performance. The parallel access member arrays provide high data transfer capacity; striping across them increases I/O request handling capability.

Parallel Access Parity RAID
Implementation Compromises

RAID Level 3 as described in **[Patterson88]** maps a fraction of a single virtual disk block to each strip. The stripe depth of a RAID Level 3 array with *N+1* members is therefore *1/N* times the size of a virtual disk block. Figure 53 illustrates two RAID Level 3 stripes using 512-byte and 2048 byte virtual disk blocks respectively.

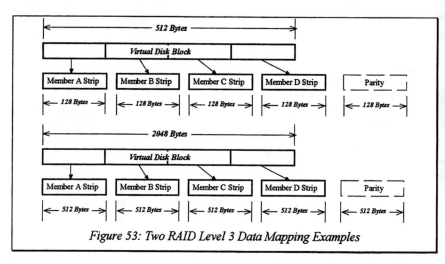

Figure 53: Two RAID Level 3 Data Mapping Examples

In the upper diagram of Figure 53, virtual disk blocks of conventional size (512 bytes[43]) are presented to the host environment. Presenting a conventional disk block size avoids difficulties that stem from lack of operating environment support for other sizes. For the five-member array illustrated, this requires a member strip size of 128 bytes. This limits implementers' options, since not all disks can be formatted with such a small block size. Even for those that can, smaller blocks mean more overhead, and hence, less efficient use of valuable media surface area.

In the lower diagram of Figure 53, member block sizes are conventional (512 bytes). Since there are four members containing data, the virtual disk block size is 2,048 bytes. While this uses member disk capacity efficiently, the usefulness of an array with

---

[43] Although other block sizes are in use in the industry, 512 byte virtual disk blocks are by far the most common.

this mapping would be limited to operating environments supporting a 2,048 byte disk block size.

Since both of these alternatives are restrictive, most parity RAID implementations *approximate* parallel access array behavior using:

⇒ a conventional member disk block size,

⇒ parallel access (full-stripe) I/O algorithms for virtual disk requests that map to full stripes of data, and,

⇒ independent access I/O algorithms (described on page 116) for small I/O request sizes (e.g., requests for less than 2,048 bytes in the lower diagram of Figure 53) and for requests in which the data affected does not map to an integral number of stripes.

This compromise allows efficient media formatting using readily available conventional disks, while presenting operating environments with the conventional virtual disk block size that most require.

Applications For Parallel Access Parity RAID

A parallel access parity RAID performs best in applications that require a high single-stream sequential data transfer rate. These applications are usually of one of two types:

⇒ processors of large data objects such as audio or video segments, CAD files, graphical images, seismic or telemetric data streams, etc., or,

⇒ non-interactive ("batch") applications that process large files sequentially.

Execution time for these applications is strongly influenced by the amount of time spent waiting for large I/O requests to complete. Since parallel access arrays provide high data transfer rates, they can substantially improve application execution time by reducing I/O wait times. To achieve this improvement, however, applications must be *tuned* to use parallel access arrays effectively. This generally means two things:

⇒ They must make *large* I/O requests (e.g., 64 Kbytes or more). If they do not, data they require may pass the disk heads in the interval between I/O requests, and the next request may incur substantial *rotational latency* waiting for the required data to rotate under the disk heads again.

⇒ They must minimize the interval between I/O requests for the same reason. Once data passes a disk head with no I/O request outstanding, it cannot be delivered for an entire disk revolution (typically 8-16 milliseconds). Applications can most easily avoid this latency by *double buffering*, or keeping two I/O requests for consecutively located data outstanding at all times. Double buffering can be difficult to implement in applications, but many file systems and other data management products either include the feature or offer it as a tuning option.

Independent Access Parity RAID

Unlike true parallel access arrays, which subdivide each virtual disk block into multiple member blocks, independent access parity RAID arrays map each virtual disk block to a single block on one member disk. As a result, execution of an application I/O request may require access to as few as one member. An independent access array's *Array Management Function* achieves disk-like behavior by careful ordering of member disk operations, sometimes combined with *logging* of operation progress to a non-volatile memory.

[Patterson88] identified two independent access RAID Levels—RAID Levels 4 and 5—differing only in the distribution of parity. A RAID Level 5 array's parity is distributed across its member disks; all of a RAID Level 4 array's parity is located on one member.

Independent Access Parity RAID
With Parity On One Member Disk

[Patterson88] used the term *RAID Level 4* to describe an independent access parity RAID array having *N* data disks with user data striped across them, and an *N+1st* disk containing only parity check data. This is identical to their description of RAID Level 3, except that RAID Level 4 stripe depth was described as an integer multiple of virtual disk block size, allowing independent simultaneous access to multiple member disks. This allows a RAID Level 4 array to execute parts of multiple application virtual disk I/O requests concurrently, as long as the data they specify is located on different member disks.

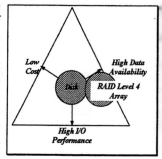

Like parallel access ones, independent access parity RAID arrays provide continued data access in the event of a single disk, path, or media failure by *regenerating* as described on page 104. Independent access parity RAID arrays, however, perform quite differently under load:

➡ Transaction read performance is substantially better than that of parallel access arrays because member disks may operate independently.

➡ Transaction write performance is extremely poor because of the complexity of parity updates.

➡ Large file read performance can be nearly as good as that of parallel access parity RAID arrays. Large file write performance can be good as well, as long as applications make large write requests.

An independent access parity RAID array with parity located on a single disk has an inherent I/O bottleneck (described on page 126). This bottleneck can be alleviated simply by distributing parity across some or all of the array's member disks, so distributed parity ("RAID Level 5") is often found in products.

Description of Independent Access
Parity RAID

Figure 54 illustrates data mapping for an independent access parity RAID array with all parity located on one disk. Mapping to a single virtual disk is illustrated, although partitioning (page 66) into multiple virtual disks is possible.

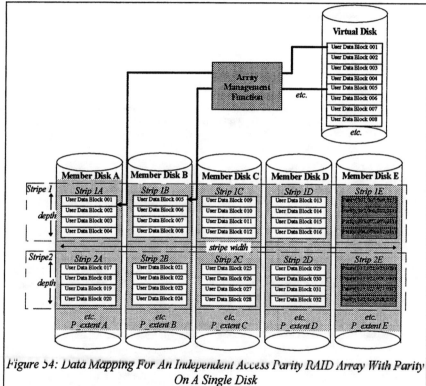

Figure 54: Data Mapping For An Independent Access Parity RAID Array With Parity On A Single Disk

Each block on the *parity disk* (Member Disk E in Figure 54) contains the parity of user data in corresponding blocks on the other disks. The parity is the `Exclusive OR` function described on page 105.

For simplicity, Figure 54 illustrates an unrealistically small stripe depth of 4 blocks (for both redundancy group stripe depth and user data extent stripe depth, in the terminology of Chapter 3). Typical stripe depths for the 2 and 4 Gbyte disks in common use today are between 100 and 200 512-byte blocks.

Both host and controller implementations of independent access parity RAID exist. Both routinely use conventional disks with no specialized features, although for large (full-stripe) I/O requests, synchronized disks would reduce rotational latency as they do for smaller requests in parallel access arrays.

Independent Access Parity RAID:
Normal Operation

A independent access parity RAID array's *Array Management Function* handles read and write requests differently because data and parity consistency of must be maintained when data is updated. For read requests, the *Array Management Function*:

1. *selects* the member or members to execute the request by converting the application request's virtual disk block addresses to one or more array members and block addresses on those members. This differs from parallel access arrays, in which all members participate in every request.

2. *schedules* member read operations for consecutively addressed strips of data on as many member disks as required. (The first and last strips may require partial strip member reads). In principle, these member operations can execute concurrently.

3. *delivers* data to the destination addresses specified in the application's virtual disk read request. In controller-based arrays, the controller usually serves as an intermediate buffer. In host-based arrays, intermediate buffering may occur, or data may be delivered directly from disks to the application's destination area.

4. *signals* completion of the request to the application. For a virtual disk read request whose data maps to multiple member disks, the *Array Management Function* must coordinate member request execution so that completion is not signaled to the application until data from all member operations has been delivered.

When an application writes data, the parity blocks that protect member blocks affected by the write must be updated. The array's *Array Management Function* must compute new parity for each affected block (possibly with hardware assist) and write it as well as the new data supplied by the application. Figure 55 illustrates a single-block write request that affects only one array member.

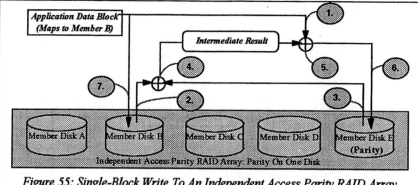

Figure 55: Single-Block Write To An Independent Access Parity RAID Array

In Figure 55, the virtual disk block to be written maps to a physical block on Member Disk B. The circled numbers (which correspond to the steps listed below) represent a likely sequence in which the member operations required to execute the application request might occur. The *Array Management Function*:

1. *acquires* the data to be written from the application.

2. *reads* the target block contents (data to be replaced) into an internal buffer.

3. *reads* the corresponding parity block's contents into an internal buffer.

4. *removes* the target block's contribution to the parity by computing the `Exclusive OR` of the two (as described on page104). This computation may be hardware-assisted, and in principle, done as data and parity are read.

5. *computes* new parity as the `Exclusive OR` of the result from the previous step and the new data supplied by the application. This computation may also be hardware-assisted, and in some implementations, done as data and parity are written.

6. *writes* new parity back to the parity disk.

7. *writes* the data supplied by the application to the target member disk.

8. *signals* completion of the request to the application (not illustrated). All virtual disk write requests involve at least two member disks, so the *Array Management Function* must coordinate member operations and delay signaling completion to the application until all member operations are complete.

In short, both the data to be replaced and the parity that protects it must be:

➡ read from disks,

➡ modified by `Exclusive OR` computation, and,

➡ rewritten,

giving rise to the phrase *read-modify-write* to describe the writing of data to an independent access parity RAID array.

For application I/O requests specifying multiple blocks that map to more than one member, these steps must effectively be performed for each member affected. In many such cases, the member operations involve strips of data in the same stripe. When this is the case, only one read and write of the parity disk are required, as illustrated in Figure 56.

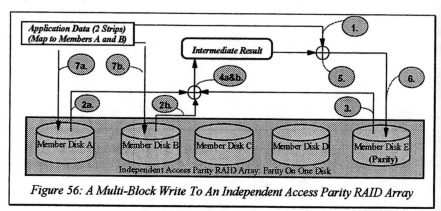

Figure 56: A Multi-Block Write To An Independent Access Parity RAID Array

In Figure 56, The sequence of operations is the same as that shown in Figure 55. Each of the numbers 2, 4, and 7, however, represents two operations (designated a & b in the diagram), one on the Member Disk A strip and one on the Member Disk B strip. Operations 3 (reading the old parity) and 6 (writing new parity) need only be done once.

Write Holes

A key challenge in implementing independent access parity RAID lies in making each *read-modify-write* operation sequence appear to applications as if it were a single write to a disk. If a disk fails while a write request is in progress, each block of data specified in the unfinished write should appear after recovery as either:

➡ either written completely or not written at all (either is correct), or,

➡ clearly marked as incorrect or unrecoverable data.

Similarly, if an application write to an independent access parity RAID array's virtual disk is in progress at the time of failure (e.g., due to an electrical power, host system, or *Array Management Function* failure, but *not* a member disk failure), then the virtual disk block should be in one of the states listed above after recovery.

In other words, after system recovery, the contents of virtual disk blocks affected by a write in progress at the time of failure may be either new data or old, with any other state marked and reported as unreadable data. More specifically, after recovery from a failure, any inconsistencies between data and parity should be marked for repair or for reporting to applications as unrecoverable.

Using Figure 56 as an example, if the member writes of new data (steps 7a and 7b) are completed before the array fails, but the parity update (step 6) is not, the array's data and parity for the affected blocks will be inconsistent after a restart. Similarly, if the parity update completes, but one or both of the member data writes does not, parity and data will be inconsistent. Depending on the specific algorithms used to perform subsequent updates, this inconsistency has a high probability of persisting, even if the data is overwritten (and hence, its parity re-computed) after recovery. If at some future time, a member disk containing user data in the affected stripes fails, its data may be incorrectly regenerated because of the lingering inconsistency. It is even possible for *bystander data*, data not active at the time of the original array failure, to be corrupted.

The interval of time during which an array is susceptible to this form of data corruption (between the start of the first member write of a virtual disk update and the completion of the last) is sometimes referred to as a *write hole*. The possibility of write holes is the difference between parallel access and independent access RAID arrays. A truly parallel access array with perfectly synchronized disks is not susceptible to this form of corruption. A quasi-parallel access array whose disks are not synchronized, however, is susceptible.

Independent access parity RAID arrays must protect against data corruption due to write holes. The general technique for doing this is for the *Array Management Function* to keep a *log* of write operations in progress in a small non-volatile memory (Both disk media and non-volatile RAM have been used for this purpose.). The contents of this log are read when the *Array Management Function* starts up. Any stripes indicated in the log as having had write operations in progress at the time of failure must have their parity re-computed so that it is consistent with on-media data before normal I/O can proceed. Even when this is done, there may still be no way to determine whether member disk contents reflect completion of writes in progress at the time of failure or not. It is true, however, that:

➡ every block contains valid user data, and,

➡ parity is consistent with user data throughout the array, so that a member failure can be sustained and the normal RAID guarantee of continued access to correct data can remain effective.

Failure Protection In Independent Access Parity RAID Arrays

As with parallel access parity RAID arrays, a disk, channel, or media failure in an independent access RAID array with all parity located on one disk affects either:

➡ the parity disk, or,

➡ one of the data disks.

If the parity disk fails, the array's ability to read and write application data is not impaired. The reduced array is effectively a striped array. Writing to a reduced array is as illustrated in Figure 49, except that parity need not be computed, because the parity disk cannot be written. All that is lost is the enhanced data availability provided by the parity disk.

If the failed disk is a data disk, the *Array Management Function* satisfies read requests that map to it by regenerating data from surviving members. Figure 57 illustrates regeneration in an independent access parity RAID array.

The only difference between Figure 57 and Figure 51 is the size of the data elements

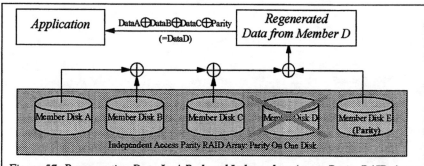

Figure 57: Regenerating Data In A Reduced Independent Access Parity RAID Array

contributing to regeneration. In Figure 51, each virtual disk block is subdivided into four sub-blocks stored on different member disks. The **Exclusive OR** of these sub-blocks with the corresponding parity sub-block regenerates the remaining sub-block so that a complete virtual disk block is delivered to the application. In Figure 57, entire blocks are input to the **Exclusive OR** computation for regeneration of a complete virtual disk block. Aside from this, regeneration is identical for independent and parallel access parity RAID arrays.

Maintaining parity consistency when data is written to a reduced independent access array is more complex, however. Figure 58 illustrates this for the case in which the data to be written maps to the failed disk.

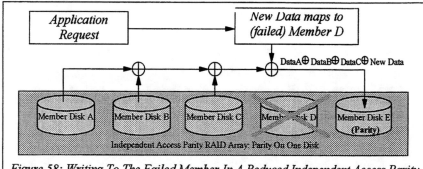

Figure 58: Writing To The Failed Member In A Reduced Independent Access Parity RAID Array

In Figure 58, data cannot actually be written to failed Member Disk D, but parity consistency can me maintained so that subsequent reads can be satisfied by regeneration.

Parity consistency is maintained by reading corresponding blocks from Member Disks A, B, and C, computing the **Exclusive OR** with them and the new data, and writing the result to the parity disk. For the 5-member array illustrated, this requires the same number of member I/O operations as normal mode application writes (3 reads and 1 write vs. 2 reads and 2 writes). Thus, reduced mode write performance should be approximately the same as normal-mode write performance when the failed disk is being updated. In arrays with more than 5 members, reduced mode updates require more member I/O operations.

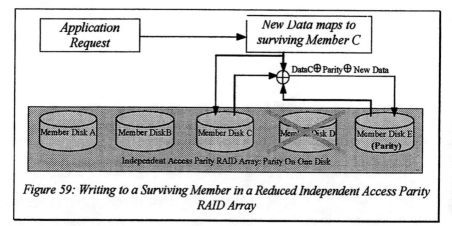

Figure 59: Writing to a Surviving Member in a Reduced Independent Access Parity RAID Array

It is also possible that the data specified in an application's write maps to a surviving disk in a reduced independent access array. Figure 59 illustrates this case. First, the data from Disk C that will be overwritten by the application's request and the corresponding parity are read, and their **Exclusive OR** is computed. The result of the **Exclusive OR** is:

$$x_p = Parity(DataA, DataB, DataC, DataD) \oplus Data3$$
$$= (DataA \oplus DataB \oplus DataC \oplus DataD) \oplus DataC$$
$$= (DataA \oplus DataB \oplus DataD) \oplus (DataC) \oplus DataC)$$
$$= DataA \oplus DataB \oplus DataD,$$

because the **Exclusive OR** of a bit stream with itself is zero. Next,

$$x_p \oplus DataC_{new} = DataA \oplus DataB \oplus DataD \oplus DataC_{new}$$
$$= Parity_{new}$$

is computed. Finally, $DataC_{new}$ and $Parity_{new}$ are written to Member Disk C and Member Disk E respectively.

Writing data that maps to a surviving member when the array is operating in reduced mode requires the same number of member operations as writing to the array in normal mode, no matter what the array size.

I/O Performance of Independent Access Parity RAID Arrays

The most apparent performance characteristic of independent access parity RAID arrays is that read and write performance are very different. Because their member disks operate independently of each other, these arrays perform well with applications that require high read request rates. Since the parity disk does not participate in read operations, the array behaves as an independent access striped array for read-only I/O loads (page 87). When applications accesses virtual disk addresses non-sequentially, a probabilistic distribution of member I/O operations usually occurs. As long as an I/O load consists of asynchronous non-sequential requests that overlap in time, it will tend to be distributed approximately evenly across member disks, minimizing the "hot spots" that can occur with independently managed disks.

For read-mostly application I/O loads, therefore, RAID Level 5 performance should approach that of a striped array. In fact, for a given usable capacity, independent access parity RAID read performance should normally be slightly better than that of a striped array because requests are distributed across one more member than they would be in a striped array of equivalent usable capacity.

Independent access parity RAID arrays are also well suited for applications that require high read data transfer rates. Dividing a sequential read load among member disks usually leads to higher performance than would be possible with a single disk.

Independent access arrays' large file write performance can be quite good, provided that application write requests align on stripe boundaries. While this is improbable in practice, write-back cache can be used to aggregate or consolidate sequential write requests until full-stripe writes are possible. Chapter 10 describes how consolidation operates.

RAID Advisory Board Definition

aggregation	The combination of multiple similar and related objects or operations into a single one. Used as a synonym for consolidation (q.v.) in the context of combining member disk data streams into an *aggregate* data stream for an array, as well as combining two or more I/O requests for adjacently located data into a single request to minimize request processing overhead and rotational latency.
consolidation	The process of accumulating the data for a number of sequential write requests in a cache, and performing a smaller number of larger write requests to achieve more efficient device utilization.

Independent Access Parity RAID
Array Transaction Write
Performance

Because of the number of member operations required to execute a single virtual disk write (at least four using the *read-modify-update* procedure described on page 119; more if the array uses a disk-based log to protect against write holes), independent access arrays' transaction write performance is significantly lower than that of a single disk of comparable performance. While some of the member operations can execute concurrently, both their number and the strict sequencing required make it virtually impossible for an independent access array to provide write performance greater than about half that of a single disk without assistance, for example, from a write-back cache. Independent access parity RAID's low write performance is called the RAID write penalty.

A write request to an independent access parity RAID array requires that both the target data and its corresponding parity be read and rewritten. Figure 60 represents the time dependencies of these member operations for the simple case where the data written maps to a single strip.

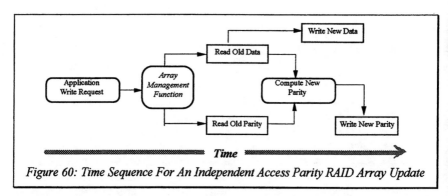

Figure 60: Time Sequence For An Independent Access Parity RAID Array Update

As Figure 60 illustrates, the *Array Management Function* first reads both the contents of the target blocks and those of the corresponding parity blocks. Since data and parity are located on different members, these operations can be concurrent. New parity cannot be computed, however, until old parity and old data have both been read (and new data has been supplied by the host). New parity cannot be written until the computation is complete. Similarly, new data cannot be written until the read of the data being replaced is complete. Thus, while some overlapping of member operations in time can occur, the minimum execution time for a write to an independent access parity RAID array includes two member I/O operations that must be sequential.

The multiple member I/Os that underlie an application write request to an independent access parity RAID array have two performance consequences:

➡️ Transaction application that include large numbers of writes exhibit poorer response with a RAID array virtual disk than with individual disks of equivalent performance.

➡️ RAID arrays to which a large number of write requests are directed saturate at a lower I/O request rate than individual disks of equivalent performance.

Because the read and write performance of independent access parity RAID arrays are so different, vendors frequently augment parity RAID with cache and write logging to improve write performance. These can improve array performance substantially, however when estimating an array's potential to meet application performance requirements it must be considered that all member operations implied by independent access parity RAID will ultimately occur. A non-volatile write-back cache can make momentary write overloads transparent, however, saturation-level array write performance is limited by the necessary *read-modify-write* cycles.

I/O Performance In Reduced Independent Access Parity RAID Arrays

When a data disk is missing from a reduced independent access parity RAID array, $1/N$ of the read requests (assuming requests that map to single members with uniform data address distribution across an $N+1$ member array) require that data be regenerated, which in turn requires an operation on each surviving member. In other words, $1/N$ of the read requests require N times as much member I/O as in normal mode. This results in $(2-1/N)$ times as many member operations for a given I/O load.

Reduced mode read performance is therefore somewhat lower than normal read performance. For writes, the performance effect of reduced operation depends upon whether the missing disk contains data or parity. If the missing disk contains parity, data is simply written to its target member; the parity computation and write can be bypassed. Performance in this case can actually be slightly higher than in normal mode, because less work is done. If a data disk is missing (whether or not it is the target for the request), then parity must be updated, which requires that all surviving member disks be read. This results in lower performance than normal mode writing for arrays of six or more members.

The Parity Disk: An Inherent Bottleneck

Locating all parity on a single disk in an independent access parity RAID array may be advantageous or not, depending on the array designer's goals. The disadvantage of locating all parity on a single disk is that two of the four member operations implied by every simple virtual disk write are directed at the single parity disk (reading the previous parity and writing the updated parity). This makes the parity disk a potential bottleneck. Distributing parity across some or all member disks, called RAID Level 5 in [Patterson88], relieves this bottleneck somewhat.

Largely due to the parity disk write bottleneck, independent access parity RAID arrays with a single parity disk are not as common as those with distributed parity. The application requirements they serve best, namely:

➡ applications whose I/O loads consist mostly of read requests, or,

➡ applications whose I/O loads consist primarily of stripe-aligned large transfers,

are usually better served by parity RAID arrays whose parity is distributed across some or all of their members.

Advantages Of A Single Parity Disk

Independent access arrays with large write-back cache may benefit from having their parity located on a single disk. Figure 61 illustrates an independent access parity RAID array in which the stripe depth is the full capacity of a member disk. In this example, Member disks A, B, C, and D are mapped directly as virtual disks P, Q, R, and S re-

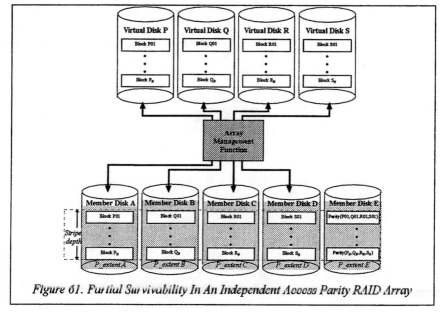

Figure 61. Partial Survivability In An Independent Access Parity RAID Array

spectively.

The mapping illustrated in Figure 61 sacrifices the I/O load balancing that would come with smaller stripe depth. If applications access files located on virtual disk P, Member Disk A is accessed, and other array members may remain idle. If most virtual disk writes complete when data is copied to a write-back cache, however, this may be a minor restriction on application I/O performance. Reads can still result in I/O load imbalance, unless there is a large read cache present and the I/O load has high locality of reference.

In applications for which certain virtual disks are of greater or lesser importance, the mapping illustrated in Figure 61 may be beneficial. For example, if Virtual Disks P and

Q contain production data, and Virtual Disks R and S contain data used by developers, then production may continue even if disks C and D were both to fail. In essence, the array would have degenerated to two independent disks.

Another advantage of mapping entire virtual disks to single array members is that it allows application I/O performance tuning techniques designed for data on independent disks to be used without modification. Database system vendors often encourage users to optimize I/O performance by locating concurrently accessed data items on different disks. Arrays with striped data mapping tend to reduce the effectiveness of this technique. While striped data mapping works well with I/O loads of uncoordinated requests, it inhibits the effectiveness of data manager-based optimization techniques. For these I/O loads, independent access parity RAID arrays with full P_extent stripe depth may outperform striped arrays with distributed parity.

While full-disk strips may be advantageous in some situations, it is not without risk. Simultaneous failure of Virtual Disk P and any other in Figure 61, for example, would mean that production could not continue. Moreover, effective use of full-disk strips requires careful configuration as well as a relatively constant assignment of specific data items to specific disks.

Independent Access RAID With Distributed Parity: RAID Level 5

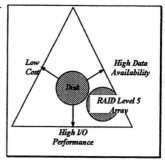

The technique most frequently used to minimize the write performance bottleneck described on page 126 is the distribution of successive parity strips across some or all array members cyclically. [Patterson88] calls this RAID Level 5. Functionally, it is equivalent to RAID Level 4, using a parity strip in each stripe to protect data stored on the remaining strips. It differs from RAID Level 4 in that its parity strips are distributed across two or more array members rather than concentrated on one. This reduces the write bottleneck, because two concurrent updates have a chance of accessing different parity disks as well as different data disks.

Description Of Independent Access RAID With Distributed Parity

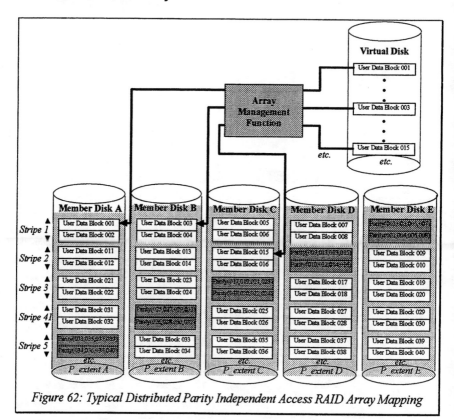

Figure 62: Typical Distributed Parity Independent Access RAID Array Mapping

Figure 62 illustrates a common data mapping for an independent access RAID array with parity distributed across all member disks. Each stripe has 4 data strips and one parity strip. Instead of all parity being on one disk, however, this array's parity strips are distributed across the array members in a cyclic pattern. Figure 62 illustrates the first five strips of each array member p_extent. Parity for Stripe 6 would stored in the sixth strip of Disk E; parity for Stripe 7 would be stored in the seventh strip of Disk D, and so forth, with the cyclic rotation repeated throughout the array's P_extents.

Figure 63 illustrates a variation of distributed parity that has been used in some disk array systems. In this example, parity is distributed across only a subset of an array's member disks,. This distribution is often coupled with a stripe depth equal to the capacity of an entire member disk. This mapping allows easy addition of member disks to an existing array (e.g., Member Disks D and E in Figure 63), since it does not require that user data be rearranged. This capability is useful in operating environments whose concept of a disk allows for dynamically changing capacity. While such environments exist, they are rare. Most operating environments' concept of a disk is a block storage space of fixed capacity. The mapping shown in Figure 63 is still useful in these environments, however, as long as the new members' capacity can be exported as a sepa-

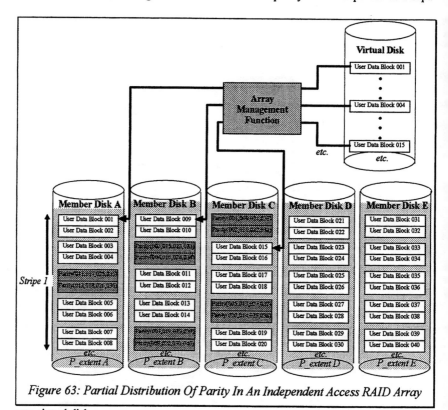

Figure 63: Partial Distribution Of Parity In An Independent Access RAID Array

rate virtual disk.

The array illustrated in Figure 63 has the same amount of usable capacity as the one in Figure 62, although the capacity distribution across member disks is different.

Normal Operation Of Independent Access Parity RAID With Distributed Parity

In independent access arrays with distributed parity, applications' virtual disk read requests to are handled as described on page 118, except that the algorithm for locating data must take the interspersed parity into account . A simple computation still suffices, however.

Similarly, for application write requests, the *Array Management Function* must locate the stripe containing the data and parity blocks for updating. The stripe's position in the array determines the disk on which parity resides. Once located, data and parity are updated as described on page 118. Figure 64 illustrates an application write request that modifies data on one array member:

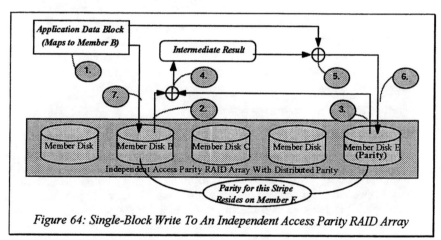

Figure 64: Single-Block Write To An Independent Access Parity RAID Array

In Figure 64, the virtual disk block to be written maps to a p_extent block on Member Disk B. The *Array Management Function* uses the stripe number to determine that parity is located on Member Disk E. The circled numbers represent a common sequence in which the member operations implied by the application request might occur. Except for determining the location of the parity dynamically based on data address, Figure 64 represents a sequence of operations identical to that illustrated in Figure 55.

If the application I/O request maps to more than one member, each affected member must be updated, along with its parity. In most cases, member requests involve blocks in the same stripe, so only one read and write of the parity disk are required as illustrated in Figure 56. When data in more than one stripe is affected, however, the *Array Management Function* must update both data and parity on multiple disks. Figure 65 illustrates this.

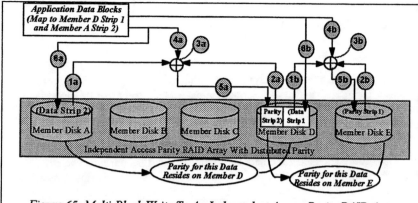

Figure 65: Multi-Block Write To An Independent Access Parity RAID Array

In Figure 65, the application data to be updated maps to successive strips in different stripes on Member Disks D and A. Since the parity for successive stripes is stored on successive members (Figure 62), parity on Member Disks E and D must be updated. Member Disk D thus participates in both a data update and a parity update for this application request.

Failure Protection in Independent Access Parity RAID Arrays With Distributed Parity

When a disk, channel, or media failure occurs in an independent access RAID array with distributed parity, both data and parity blocks may become inaccessible. If the data specified in an application virtual disk read request maps to a surviving array member, it is delivered as if the array were intact. If the address maps to the failed member, the *Array Management Function* regenerates the data by reading corresponding blocks from surviving members and computing the **Exclusive OR** of their contents. Figure 66 illustrates regeneration.

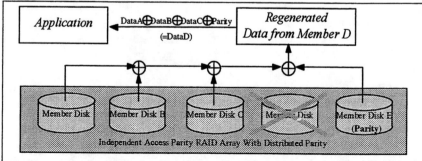

Figure 66: Regenerating Data In A Reduced Independent Access Parity RAID Array

Application writes to a reduced independent access RAID array with distributed parity are slightly more complex to describe than those to an array with a single parity disk (page 122). When application data maps to a surviving member, there are two possibilities:

➡ *The corresponding strip on the failed member contains parity.* In this case, writing in reduced mode is as illustrated in Figure 64, except that parity need not be computed, since it cannot be written.

➡ *The corresponding strip on the failed member contains user data.* In this case parity consistency is maintained by reading the contents of corresponding strips on all surviving members, computing the **Exclusive OR** of their contents and the new data, and writing the result to the parity member.

When the data to be written maps to the failed member disk:

➡ Corresponding blocks from all surviving members which store user data (i.e., not including the member that stores the parity) are read into *Array Management Function* internal buffers.

➡ Updated parity is computed by **Exclusive OR** of the all the data blocks read in the previous step and the new data to be written.

➡ The updated parity overwrites the previous parity.

Figure 67 illustrates this sequence of events.

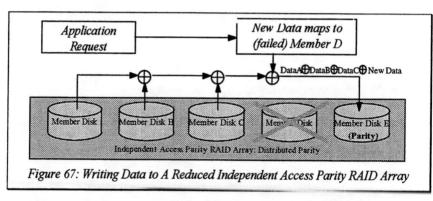

Figure 67: Writing Data to A Reduced Independent Access Parity RAID Array

In this case, the application's data itself is never actually written to a disk. On subsequent read requests, however, it can be regenerated correctly by reading corresponding blocks from all surviving members and computing the **Exclusive OR** of their contents.

Some implementations use a variation of this technique in which application data targeted for a failed disk is written instead over the parity that would ordinarily protect it. This requires each block that would normally store parity be flagged to reflect whether its contents are actually parity or are data written since the array became reduced. This technique allows data updated after the array becomes reduced to be read directly instead of regenerated.

Restoring Protection: Rebuilding

Whichever technique is used, data continues to be available to applications when a parity RAID array member disk fails. What is lost is the enhanced data reliability and availability provided by a fully functional parity RAID array. In order to restore full data protection:

➡ the failed disk must be replaced by a functional one, and,

➡ the contents of the replacement disk must be made consistent with the contents of the remaining array members.

Making a replacement disk's contents consistent with those of the remaining array members requires:

➡ reading corresponding strips from each of the surviving original member disks,

➡ computing the *Exclusive OR* of these strips' contents, and,

➡ writing the result to the replacement disk.

This process is called rebuilding, or reconstruction. Rebuilding is time-consuming (it can last up to several hours for large arrays), so parity RAID systems must be capable of operating while it is occurring. Operation while rebuilding tends to increase rebuild time, but provides the compensating benefit of continuous data availability to applications.

If an array must be made idle before a disk can be replaced (i.e., if the disk must be *warm-* or *cold-swapped*), applications that use it must also be halted while the replacement is effected. Implementations that allow *hot-swapping* or *automatic-swapping* of disks are generally preferable. Many array systems incorporate spare disks which are not used during normal operation, but which are automatically swapped in as replacements by the *Array Management Function* when a member disk fails.

Independent Access Parity RAID
With Very Large Stripe Depth

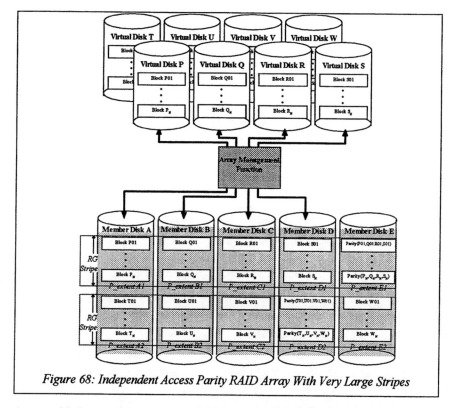

Figure 68: Independent Access Parity RAID Array With Very Large Stripes

Arrays with large write cache sometimes use independent access parity RAID data mapping with very large stripe depths to achieve partial survivability of multiple disk failures. Figure 68 illustrates a five-member array in which virtual disk capacity is equal to redundancy group stripe depth. In this example, single-strip P_extents A1, B1, C1, D1, A2, B2, C2, and E2 all map to separate virtual disks.

Mapping with a very large stripe depth sacrifices much of the I/O load balancing that would come with smaller stripe depth. If most updates cause data to be written to a write-back cache, this may be transparent to applications.

In applications for which different disks are clearly of greater or lesser importance, the mapping illustrated in Figure 68 may offer some positive benefits. For example, if Virtual Disks P, Q, T, and U contain production data, and Virtual Disks R, S, V, and W contain data used by developers, then production may continue even if member disks C and D both fail. In essence, the array would have degenerated to two independent disks, exported as four virtual disks.

Another advantage of single-strip virtual disks is that direct mapping entire virtual disks to single array members allows application performance tuning techniques designed for individual disks to be used. Many database systems include extensive facilities that allow the system manager to tune the database for improved I/O performance, basically by locating specific data items on specific disks. Striped data mapping tends to reduce the effectiveness of these facilities. While striped data mapping works well in almost all cases to balance an I/O load of uncoordinated requests, I/O loads from data managers that assume that their databases are stored on individual disks may tend to perform worse with striped arrays. For these I/O loads, mapping an entire virtual disk to a single member disk may actually offer better performance than RAID Level 5 with smaller stripes.

While full-volume strip data mapping may offer advantages in some installations, it is not without risk. Simultaneous failure of Member disk 1 and any other member in Figure 68, for example, would mean that production cannot continue. Moreover, using this technique effectively requires careful system configuration as well as a relatively constant assignment of data to disks.

Applications for Independent Access Parity RAID

Because their members operate independently, independent access arrays generally perform best with I/O request-intensive I/O loads. In principle, if the entire I/O path between an independent access parity RAID array's member disks and host is unrestricted, read data rates for large I/O requests can be very high. Parallel access RAID arrays with synchronized disk rotation, however, provides both higher data transfer rate per disk and equal read and write performance for these applications.

Independent access parity RAID arrays are most suitable for applications in which:

➡ data availability is worth protecting, but the cost of disk mirroring is excessive,

➡ transaction read request rates are high,

➡ there is small percentage of writes in the I/O load.

Inquiry-type transaction processing, group office automation, on-line customer services departments, etc. are all examples of applications where independent access parity RAID can be used effectively. High-speed data collection from a process, or credit bureau applications in which balances are continually updated are not particularly suitable for independent access parity RAID.

When independent access parity RAID technology is combined with cache to improve its write performance, the resulting array systems can be used in almost any application where general purpose disks would be suitable. Without some form of write assist, however, independent access parity RAID arrays perform best in applications whose I/O loads are either:

➡ light (i.e., have a low I/O request rate compared to the array's capability), or,

➡ dominated by read requests.

Chapter 6: RAID Level 6

Protection Against Two Simultaneous Disk Failures

RAID Level 6, defined in a subsequent paper by the Berkeley researchers ([Katz89]), is an evolutionary development of the independent access parity RAID (RAID Levels 4 and 5) concept that greatly improves data availability. In essence, a RAID Level 6 array is a parity RAID array with two independently computed sets of check data protecting each user data block. Assuming that each checksum requires no more storage capacity than the data it protects on each member disk, a RAID Level 6 array with *N* member disks of user capacity requires *N+2* member disks.

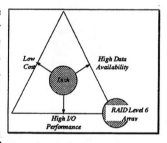

In a RAID Level 6 array, two check data blocks in separate p_extents must be updated for each data block written. This creates a write penalty similar to the independent access parity RAID write penalty (page 125) but twice as large in magnitude. To be practical, RAID Level 6 implementations must include some form of write performance assist, such as update logging or write-back cache, to mitigate this write penalty.

The user benefit of RAID Level 6 is extremely high data availability. In order for data to become inaccessible due to disk failure, three disks in a RAID Level 6 array must fail within the mean time to repair (MTTR) interval. This eventuality is literally thousands of times less likely than the simultaneous failure of the two disks in a mirrored array.

Description of RAID Level 6

RAID Level 6 requires two independent check data computations. Independence of the check data computations can be achieved either by using two different computation algorithms covering the same user data, or by using one algorithm covering two different overlapping subsets of user data.

Two check data computation algorithms covering the same data is known as one-dimensional redundancy. The term *P+Q parity*, indicating that two check data computation algorithms are in use, is also used. Figure 69 illustrates a virtual disk-to-member disk mapping for a RAID Level 6 array using P+Q parity.

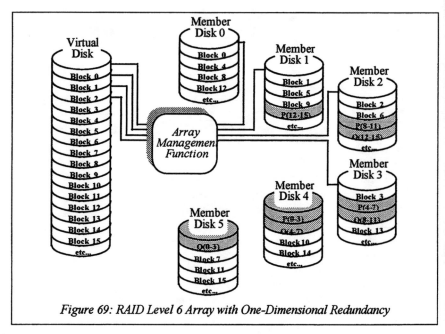

Figure 69: RAID Level 6 Array with One-Dimensional Redundancy

In Figure 69, each stripe consists of four data blocks and two check data blocks (labeled *P* and *Q*). P and Q represent two independent check data computation algorithms. Simply replicating the `Exclusive OR` function on two disks does not provide general protection against double disk failure because failure of two disks containing user data would make regeneration impossible. Reed-Solomon error correction codes similar to those used for disk drive error correction can be used to compute Q-parity.

Using a single check data computation algorithm to cover different overlapping subsets of the data is called two-dimensional redundancy. Figure 70 illustrates RAID Level 6 data protection using two-dimensional redundancy as outlined in **[Gibson92]**.

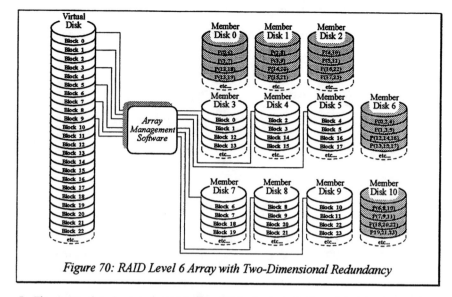

Figure 70: RAID Level 6 Array with Two-Dimensional Redundancy

In Figure 70, data is stored on Member Disks 3, 4, 5, 7, 8, and 9. Member Disk 6 holds the **Exclusive OR** of the contents of Member Disks 3, 4, and 5. Member Disks 3, 4, 5, and 6 are effectively a parity RAID array, as are Member Disks 7, 8, 9, and 10. Similarly, Member Disk 0 holds the **Exclusive OR** of the contents of Member Disks 3 and 7. Member Disks 0, 3, and 7 effectively comprise a separate parity RAID array, as do Member Disks 1, 4, and 8, and Member Disks 2, 5, and 9. The net result is that each user data block is protected by two parity blocks. In this case, since each parity block protects a different set of user data, the **Exclusive OR** function can be used for both horizontal and vertical parities.

In a RAID Level 6 array with two-dimensional redundancy, MxN data disks require $M+N$ parity disks. For small arrays such as that illustrated in Figure 70, two-dimensional redundancy is costly in terms of number of parity disks required. For large arrays, however, efficiency improves. An array with 100 data disks would require 20 parity disks, for example. This compares favorably with many of today's parity RAID array systems, but offers substantially improved protection against disk failures.

Two-dimensional redundancy has the apparent advantage that parity is simple to compute. With application-specific integrated circuits (ASICs), however, more complex parity computations such as Reed-Solomon can be implemented with adequate performance at low cost. As a result, RAID Level 6 implementations are tending toward one-dimensional check data techniques.

Like the one-dimensional redundancy illustrated in Figure 69, two-dimensional redundancy incurs a substantial write penalty.

RAID Level 6 Normal Operation

During normal operation, RAID Level 6 read and write processes are very similar to those of independent access parity RAID (page 118). Just as parity RAID balances read-only I/O loads across one more disk than a striped array of equivalent usable capacity, a RAID Level 6 array balances read-only I/O loads across two more disks, providing very good read performance in principle.

For application writes to the virtual disk, the performance of RAID Level 6 is lower than that of independent access parity RAID, because the *read-modify-write* cycle must accommodate both user data and two corresponding check data blocks. The inherent write performance of RAID Level 6 arrays is therefore extremely low. RAID Level 6 implementations include write performance assists, such as update logging and write-back cache, to mitigate the write penalty.

Failure Protection in RAID Level 6 Arrays

When a disk fails in a RAID Level 6 array, either a data strip or one of the two parity strips for each stripe becomes unavailable. Regeneration in this case is identical to regeneration in an independent access parity RAID array (described on page 121).

The benefit of RAID Level 6 is realized when a second disk fails before the first failed disk has been completely replaced. When this occurs, it is still possible to deliver data to applications by regenerating it from the contents of the remaining members in the stripe. Since the two parity computations are independent, regeneration may be thought of as the solution to a system of two equations in two unknowns, where the

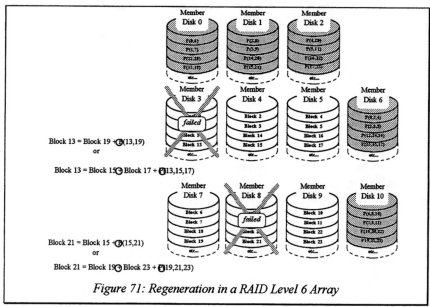

Figure 71: Regeneration in a RAID Level 6 Array

unknowns are the correct data block contents.

Figure 71 illustrates regeneration in a RAID Level 6 array with two-dimensional redundancy. In Figure 71, user data from failed Member Disk 3 can be regenerated either from horizontal parity RAID (using Member Disk 4, 5, and 6 contents) or from vertical parity RAID (using Member Disk 0 and 7 contents). Similarly, user data from failed Member Disk 8 can be regenerated either from Member Disks 7, 9, and 10, or from Member Disks 1 and 4. If any two disks in a column should fail, horizontal parity could be used to regenerate user data; if two disks in a row should fail, two disks in a column could be used for regeneration.

Application of RAID Level 6

The tolerance of RAID Level 6 arrays for two simultaneous disk failures provides extremely high data reliability—computed MTDLs for arrays of moderate size are literally in the trillions of hours—but the complexity of implementation and the severe write performance penalty have limited implementation of this technology to large-scale complex arrays (see page 41). Figure 72 illustrates the sequence of events required to execute an application write request to a RAID Level 6 array.

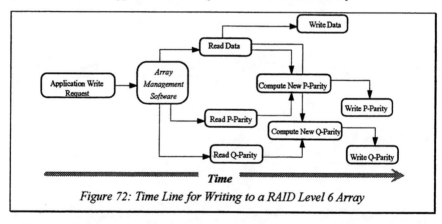

Figure 72: Time Line for Writing to a RAID Level 6 Array

As Figure 72 illustrates,[44] there can be considerable concurrency in the member operations required to execute an application write to a RAID Level 6 virtual disk. The user data to be replaced, as well as both check data protecting it, can be read concurrently. Similarly, once new check data are computed, both can be written concurrently with the new user data. It is easy to see why write-back cache can substantially improve the responsiveness of a RAID Level 6 array, however, the fact remains that all member write operations and such of the member reads as cannot be satisfied from read cache must ultimately be executed, possibly limiting the I/O request handling capacity of RAID Level 6 in write-intensive applications.

---

[44] The time line of Figure 72 assumes that both P and Q check data computation algorithms have the property that a user data block's contribution to check data can be "backed out" using only the user data and the check data. For check data computation algorithms which require complete re-computation using all user data, more member reads would be required.

As the industry and the user base gain experience and comfort with RAID arrays, as typical array sizes become larger, and most important, as user demands for ultra-reliable on-line storage increase, RAID Level 6 implementations may be expected to become more common across a broader market range.

Chapter 7: *RAID* Advisory Board Conformance

Verified RAID Functionality

The *RAID* Advisory Board formerly licensed vendors to use designators like the one illustrated below to denote disk system data protection and mapping characteristics.

RAID Level *n* Conformance

where one or more of the Berkeley RAID Levels would appear in place of *n*.

This program has been replaced by a more comprehensive classification program, which deals with all aspects of disk system resiliency. Since the licensing term was product lifetime, however, RAID Level conformance designators may still be found in vendor literature.

RAID Advisory Board Functional Requirements for Striped Arrays

A *RAID Level 0 Conformance* designator attached to a product means that the product has been determined to exhibit the following characteristics

1. The disk system's arrays respond to application read and write requests as if they were disks.

2. The disk system's arrays *stripe* data across member disks using the model described in Chapter 3.

3. The disk system's arrays are able to transfer data concurrently to or from all affected members when executing application requests.

4. The disk system is capable of concurrently executing as many virtual disk I/O requests as it has array members.

Striped Array Optional Features

Disk systems that support striped arrays may have some or all of the following attributes, but these attributes are specifically *not* implied by use of *the RAID Level 0 Conformance* designator.

1. The maximum and minimum number of supported members per array and number of arrays supported per disk system.

2. The ability for the user to define stripe depth, and the range of stripe depths supported.

3. Support for *partitions*, or multiple virtual disks in a single array.

4. Coexistence of striped arrays and other types of arrays in a single disk system.

5. Support for multiple disk types or capacities in a single array.

RAID Advisory Board Functional Requirements for Mirrored Arrays

A *RAID Level 1 Conformance* designator attached to a product means that the product has been determined to exhibit the following characteristics

1. The disk system's arrays respond to application read and write requests as if they were disks.

2. The disk system's arrays maintain two or more identical copies of user data on separate member disks.

3. Upon failure of as many as all but one disk in an array, the disk system continues to satisfy application I/O requests as if there were no failure.

4. Substitution of a replacement disk for any failed array member (including rebuilding of the failed disk's contents) is possible, while the array is in use by applications.

5. The *Array Management Function* either (a.) guarantees that array member contents are always mutually consistent, or (b.) is able to restore consistency after a failure. In the latter case, the restoration mechanism can operate while the array is in use by applications.

Mirrored Array Optional Features

Disk systems that support striped arrays may have some or all of the following attributes, but these attributes are specifically *not* implied by use of the *RAID Level 1 Conformance* designator.

1. More than 2 mirrored array members.

2. More than one mirrored array per disk system.

3. Different disk types in the same array.

4. Concurrent operation of mirrored arrays and other RAID array types.

5. Partitioning an array into multiple virtual disks.

6. Any particular algorithm for deciding which member disk(s) will satisfy read requests.

7. Any particular failed disk replacement mechanism (from *cold swap* to *automatic swap*).

8. Any particular mechanism for ascertaining that members are consistent or restoring consistency after an *Array Management Function* loss of state.

9. Any other availability enhancing mechanisms (in addition to disks and I/O ports) such as power supplies, cooling fans, intelligent controllers, etc.

10. Any other performance enhancing mechanisms, such as cache.

RAID Advisory Board Functional Requirements for RAID Level 3 Arrays

A *RAID Level 3 Conformance* designator attached to a product means that the product has been determined to exhibit the following characteristics

1. The disk system's arrays respond to application read and write requests as if they were disks.

2. The disk system's virtual disks behave as FBA disks with respect to single-block I/O operations. In particular, only complete virtual disk blocks are read or written.

3. Upon failure of any single disk or a path to it, arrays continue to satisfy I/O requests as if there were no failure.

4. Virtual disk read and write performance are approximately equal for stripe-aligned I/O requests for one stripe of data or more.

5. Substitution of a replacement disk for any failed array member (including rebuilding of the failed disk's contents) is possible, while the array is in use by applications.

6. The *Array Management Function* either (a.) guarantees that array member contents are always mutually consistent, or (b.) is able to restore consistency after a failure. In the latter case, the restoration mechanism can operate while the array is in use by applications.

RAID Level 3 Optional Features

Disk systems that support striped arrays may have some or all of the following attributes, but these attributes are specifically *not* implied by use of *the RAID Level 3 Conformance* designator.

1. Rotational synchronization of member disks.

2. More than one array per disk system.

3. Different disk types in the same array.

4. Concurrent operation of RAID Level 3 arrays and other RAID array types.

5. Partitioning an array into multiple virtual disks.

6. Any particular algorithm for deciding which member disk(s) will satisfy read requests.

7. Any particular failed disk replacement mechanism (from *cold swap* to *automatic swap*).

8. Any particular mechanism for ascertaining that member contents are consistent or for restoring consistency after an *Array Management Function* loss of state.

9. Any other availability enhancing mechanisms (in addition to disks and I/O ports) such as power supplies, cooling fans, intelligent controllers, etc.

10. Any other performance enhancing mechanisms, such as cache.

RAID Advisory Board Functional Requirements for RAID Level 4 Arrays

A *RAID Level 4 Conformance* designator attached to a product means that the product has been determined to exhibit the following characteristics:

1. The disk system's arrays respond to I/O requests as if they were disks, including disk-like single-block write behavior which performs correctly in the presence of host system failures (i.e., there is protection against the *write hole* described on page).

2. Upon failure of any disk or a path to it, the disk system's arrays continue to satisfy I/O requests as if there were no failure.

3. Substitution of a replacement disk for any failed array member (including rebuilding of the failed disk's contents) while the array is in use by applications is possible.

4. The disk system's arrays can simultaneously execute as many I/O requests as there are members that contain user data.

5. The *Array Management Function* either (a.) guarantees that array member contents are always mutually consistent, or (b.) is able to restore consistency after a

---

failure. In the latter case, the restoration mechanism can operate while the array is in use by applications.

6. Check data for an entire redundancy group can be concentrated in a single *p_extent* (i.e., on a single member disk).

RAID Level 4 Optional Features

Disk systems that support striped arrays may have some or all of the following attributes, but these attributes are specifically *not* implied by use of *the RAID Level 4 Conformance* designator.

1. Rotational synchronization of member disks.

2. More than one array per disk system.

3. Concurrent operation of RAID Level 3 arrays and other RAID array types.

4. Partitioning an array into multiple virtual disks.

5. Any particular algorithm for deciding which member disk(s) will satisfy read requests.

6. Any particular failed disk replacement mechanism (from *cold swap* to *automatic swap*).

7. Any particular mechanism for ascertaining that members are consistent or restoring consistency after an *Array Management Function* loss of state.

8. Any other availability enhancing mechanisms (in addition to disks and I/O ports) such as power supplies, cooling fans, intelligent controllers, etc.

9. Any other performance enhancing mechanisms, such as cache or logging.

10. Different disk types in the same array.

11. Ability to add disks to an existing array without requiring re-initialization.

RAID Advisory Board Functional Requirements for RAID Level 5 Arrays

A *RAID Level 5 Conformance* designator attached to a product means that the product has been determined to exhibit the following characteristics

1. The disk system's arrays respond to I/O requests as if they were disks, including disk-like single-block write behavior which performs correctly in the presence of host system failures (i.e., there is protection against the *write hole* described on page 120).

2. Upon failure of any disk or a path to it, the disk system's arrays continue to satisfy I/O requests as if there were no failure.

3. Substitution of a replacement disk for any failed array member (including rebuilding the failed disk's contents) while the array is in use by applications is possible.

4. The disk system's arrays can simultaneously execute as many I/O requests as there are members that contain user data.

5. The *Array Management Function* either (a.) guarantees that array member contents are always mutually consistent, or (b.) is able to restore consistency after a failure. In the latter case, the restoration mechanism can operate while the array is in use by applications.

6. The check data in a redundancy group can be distributed across at least two *p_extents* (array members).

RAID Level 5 Optional Features

Disk systems that support striped arrays may have some or all of the following attributes, but these attributes are specifically *not* implied by use of *the RAID Level 5 Conformance* designator.

1. Rotational synchronization of member disks.

2. More than one array per disk system.

3. Concurrent operation of RAID Level 3 arrays and other RAID array types.

4. Partitioning an array into multiple virtual disks.

5. Any particular algorithm for deciding which member disk(s) will satisfy read requests.

6. Any particular failed disk replacement mechanism (from *cold swap* to *automatic swap*).

7. Any particular mechanism for ascertaining that members are consistent or restoring consistency after an *Array Management Function* loss of state.

8. Any other availability enhancing mechanisms (in addition to disks and I/O ports) such as power supplies, cooling fans, intelligent controllers, etc.

9. Any other performance enhancing mechanisms, such as cache or logging.

10. Different disk types in the same array.

11. Ability to add disks to an existing array without requiring re-initialization.

Part 3: High-Performance Failure-Tolerant Disk Systems

While they offer significant data reliability and availability advantages compared to individually managed disks, RAID arrays do not by themselves provide fully failure-tolerant data access. Moreover, RAID arrays (particularly the more economical parity RAID arrays) have I/O performance characteristics that make it difficult to simply substitute them for independent disks.

Most of the interesting development work in disk systems today is concerned with integrating RAID data protection and mapping techniques with related technologies to provide both higher I/O performance and more robust data availability than has heretofore been available from disk systems. This part describes some techniques that are commonly combined with RAID to create high-performance failure-tolerant on-line disk systems.

Chapter 8: Hybrid RAID Arrays

Using More Than One Type of RAID in an Array

One technique frequently used to improve RAID array I/O performance is to combine multiple types of RAID protection and mapping in the same array. This combination can be thought of as implementing two separate layers of *Array Management Function*. The lower layer manages physical disks and presents virtual disks to the upper layer. The upper layer manages the virtual disks presented to it, and presents the result to applications. Figure 73 illustrates such an array.

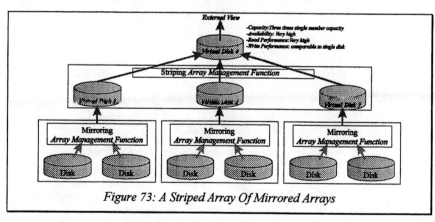

Figure 73: A Striped Array Of Mirrored Arrays

In Figure 73, the lower *Array Management Function* layer presents two-member mirrored arrays labeled Virtual disks 1, 2, and 3 to the upper *Array Management Function* layer, which stripes data across them and presents a single virtual disk to applications. The result is functionally equivalent to the multi-disk mirrored arrays described in Chapter 4. The layered implementation offers more flexible implementation possibilities, however. For example, the mirroring *Array Management Function* might be implemented in an intelligent controller, with a host-based striping *Array Management Function*. This would allow aggregation of multiple disk systems' data transfer capacities for large file applications, or aggregation of I/O request capacities for transaction applications.

Even for the integrated multi-disk mirrored arrays described in Chapter 4, whose data protection and mapping may not be formally layered, thinking of the striping and mirroring functions separately can aid in understanding how each of the two affects I/O performance.

This chapter presents two examples of hybrid arrays: the striped array of mirrored arrays illustrated in Figure 73, and striped arrays whose members are parity RAID (RAID Level 3 or RAID Level 5) arrays.

Combining Striping with Mirroring for High I/O Performance *and* High Data Availability

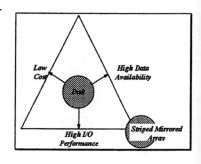

The combination of RAID Level 0 and 1, variously called *RAID 0+1, RAID 0&1, RAID 10,* and other names by vendors, combines RAID Levels 0 and 1 in a single array that provides:

➡ enhanced data availability through disk mirroring, and,

➡ enhanced I/O performance through disk striping.

The result is storage with both high I/O performance and high data availability, albeit at a relatively high inherent cost.

Description Of Data Mapping In Striped Mirrored Arrays

Figure 74 illustrates a common data mapping for a striped array of mirrored arrays. In Figure 74, Member Disks 0 and 1 comprise a two-member mirrored array, labeled **Virtual Member 0**. Similarly, Member Disks 2 and 3 comprise mirrored array **Virtual Member 1.** Each mirrored array provides disk failure-tolerant storage capacity approximately equal to that of the smaller of its members. and

Virtual Members 0 and 1 are members of a striped array labeled **Virtual Disk**, whose capacity is approximately twice that of the smaller of *its* two members.

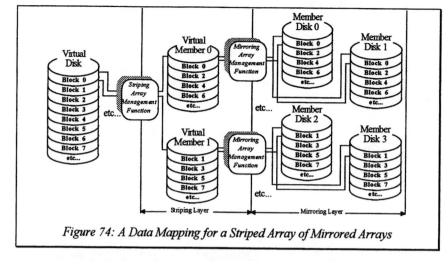

Figure 74: A Data Mapping for a Striped Array of Mirrored Arrays

The striping (upper layer, shown on the left side of Figure 74) *Array Management Function* balances application I/O load across Virtual Members 0 and 1. Member read operations directed at Virtual Members 0 and 1 by the striping *Array Management Function* can be further balanced across each mirror set's two members by a sufficiently sophisticated mirroring (lower layer, shown on the right side of Figure 74) *Array Management Function*. Member write operations must be replicated on both member disks. The result is mirroring data availability combined with striping I/O load balancing.

Normal Operation of Striped Mirrored Arrays

When an application I/O request is delivered to an array such as that illustrated in Figure 74, the striping *Array Management Function* breaks it down into the member operations implied by the striped data mapping (described on page 85). These member operations are delivered to the mirroring *Array Management Function*. The mirroring *Array Management Function* executes each member operation as if it were an application request. (Mirrored array I/O request processing is described on page 94.)

Failure Protection

The Mean Time To Data Availability loss (MTDA) of a striped mirrored array with $2n$ physical member disks is about $1/n$ times that of a two-member mirrored array.[45] If a disk fails, failure of its mirrored partner prior to replacement will make data unavailable. Depending on the nature of the failure, data loss may also occur. No *other* member disk failure will cause data loss, however. This is superior to a parity RAID array,

---

[45] This takes into account only the contribution of disk failure to MTDA. In practice, other components may fail in a way that can cause data or accessibility loss (e.g., a bus that begins to broadcast erroneously during data transfer, a controller failure, etc.). Site disasters (e.g., fire, flood) may also destroy data or block access to it.

where for the duration of a disk outage (MTTR, which is longer than for a mirrored array because of the larger amount of I/O required to rebuild a failed member), failure of *any* remaining array member makes data unavailable. A mirrored array's data reliability is typically so high (approximately member MTBF[2]) that even when several are combined into a striped mirrored array, net data availability is still measured in tens of millions of hours for arrays of typical modern disks.

When a replacement disk becomes available, the mirroring *Array Management Function* can restore protection by rebuilding the failed disk's contents. It copies data from the surviving member to the replacement disk. Rebuilding is functionally transparent to applications (data remains accessible for reading and writing), however it creates a heavy I/O load, and so application performance during rebuilding is usually significantly degraded. Figure 75 illustrates member rebuilding in a striped mirrored array.

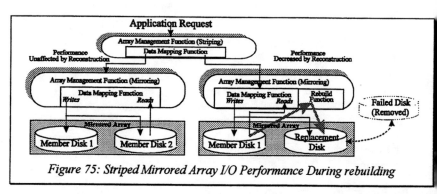

Figure 75: Striped Mirrored Array I/O Performance During rebuilding

The striping *Array Management Function* in Figure 75 tends to direct about half of application I/O requests to each of its virtual members. Those directed to the left member in the figure are further redirected by the mirroring *Array Management Function*:

➡ to one of the two member disks if the request is a read (the mirroring *Array Management Function* may have a preferred member, or it may use a selection algorithm that tends to balance load between the two),

➡ to both of the member disks if the request is a write.

The same occurs with application requests directed to the mirrored array on the right, however, that virtual member's *Array Management Function* is simultaneously rebuilding the failed disk's contents onto the replacement disk by reading Member Disk 0's entire contents and copying them to Member Disk 1. Application I/O requests must be interspersed with this (essentially continuous) stream of work. Even if application I/O is given absolute priority, waiting for completion of the rebuilding I/O operation in progress at the time an application I/O request is received results in longer application response times. During rebuilding, application requests requiring operations on the mirrored array on the right in Figure 75 will generally take longer to complete than those that result only in operations on the mirrored array on the left.

I/O Performance Of Striped Arrays
Of Mirrored Arrays

Primary and secondary load balancing effects combine to give striped arrays whose members are mirrored arrays high I/O performance:

➡ *Primary*: The striped data mapping balances the I/O load across members. For I/O request-intensive applications, load balancing occurs because concurrent application I/O requests for relatively small amounts of data tend to distribute evenly across the array's (virtual) members. For data transfer-intensive applications, load balancing occurs because large application I/O requests are broken down into multiple member operations which are executed concurrently by multiple virtual members.

➡ *Secondary*: When the I/O load is high, I/O queues may build up at the virtual members of the striped array. A sophisticated mirroring *Array Management Function* can further balance heavy I/O loads by choosing its least busy member disk to satisfy each read request. Of course, this effect does not occur for write requests, which must be replicated on each mirrored array member.

Between them, these effects can significantly improve performance for I/O-intensive applications which meet the one of basic requirements for I/O load balancing:

➡ I/O request-intensive applications with I/O loads of asynchronous I/O requests, or

➡ data transfer-intensive applications which make large double-buffered requests.

Figure 76 illustrates load balancing in a striped array of mirrored arrays.

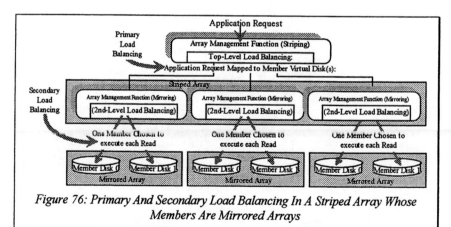

Figure 76: Primary And Secondary Load Balancing In A Striped Array Whose Members Are Mirrored Arrays

Applications For Striped Mirrored
Arrays

Adding striping to multiple mirrored arrays requires no more physical disks or connections than mirroring alone. The sole incremental cost of striping (if any) is that of its

Array Management Function. This usually means that striping mirrored arrays is an excellent bargain for any data whose value and volume justifies placing it on mirrored disk storage.

There are probably more configuration options available for striped mirrored arrays than for any other form or RAID. Often, it is possible to use host-based striping to combine virtual disks presented by controller-based mirrored arrays into an array. Some vendors offer both striping and mirroring capability within their disk systems. Finally, some system vendors offer host-based software packages for both striping and mirroring.

Striping Mirrored Arrays vs. Mirroring Striped Arrays

The configuration used as an example in the foregoing discussion is a striped array whose (virtual) members are mirrored arrays. From a performance standpoint, this is equivalent to a mirrored array whose members are striped arrays. Figure 77 illustrates the latter configuration. The I/O performance of the two configurations is essentially equivalent, since an application's I/O request to the array results the same number of I/O operations on the same physical members in both cases, so similar load balancing occurs.

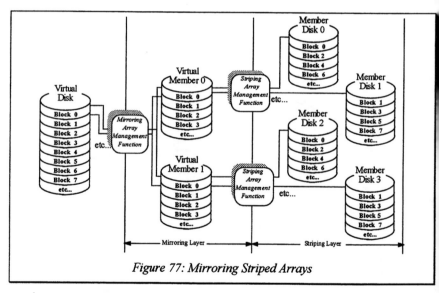

Figure 77: Mirroring Striped Arrays

From an availability standpoint, however, there is a significant difference between the array illustrated in Figure 74 and that in Figure 77. As discussed in Chapter 4 (page 83), the failure of a single member disk effectively renders an entire striped array inoperative and the data stored on it inaccessible. Failure of any physical disk in Figure 77 is tantamount to failure of the striped array of which it is a member. While this does not interrupt service to applications from the upper **Virtual Disk**, it increases the number of disks any one of whose failure *would* cause data to become unavailable. When the array illustrated in Figure 74 is operating in reduced mode, one specific disk, the second member of the same mirrored array whose first member has failed, must fail in order to interrupt data access. In the array illustrated in Figure 77, however, a failure of either of the disks in the alternate mirrored array would make data unavailable.

Rebuilding time after a failed disk has been replaced is also substantially greater for a mirrored array of striped arrays than for a striped array of mirrored arrays. In the former case, data from the entire striped array must be copied from the surviving striped array to the one created by combining the replacement disk with the failed array's remaining member(s). In the latter case, however, only the data from one physical disk must be copied during a rebuilding operation.

For these reasons, striping of mirrored arrays is generally the preferable solution. Mirrored arrays of striped arrays are sometimes used as a matter of expediency, as for example, when a vendor's disk system supports striped arrays but not mirrored ones. A host-based mirroring capability can provide data protection by mirroring two striped arrays belonging to the same or different disk systems.

Combining Striping With Parity RAID For More Symmetrical Read and Write Performance

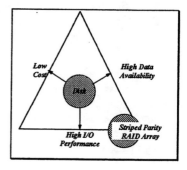

The terms *RAID 30* and *RAID 50* are sometimes used to describe disk arrays in which striping and parity RAID *Array Management Functions* are combined in a single array. For applications requiring large storage capacity, these arrays can simultaneously provide parallel access parity RAID-like data transfer performance and independent access striping-like I/O request rates at an inherent cost comparable to that of parity RAID.

Data Mapping in Striped Arrays with Parity RAID Arrays as Members

Figure 78 illustrates an example of a data mapping scheme that combines a parity RAID lower level mapping with a striping upper level.

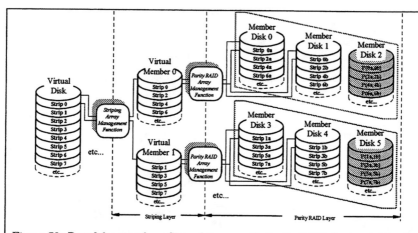

Figure 78: Data Mapping for a Striped Arrays with Parity RAID Arrays as Members

In Figure 78, Member Disks 0, 1, and 2, and Member Disks 3, 4, and 5 each comprise parity RAID[46] arrays presented to the upper level *Array Management Function* as **Virtual Members 0** and **1**. The six member disks provide the equivalent of four

---

46 Figure 78 is conceptual, with small numbers of members used for simplicity of presentation. In actual implementations, greater economy can be achieved if the lower-level parity RAID arrays have larger numbers of members.

physical disks of highly reliable storage capacity. The stripe depth of the parity RAID arrays is the size of one member strip (e.g., Strip 0a). Each parity RAID array has a potential data transfer rate about equivalent to the spiral data transfer rate of two physical disks (provided that adequate data transfer capacity is available).

Virtual Members 0 and **1** are organized as a striped array presented to the operating environment as **Virtual Disk**. The capacity of **Virtual Disk** is the sum of the capacities of its two member arrays. The striped array's stripe depth in this example is the size of a member array's strip (e.g., Strip 0).

The striping *Array Management Function* balances application I/O loads across **Virtual Members 0** and **1**. Each member I/O request directed at **Virtual Member 0** or **1** is processed by the parity RAID *Array Management Function*, and satisfied by parallel data transfers to or from the parity RAID array's data disks. The result is disk failure-tolerant storage with both high data transfer capacity and high I/O request rate at a parity RAID-like inherent hardware cost.

Normal Operation

When an application I/O request is delivered to this array, the striping *Array Management Function* breaks it down into as many member operations as required (as described on page 85), and makes these requests to the parity RAID virtual members.

Each operation directed to one of the parity RAID *Array Management Functions* is processed as if it had come directly from an application. (parity RAID I/O request processing is described on page 108.)

The parity RAID layer of this array enhances data availability by protecting against loss of data availability due to member disk failure. The striping layer improves I/O request handling capability (compared to that of parity RAID alone). The underlying parity RAID arrays' member disks provide high data transfer performance.

Failure Protection

The data availability of a striped array of n parity RAID virtual members is equal to $1/n$ times that of one of its member arrays. The data availability of parity RAID arrays is typically so high, however, that the net data availability provided by this configuration is still well beyond that of individually managed disks.

Failure of a physical disk in a striped array of parity RAID virtual members affects neither the array's ability to deliver data to applications, nor its performance (except during rebuilding).

As soon as a replacement disk is provided, the lower-layer parity RAID *Array Management Function* may restore full data protection by rebuilding data from the surviving members of the parity RAID array that experienced the failure. Rebuilding is usually functionally transparent to applications, but the I/O load it imposes can significantly impact responsiveness for application I/O requests that map to the affected virtual member array during rebuilding, as illustrated in Figure 79.

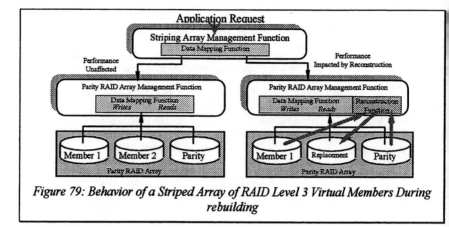

Figure 79: Behavior of a Striped Array of RAID Level 3 Virtual Members During rebuilding

For a large number of I/O requests with randomly distributed data addresses, the striping *Array Management Function* in Figure 79 directs an average of half to each virtual member. Those directed to the left member are subdivided equally by the parity RAID *Array Management Function* as described on page 108.

Requests directed to the parity RAID array on the right in Figure 79 are also subdivided, however, the rebuilding function is simultaneously reading both surviving member disks' entire contents, computing their **Exclusive OR**, and writing the result to the replacement disk. Because of the I/O load this imposes, application requests for data that maps to this virtual member tend to take longer to complete than requests for data that map to the member on the left.

I/O Performance in Striped Arrays with Parity RAID Arrays As Members

The high I/O performance of this type of array stems from two sources:

➡ The upper (striped) array balances the I/O load. For I/O request-intensive applications, load balancing occurs because concurrent I/O requests for relatively small amounts of data tend to map evenly across the member disks. The I/O request handling capacity of these arrays is equivalent to that of n physical disks[47] with a perfectly balanced I/O load.

➡ Each of the parity RAID virtual members transfers data at a rate equal to the sum of *its* data disk transfer rates. The result is that the data transfer portion of every I/O request executes at the aggregate transfer rate of a parity RAID member array. For large transfers, if the parity RAID arrays' member disks are not rotationally synchronized, the increased aggregate rotational latency of unsynchronized

---

[47] whose performance is equivalent to that of the actual array member disks.

disks working in tandem must be balanced against the improved data transfer performance.

In combination, these effects can significantly improve I/O performance for I/O-intensive applications which meet one of the basic requirements for I/O load balancing:

➡ I/O request-intensive applications whose I/O loads consist of asynchronous I/O requests, or

➡ data transfer-intensive applications which make large requests and are (at least) double buffered.

Figure 80 illustrates load balancing in a striped array with parity RAID virtual members.

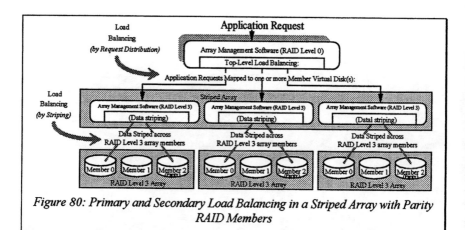

Figure 80: Primary and Secondary Load Balancing in a Striped Array with Parity RAID Members

Applications for Striped Arrays with Parity RAID Arrays As Members

Like the combination of striping with mirroring, combining striping with parity RAID uses no more physical disks per unit of application storage capacity than parity RAID arrays alone. The incremental inherent cost, if any, is the cost of the striping *Array Management Function*. This makes this combination an excellent choice for data which must be highly available and whose volume, cost constraints, and I/O performance requirements (high data transfer rate) indicate multiple parity RAID arrays as the basic storage technology. As with combinations of striping and mirroring, it is often possible to combine controller-based parity RAID arrays using a host-based striping *Array Management Function*.

Chapter 9: RAID and Parallel Processing

Parallel Operations That Make RAID Systems More Effective

An application I/O request to a modern disk system is the beginning of a complex multi-step process, in which multiple computing, data movement, and other resources participate. The primitive functions that make up an I/O operation are simple and highly structured. Moreover, their time relationships to each other, while sometimes complex when viewed as a whole, can be expressed as a dependency matrix.

Time Line for an I/O Request

The time line in Figure 81 represents the major primitive functions required to execute a read request to a disk attached to an intelligent controller.[48] The time line is shown primarily from the controller point of view, treating host (steps 1, 2, and 11) and device functions (steps 5, 6, and 7) as though they were atomic, although these functions might be similarly subdivided if the I/O request viewed from the host's or the device's perspective.

---

[48] For simplicity, all primitive functions represented in this chapter are shown as being of equal duration. In reality, there is obviously wide variation in execution times.

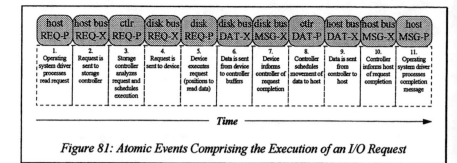

host REQ-P	host bus REQ-X	ctlr REQ-P	disk bus REQ-X	disk REQ-P	disk bus DAT-X	disk bus MSG-X	ctlr DAT-P	host bus DAT-X	host bus MSG-X	host MSG-P
1. Operating system driver processes read request	2. Request is sent to storage controller	3. Storage controller analyzes request and schedules execution	4. Request is sent to device	5. Device executes request (positions to read data)	6. Data is sent from device to controller buffers	7. Device controller of informs request completion	8. Controller schedules movement of data to host	9. Data is sent from controller to host	10. Controller informs host of request completion	11. Operating system driver processes completion message

Time ──────►

Figure 81: Atomic Events Comprising the Execution of an I/O Request

The steps represented in Figure 81 are as follows:

1. (**REQuest-Processing**) Trusted operating system components analyze the validity and appropriateness of applications' I/O requests and translate them into the form required for transmission to the controller. *Validation* includes verifying both the correctness of memory and device addresses specified in the application's request and the application's right to access data at those addresses.[49]

2. (**REQuest-Xmission**) An I/O request packaged for transmission to a storage controller is a concisely encoded packet of data (10-50 bytes is common) containing the essential details of the request. These packets are transmitted over the host I/O bus to the disk controller that will carry out the instructions they contain. Host driver software and I/O bus adapters typically cooperate to manage *queues* of I/O request packets, interspersing them with data according to the rules of the host I/O bus protocol.

3. (**REQuest-Processing**) Upon receipt of an I/O request packet, the disk controller determines that it is a new I/O request (rather than data sent in response to a previous request or a status message). Like the host, the controller validates the request and inserts it into its queue of outstanding work for the addressed device. If the request is made to a RAID array's virtual disk, the storage controller converts it into one or more member disk operations and schedules those for execution.

4. (**REQuest-Xmission**) The disk devices used in modern disk systems are intelligent in their own right, and can process I/O requests autonomously. SCSI-2[50] protocols assume that devices have this capability. The model represented in Figure 81 assumes that a read request can be sent to a disk as one I/O request packet on the device channel, and executed completely by the device without controller assistance.

---

49 This discussion deals with I/O requests addressed to physical or virtual storage devices. Most application I/O requests are made indirectly through a file or database system, which imposes structure and file semantics on the flat logical block space of a disk or tape. Requests made in a file system context are subject to other access controls, which are applied before physical I/O is requested.

50 Small Computer System Interconnect—the standard bus most frequently used to connect storage devices to controllers, and also very often used as a host to controller interconnect.

5. (REQuest-Processing) To process an I/O request, a device must analyze the request and prepare itself for data transfer. For disks, preparation for data transfer means positioning the read/write heads at the data to be transferred by *seeking* and *rotating* as necessary.

6. (DATa-Xmission) When prepared, the device transfers data to the controller over the device channel. The controller typically receives the data into buffers from which it is relayed to the requesting host. From the device's perspective, this may be a complex sequence of its own primitive functions, involving internal buffering and processing. The model of Figure 81 treats the device action as a primitive function, however, since that is generally how controllers must view I/O requests to intelligent disk devices.

7. (MeSsaGe-Xmission) When its transfer of data to the controller is complete, the device sends a status message indicating that all data was successfully delivered (from the device's standpoint). For most bus protocols, this message is a separate device channel transaction from the data transfer.

8. (DATa-Processing) When it has received the requested data (signaled by device status message(s)), the controller schedules its transmission to the requesting host. Since a controller normally moves data between several devices and a host on a single host I/O bus, it typically has a queue of pending data and messages. The operation of transmitting the data for the new read request is added to that queue to await its turn to be executed.

9. (DATa-Xmission) The controller transmits the data for the read request to the host. The example of Figure 81 assumes that the amount of data requested is small enough to be sent with a single host I/O bus transaction. Larger I/O requests often require multiple bus transactions.

10. (MeSsaGe-Xmission) Most host I/O bus protocols require that data sent to the host be followed by a status message indicating that the host's request has been successfully executed (or otherwise). This is typically a separate bus transaction. Some protocols require more than one bus transaction at this stage.

11. (MeSsaGe-Processing) On receipt of the controller's status message, the host (usually an I/O driver operating system component) notifies the originating application that its data is available. This usually makes the application eligible to continue execution, using the data delivered in response to its I/O request.

Concurrent Use of Resources

In the example represented in Figure 81, each step requires that the preceding step be complete. This leaves little opportunity for parallel operation. It is important to note, however, that different disk system resources are used at different stages of I/O request execution, and that resources are idle for part of the execution time.

One of the primary functions of storage controllers is to attach multiple devices to host computers using one or two host I/O bus addresses. If multiple requests for data from

---

different devices were present at the same time, a controller could, in principle, process them concurrently. This is illustrated in Figure 82:

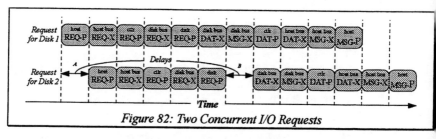

Figure 82 represents two sequences of primitive functions, each comprising a request made to a different disk attached to the same controller.[51] The requests might come from different hosts, from different application processes timesharing a host, or from a multi-threaded application, in operating environments that support the latter capability.

Unless the host is a multiprocessor system, the application requests can not be processed at quite the same time (since a single processor can only execute a single instruction stream), but it is conceivable (and even common) that as soon as one request has been processed and scheduled for transmission to the controller, the host becomes free to handle a second request on behalf of a different application. The second application may have been ready to make its I/O request at the same time as the first; however, with only one host processing resource, one of the two must wait. This forced wait is represented by delay A in Figure 82. From that point until the point marked as delay B in Figure 82, the two requests can be processed *in parallel* (concurrently in time) because they are using different resources at each point in time. Delay B occurs because both requests require the disk bus at the same time, and only one can use it. The net result is that execution of both applications' requests takes only slightly more time than execution of either one alone (13 units of time to process two I/O requests, compared to 11 units of time for one).

Measures Of I/O Performance
Response Time and Throughput

Together, Figure 81 and Figure 82 illustrate the difference between the two most common measures of I/O performance, *response time* and *throughput*. Response time is the time between an application's making an I/O request, and completion of the request's execution, including delivery of data and status message, and any host processing required to signal the application that its request is complete and make it executable. Assuming for simplicity that each primitive function represented in Figure 82 is of equal duration, execution of an I/O request requires 11 units of time. An application I/O request made to an idle I/O system will receive its response eleven units of time later.

---

[51] For simplicity, all primitive functions are represented as taking equal time, although in practice, this is not the case.

The *average* I/O response time for a large number of requests is important to designers of transaction applications. A single transaction from the system user's point of view (sometimes called a *business transaction*) may require the execution of dozens or hundreds of I/O requests as databases are searched, records updated, and results logged. The response time for a business transaction in an otherwise idle system is the sum of the response times for the I/O requests needed to accomplish it plus the time required for processing. For business transactions which require hundreds of I/O requests, a few milliseconds longer average I/O response time can add seconds to user response time.

In Figure 81, one I/O request is executed in eleven units of time. In Figure 82, two I/O requests are executed in a total of 13 units of time—an increase of 70% in units of work accomplished per unit time. From the point of view of the application making the request for Disk 2, however, I/O performance is not as good. Response to its request requires 13 units of time, rather than eleven.

Another way to look at responsiveness using Figure 82 is to observe that the average of the two I/O request execution times is 12 units. It is easy to imagine how execution of more than two concurrent I/O requests using the same set of resources would result in even longer average response times, even though disk system resources would be used more completely, and more I/O requests would be executed per unit of time.

For systems that share their resources among multiple I/O requests, *throughput*, the number of requests executed per unit time, is greatest when all of the resources are constantly in use. The best way to assure that a resource will be used constantly is to build up a queue of work for it to do, so that each time the resource completes a work item, the next item can be started on immediately. In Figure 82, the **REQ-P** and **DAT-X** primitive I/O functions in Disk 2's time line represent queues of work items for the host processor and disk bus respectively.

Building up queues of primitive I/O functions (represented by Delays A and B in Figure 82) implies that the application I/O requests of which they are part experience elongated response times. Thus, getting the greatest possible throughput from a disk system usually implies (sometimes significantly) longer response times for individual application I/O requests. Application system designers usually face the challenge of configuring disk systems whose resources are used heavily enough to be cost-justified, but not so heavily that the system becomes unresponsive due to queuing of work items for over-utilized resources.

Fairness in Multi-Device Shared Resource Systems

In the example of Figure 82, the request for Disk 1 is serviced first in both cases where there is contention for a resource. As illustrated, Disk 1's request is implicitly given priority. Figure 83 illustrates another possible scenario.

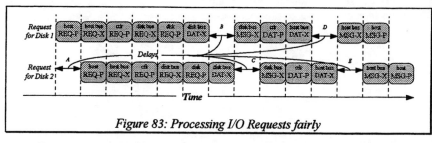

Figure 83: Processing I/O Requests fairly

Figure 83 represents the same two I/O requests as Figure 82. In this case, however, each time there is contention for a resource, a "fairness" algorithm determines which of the two requests' primitive functions is granted use of the resource first. The fairness algorithm illustrated in Figure 83 grants any resource for which there is contention alternately to the two host I/O requests being processed (In practice, more sophisticated algorithms are typically used.).

Thus, when both requests require the host processor at the same time, Disk 1's request is processed first, and Disk 2's request is delayed (*Delay A*). When both requests require access to the disk I/O bus simultaneously, Disk 2's data transfer is granted first use of the bus, and Disk 1's ending message to the controller is delayed (*Delay B*). Disk 1's request for the disk bus is granted next, however, and Disk 2's ending message is delayed (*Delay C*). The data transfer for Disk 2's request causes the ending message to the host for Disk 1's request to be delayed (*Delay D*), and Disk 1's ending message to the host delays Disk 1's ending message.

Figure 83 represents a somewhat realistic sequence of events for multi-device storage controllers, which can process several I/O requests concurrently. Intelligent controllers *decompose* each application I/O request into primitive functions according to the resources required, and schedule execution of multiple requests' primitive functions (which are independent of each other) so as to maximize use of controller resources such as processors, I/O interfaces and buses, disks, and internal data paths. As can be seen from Figure 83, a well-designed controller can significantly enhance I/O *throughput*, but it usually increases individual request response times slightly (compared to disks attached directly to a host adapter). Well designed fairness algorithms tend to increase the response time for all requests by equal or proportional amounts.[52]

Figure 83 illustrates the difficulty of designing fairness algorithms that produce the desired effect. While the round-robin algorithm is nominally fair, in the example illustrated it increases both average and maximum response time (compared to Figure 82).

---

[52] Some I/O protocols allow a host to direct a controller to favor certain requests over others, usually by assigning a higher priority to them.

RAID and Parallelism

Because RAID I/O algorithms consist essentially of translating each application I/O request to a virtual disk into one or more member I/O operations, RAID arrays work particularly well with disk systems capable of executing several primitive I/O functions in parallel. The overall effect of parallel execution in a RAID array is to minimize the elapsed time to execute an application request, thereby more closely approximating, or even improving upon the performance of an equivalent individual disk, while still providing RAID data availability benefits.

Figure 84 illustrates parallel operations using a controller-based two-member striped array with a stripe depth of 100 disk blocks, and shows the execution timeline for an application request to read 200 blocks (assumed for simplicity to be strip-aligned). The controller's *Array Management Function* decomposes the application's request for 200 virtual disk blocks into requests for 100 blocks from each array member.

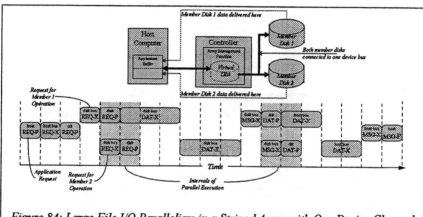

Figure 84: Large File I/O Parallelism in a Striped Array with One Device Channel

In Figure 84, execution times for the data transfer primitive functions have been lengthened to reflect the fact that transferring such a large amount of data would typically be a significant portion of overall request execution time. Moreover, controller-to-host data transfer is represented as a shorter time than device-to-controller data transfer, since host I/O buses are often capable of higher data transfer rates.

The two member operations represented in Figure 84 can execute independently of each other. Since each member operation results in data being sent to a different area of the application's buffer, the order in which their respective primitive functions execute is immaterial. With sufficient resources, both member operations could be partly or completely concurrent. As an example, Figure 85 represents the same application read request made to a striped array whose members are connected to separate disk I/O buses so that they can transfer data concurrently.

The primitive functions of the two member operations illustrated in Figure 85 (e.g., DAT-X and MSG-X) can execute concurrently. Some delay may still occur if data from both member disks are ready for transmission to the host at the same time, but it is clear from the diagram that significant reduction in application response time is possible if sufficient resources (disk I/O buses in this case) are available.

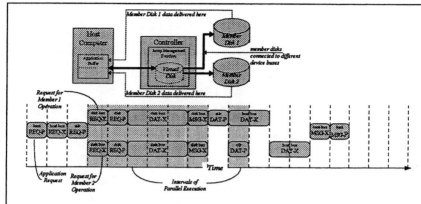

Figure 85: Large File I/O Parallelism in a Striped Array with Multiple Device Channels

Figure 85 represents an I/O request that has elsewhere (e.g., page 43) been characterized as *data transfer-intensive*, or large file I/O, because the amount of data requested makes data transfer time large compared to the time required by the request's other primitive functions. From Figure 85, one might infer that further performance improvement might be achieved by:

➡ reducing disk-to-controller data transfer time adding more disks on separate channels and reducing stripe depth to shorten individual member I/O times,

➡ reducing controller-to-host data transfer time by using a higher-performing host I/O bus, and,

➡ reducing disk-to-controller data transfer time, by using disks and device channels with higher data transfer capacity.

The first of these possibilities increases the system's parallelism. The second and third may be characterized as reducing service time for individual primitive functions.

Parallel Execution and Transaction I/O

The foregoing example illustrates how parallel operations can improve large data transfer performance. Parallel operations can also benefit transaction I/O loads. Transaction I/O loads, described on page 45, are characterized by:

➡ a large number of I/O requests per unit of time (so that requests overlap in time),

➡ I/O requests that are somewhat uniformly distributed among disks,

➡ non-sequential access to data, and,

➡ relatively small amounts of data accessed in each request.

As described on page 32, the striped data mapping in most RAID arrays improves I/O performance through its tendency to *balance*, or evenly distribute the I/O load across the array's physical resources (particularly its disks). Balancing means that demands on the array's resources are distributed more or less evenly across them; parallel execution, as illustrated in Figure 83 through Figure 85, maximizes resource utilization.

Some forms of improved individual resource performance (e.g., faster disk positioning or controller I/O request processing) would be of minimal benefit to large file I/O performance, since the fraction of total application I/O request execution time spent processing and positioning is small compared to the data transfer time. With transaction I/O loads, data transfer performance is less of a concern, but parallel execution can still improve I/O performance substantially. Figure 86 represents three overlapping small application I/O requests made to an independent access striped array with all of its member disks attached to a single device channel.

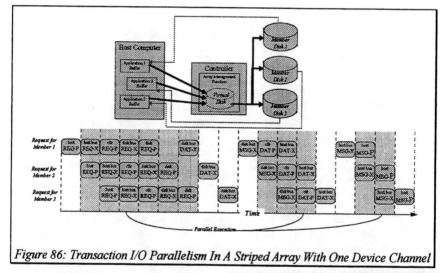

Figure 86: Transaction I/O Parallelism In A Striped Array With One Device Channel

In Figure 86 (which is highly idealized), a significant amount of parallel execution (represented by shaded background) is illustrated, even with a single device channel. This occurs because so high a percentage of each member request's execution time is taken up with primitive functions other than moving data between disk and controller buffers, using resources which are either

➡ replicated (e.g., disks, which allow concurrent disk REQ-P functions), or,

➡ not otherwise occupied at the instant they are required.

With transaction I/O, the degree of parallel execution that can be achieved without multiple disk buses is much greater than in the large file I/O case (Figure 84). Nonetheless, transaction I/O also benefits from additional resources that further increase the potential for parallel execution, as illustrated in Figure 87.

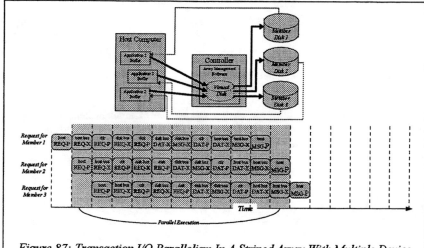

Figure 87: Transaction I/O Parallelism In A Striped Array With Multiple Device Channels

In Figure 87, each member disk is attached to a separate device channel, so that concurrent data and status message transfers between different disks and the controller are possible. This eliminates delays due to devices waiting for a device channel to become available. At least some parallel activity is occurring for almost the entire application request execution time. In fact, the non-parallel activity (initial host processing of the application requests; a single-processor host is assumed), is arguably beneficial, since it offsets the I/O request arrivals at the controller in time, minimizing overlaps that could cause delays waiting for the controller's processor to be available.

Together, Figure 86 and Figure 87 illustrate that the best way to improve the I/O performance of a striped array subjected to transaction I/O loads is to add additional resources in the form of disks, preferably, but not necessarily, attached to additional device channels. The performance goal for a transaction I/O load is usually to maximize throughput while maintaining a reasonable average response time. Adding disks without additional disk buses tends to improve response time because with a transaction I/O load, the device channels are idle most of the time. As the intensity of the I/O load increases, however, there is a greater probability that when a device channel is required, it will be busy executing another primitive function, and a queue will develop.

Additional Resources that Promote
Parallel I/O Request Execution

The foregoing sections demonstrate the value of multiple disks and device channels that can operate in parallel to increase I/O performance in two different ways:

➡ For large file I/O loads, spreading application request execution across multiple disks attached to separate device channels shortens data transfer time, improving responsiveness.

➡ For transaction I/O loads, multiple disks allow multiple I/O requests to execute concurrently, improving throughput (without substantially reducing response time for individual requests). In this case, separate device channels for each disk are less important than with large file I/O, although they can result in further performance improvement (as well as improved failure tolerance).

Disks and device channels are the two most obvious resources which can be beneficially replicated for parallel execution. Other resources, particularly within the disk controller, can also be augmented or replicated to improve I/O performance. Figure 88 illustrates a typical controller architecture in which both processing and data movement resources can be added to increase the disk system's I/O performance potential.

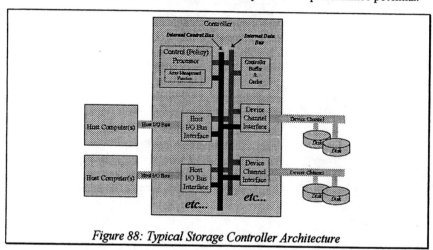

Figure 88: Typical Storage Controller Architecture

The backbone of the controller architecture represented in Figure 88 is a very high-performance internal bus used for moving data between controller components. Because a controller's internal data movement requirements (high speed, large blocks) differ from its internal control flow requirements (small messages or signals requiring fast response), a controller's internal data buses is often augmented with a second bus optimized for sending control signals between controller components. Four types of controller components are generally connected to one or both of these internal buses:

➡ **Device channel interfaces.** These consist of the logic necessary to control and communicate with a device channel. Each manages the work load for a device channel, converting data between the channel's format and protocols and those internal to the controller, as the data moves between controller internal buffers and devices. Device channel interfaces usually consist of specialized interconnect circuits, logic to sequence work flow, and a small buffer ("FIFO") to smooth momentary speed mismatches between the controller's internal bus and the device channel. In some implementations, a microprocessor is used for sequencing. More often, the interconnect circuits and work flow sequencing functions are integrated in a single package. In most controllers, each device channel is controlled by a separate device channel interface.

➡ *Host I/O bus interfaces.* These perform the interface and work flow sequencing function for the host I/O bus. Like device channel interfaces, they usually consist of specialized bus connection logic, logic to sequence work flow, and a FIFO. Host I/O bus interfaces complete the data transfer path through the controller by moving data between internal buffers and the host I/O bus. Today, most controllers attach to a single host I/O bus, although increasingly, disk systems are being designed for clustered computing environments in which a set of storage devices is connected to multiple hosts. Multiple host I/O buses can increase single-stream I/O performance between a controller and host, but more importantly, they increase failure tolerance and allow connection to multiple hosts.

➡ *Control processors.* In addition to simple, repetitive bus interface operations, controllers perform more complex functions, such as application I/O request analysis, primitive function scheduling, resource allocation, status message generation, and error handling. The complexity of these functions requires general purpose processing. Virtually all storage controllers today use embedded general purpose processors for control. Most contain a single control processor, but closely-coupled multiprocessors may be designed in to improve throughput under heavy load by allowing multiple primitive functions to be executed in parallel.

➡ *Internal buffers and cache memory.* Because device and host I/O interface data transfer rates are different, and because data and control information from multiple I/O requests are often interspersed on a host I/O bus, disk controllers require buffers to compensate for short-term speed differences among their components. For read requests, buffers hold blocks of data received from disks until they can be transmitted to the host. For write requests, buffers are used to fetch blocks of data from the host "just in time" as the target disk(s) require them.

In high-performance disk systems, controller buffers (typically hundreds of Kbytes) are sometimes augmented by a much larger cache (typically hundreds of Mbytes), in which data passing through the controller is held for relatively long periods. *Read cache* holds data recently read or written in anticipation that it will soon be required again by the host, at which time it can be delivered immediately from the controller's cache, without waiting for the storage device to prepare itself and transfer data. Write cache holds data written by applications so that the application can regard its I/O request as complete and continue to execute, without waiting for service from the target device. Write cache with a policy of informing the host that its write requests are complete, and holding data for later writing is called *write-behind* cache. To preserve disk system data integrity, write-behind cache should be protected against power failure and other disk system failures so that these events do not cause loss of data (in the sense that data successfully "written" by an application never appears on disk media if a failure occurs while it is still in the cache). A write-behind cache with such protection is called a *write-back* cache.

The amount of buffer memory or cache in a controller may be increased to improve performance; indeed, some implementations offer multiple Gbytes of cache memory. To protect against rare failures of the cache itself, some controllers replicate cache contents in a manner analogous to the replication of on-disk data provided by mirroring. This feature is called *dual-copy* cache or *mirrored* cache.

As vendors have sought to produce disk systems with increasingly higher performance, the architecture illustrated in Figure 88 has proven remarkably durable. Adding device channel interfaces has proven to be the most popular way to expand a controller line's applicability; accommodation of large amounts of cache is a close second. Larger cache capacity increases the fraction of I/O requests that can be satisfied without recourse to disks, and the time it entails.

More recently, controllers with multiple host interfaces have begun to appear, although today this feature is used at least as much for connecting to multiple hosts as for increasing performance between a single controller-host pair. Finally, for transaction I/O loads, additional control processors can increase request handling capability.

Replicating storage controller components allows multiple primitive I/O functions to execute concurrently. This tends to increase throughput potential for transaction I/O loads, and shorten response times for large file I/O loads. To shorten individual I/O requests' response times in transaction I/O loads, it is necessary to increase the speed with which primitive I/O functions are carried out. This can only be achieved through the use of higher-performing disk system components, such as controller internal data bus, control processor, and cache, host and device channel, and devices themselves.

More Complex Scenarios: Parity
RAID

Application requests in the preceding striped array examples have the property that the member I/O operations of which they consist are independent of each other; that is, each member operation may execute to completion without waiting for any other member operation to complete. The controller need only synchronize member operations in the sense that all of them must finish before completion of the application I/O request is reported to the host. This is not the case with application requests to mirrored arrays or independent access parity RAID arrays, however. For these arrays, an application write request entails a series of member read and write operations, some of which require that previous ones be completed. Figure 89 (adapted from Figure 64 on page 131) shows the controller portion of the primitive I/O function sequence required to execute an application write request to an independent access parity RAID array.[53]

---

[53] Some primitive I/O functions, such as movement of data between controller and host, are omitted for clarity.

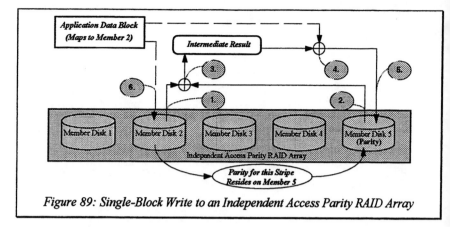

Figure 89: Single-Block Write to an Independent Access Parity RAID Array

In Figure 89 there is a degree of mutual dependency among the primitive functions. In particular,

➡ Step 3 cannot be executed until both step 1 and step 2 are complete.

➡ Step 4 requires the data delivered by steps 1, 2, and 3.

➡ Step 5 cannot be executed until step 4 is complete.

➡ Step 6 cannot be executed until step 1 is complete. [54]

On the other hand, there are also primitive I/O functions that are independent of each other.

➡ Steps 1 and 2 can execute concurrently.

➡ Steps 5 and 6 can execute concurrently.

These pairs of primitive functions can execute concurrently as long as they use separate hardware resources. Fortunately, this is the case for all but the smallest RAID systems. A user data block and the check data that protects it must be on separate disks for RAID algorithms to provide failure protection. For availability reasons, most RAID systems require or recommend that the member disks of any single array be attached to separate device channels.

For RAID systems which do allow a single array's member disks to be attached to the same device channel, steps 1 and 2 or steps 5 and 6 might require use of the device channel at the same time. When this occurs, one or the other of these primitive functions would be forced to wait for the shared resource to become available, adding to the application request's I/O response time. For transaction I/O loads with relatively small average request sizes, the increase in response time is usually minimal, since the device channel is typically occupied with data or message transfer for relatively short periods compared to the time required for device preparation (seeking and rotation). For the largeer member requests typical of large file I/O loads, however, primitive

---

[54] There are other dependencies, such as the need to hold a copy of the data delivered by step 1 until step 5 is complete so that the operation can be undone if necessary, but the examples given are sufficient for illustration purposes.

functions would almost certainly have to be queued to wait for a single device channel. Thus, parity RAID arrays with two or more members attached to the same device channel are a relatively poor choice, not only for failure tolerance (a single device channel failure causes loss of data access), but also for large file I/O performance.

Still More Parallelism: Very Large I/O Requests

In disk systems with intelligent controllers, the data transfer portion of I/O request execution is a two-step process. For a read request, for example,

➡ data is transferred from the device to the controller's buffer, and,

➡ data is transferred from the controller's buffer to the host.

This two-stage architecture increases application I/O response time compared that of to directly attached disks. For the small I/O requests that characterize transaction I/O, this increase in I/O response time is negligible. For large I/O requests, however, where data transfer time is a large fraction of total request execution time, the difference can be substantial. Moreover, such I/O loads implicitly require that controllers be equipped with large buffers. Figure 90 represents a timeline for a very large read request.

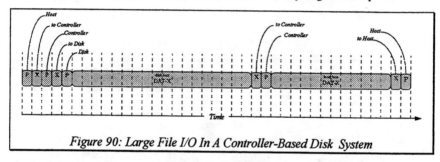

Figure 90: Large File I/O In A Controller-Based Disk System

As does Figure 85, Figure 90 represents a host I/O bus with higher data transfer capability than the device channel. What is clear in Figure 90 is that serial nature of the entire disk-to-controller data transfer and the controller-to-host data transfer adds substantially to application I/O response time. Moreover, the controller's buffer must be large enough to hold all the data for the application's I/O request at one time.

Parallel execution using multiple resources can both improve I/O response time and reduce controller buffer requirements in this situation. Most controllers execute large application I/O requests by subdividing them into multiple requests to the target disk(s), and allowing execution of these to overlap. This is illustrated in Figure 91.

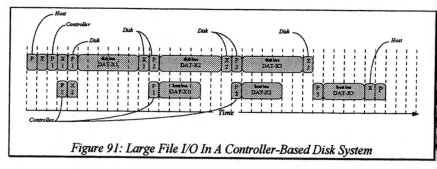

Figure 91: Large File I/O In A Controller-Based Disk System

Figure 91 illustrates Figure 90's large data transfer divided into three smaller sub-operations, denoted X1, X2, and X3. As soon as the data for sub-operation X1 is available to the controller, it is transferred to the host. The transfer to the host can occur concurrently with the disk-to-controller transfer portion of sub-operation X2, since the two use different resources (host I/O bus, and device channel respectively). All except the first and last sub-operations of an arbitrarily large transfer can be overlapped in this way. While there is additional controller processing overhead in creating and managing multiple sub-operations, that is small compared to the total data transfer time for a large request. The application's I/O request is complete in a little more than one sub-operation time after the last data is moved from disk to controller, rather than in the time required to transfer all of the requested data to the host. Moreover, the controller buffering requirement is reduced to the amount of storage required by data for two of the sub-operations because as soon as the data from a sub-operation has been transferred to the host, the buffer containing it can be reused.

Because of the controller overhead to create "extra" disk operations, segmentation of an application request into sub-operations only improves performance if a large amount of data is being transferred. Most storage controllers have an I/O request size threshold below which data transfers are done in one segment, and above which segmentation like that described above takes place.

Combining Disk Systems For Increased Performance

For applications that require higher performance or more storage capacity than a single disk system can provide, many computer systems support the combination of multiple disk arrays using a host-based *Array Management Function*. Host-based *Array Management Functions* are often used to create striped or mirrored arrays whose "members" are controller-based arrays of some kind. Figure 92 (adapted from Figure 14 on page 37) illustrates one combination of host-based and controller-based arrays.

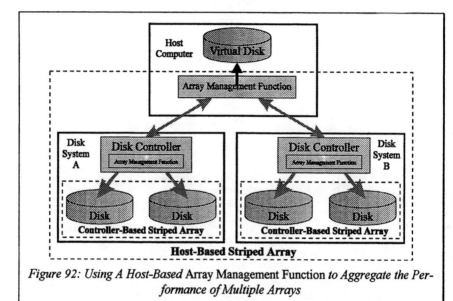

Figure 92: Using A Host-Based Array Management Function *to Aggregate the Performance of Multiple Arrays*

Figure 92 represents a computer with two disk systems. The disks in each disk system are managed as striped arrays, each seen by the host as a single virtual disk. In this system, it is possible that either a disk system or the I/O bus connecting it to the host is the limiting factor on I/O performance. By using the host-based striping *Array Management Function* to create a striped array whose members are striped array virtual disks, the performance potential of the two controller-based striped arrays can be aggregated into a single I/O stream. Large file I/O can be performed at the combined data transfer rate of both disk systems, and transaction I/O can be balanced across both sets of physical disks. In principle, this performance aggregation is possible with any system that supports multiple disk systems and a host-based *Array Management Function*. and can be used to increase I/O performance beyond the capability of the highest-performing disk system available.

Chapter 10: RAID and Cache

Using Write-Back Cache To Improve RAID Array I/O Performance

Cache has proven to be a highly effective tool for improving I/O performance in general, and that of RAID arrays in particular. This chapter reviews the sources of undesirable parity RAID I/O performance characteristics and describes how cache can be employed to overcome them. This chapter is based on material originally published in Computer Technology Review (**[Massiglia95a]**, **[Massiglia95b]**, and **[Massiglia95c]**), adapted by permission.

Parity RAID I/O Performance

Parity RAID array performance is extremely sensitive to the percentages of reads and writes in I/O request loads To appreciate why, one need only analyze what a parity RAID *Array Management Function* must do to process an application I/O request. For read requests, data must be read from whichever member disk(s) it resides on and delivered to the application. For write requests, however, not only must the requested data be overwritten, but the check data that protects it must be updated as well. Each application write request, therefore results in multiple member operations.

If an application request to write a large amount of data results in modification of an entire *stripe*, all member disks can be written concurrently, resulting in a shorter application request execution time. Figure 93 illustrates this. When complete stripes are written, parity can be pre-computed or computed as user data is written. In either case, parity can be written concurrently with user data, or shortly after.

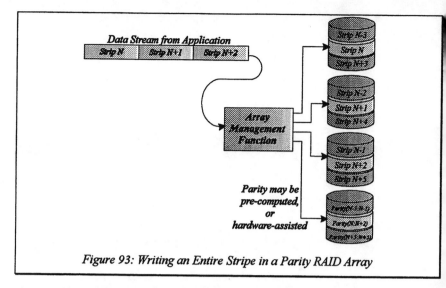

Figure 93: Writing an Entire Stripe in a Parity RAID Array

Arrays which transfer data *only* in full stripes are known as parallel access arrays (page 108). Few parity RAID arrays are strictly limited to full-stripe data transfers; more often, member disks are independently accessible, and the *Array Management Function* opportunistically writes complete stripes when the I/O load permits, and partial stripes when it does not. When combined with distribution of parity across some or all of an array's disks, this is commonly known as RAID Level 5. Purely parallel access RAID arrays have limited applicability (Although for applications which *only* transfer large sequential data streams, they are usually the highest-performing array option.), and are not as frequently encountered in practice.

Independent access parity RAID arrays which opportunistically write complete stripes perform acceptably for most data transfer intensive applications. To take advantage of full-stripe write performance, however, applications must make very large I/O requests (typically hundreds of Kbytes per request). Such applications are not common, so optimal use of these arrays often requires application modification, or *tuning,* which can be expensive and error prone. Thus, the high data transfer performance potential of parallel access RAID may be difficult to achieve.

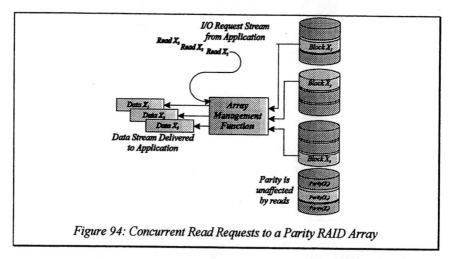

Figure 94: Concurrent Read Requests to a Parity RAID Array

A more common type of application I/O load is *transaction-intensive*. Transaction-intensive I/O loads consist of I/O requests that occur at high enough frequency to make it common for several to overlap in time. Individual requests in these I/O loads are typically small (1-16 Kbytes per request is common), and the data accessed tend to be distributed across a range of disk array data addresses. Small random read and write requests typically access partial stripes of data.

If two or more application read requests that overlap in time specify data addresses that map to different member disks, they can often execute concurrently (up to the number of members in the array). This results in shorter execution time for the whole request stream, although individual request's execution time is not affected.

Application write requests which result in data being written to part of a stripe (e.g., to a single member) require multiple member read and write operations, as discussed in Chapter 5. Figure 55 (page 119), repeated here for convenience as Figure 95, illustrates the main steps in a partial stripe update to an independent access parity RAID array. Both the elapsed time and the I/O resources required are considerably greater than they would be if the same request were made to an individual disk. This increased resource consumption and longer elapsed time are collectively known as the parity RAID *write penalty*.

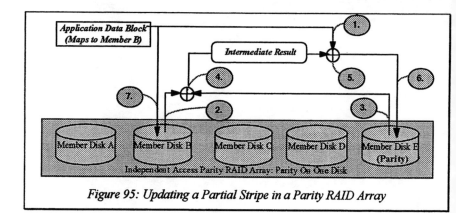

Figure 95: Updating a Partial Stripe in a Parity RAID Array

I/O Performance Limits Parity RAID Arrays' Applicability

Parity RAID I/O performance differs from that of a single disk in two respects:

➡ it is sensitive to application I/O request sizes, and,

➡ it is sensitive to application read:write mix.

These sensitivities mean that for optimal (in many cases, acceptable) I/O performance, the type of parity RAID array must be matched to the expected type of I/O load:

➡ Strictly parallel access arrays (RAID Level 3) work best with applications that read or write large amounts of data sequentially using large I/O requests.

➡ Independent access arrays (RAID Level 5) work best with transaction-intensive applications whose I/O loads consist mostly (70% or more) of read requests.

➡ Neither type of parity RAID array works well with transaction-intensive I/O loads consisting predominantly of write requests.

➡ Where cost is not a consideration, striped arrays with mirrored virtual members (Chapter 8, page 151)perform well for most I/O loads.

The need to match array type and I/O load characteristics makes determining the 'right' type of parity RAID array for general use difficult. If a disk array is to be used for a single application throughout its service life, and if the application's I/O load characteristics are known and remain constant, then a clear choice can be made. Most on-line storage, however, is used for multiple applications, either concurrently, at different times of the day or week, or at different times during its service life. Moreover, few applications' I/O characteristics are constant over time. The combination of these factors makes it difficult to choose a parity RAID array that is:

➡ optimal for the application(s) for which it is purchased,

➡ flexible enough to perform acceptably if that application's I/O load changes, and,

➡ flexible enough to be used with other applications when requirements change.

Inflexibility makes it difficult to take advantage of parity RAID's cost and availability benefits. Whereas individual disks can be moved freely among applications with predictable performance implications, the same is not as true of parity RAID arrays. An array optimized for data transfer, for example, generally performs poorly in transaction-intensive applications.

Improving Parity RAID I/O Performance: Requirements

A central question for parity RAID array developers has therefore been whether the strong dependency of array performance on I/O load characteristics could be reduced, making a single type of RAID array suitable for a wider range of applications. To achieve this, parity RAID array performance would have to improve in three ways:

➡ **Reduced *write penalty*.** The difference between read and write performance, due primarily to the partial stripe *read-modify-write* update cycle, would have to be reduced to insignificance. Applications (including system applications such as paging and swapping) cannot easily be designed for I/O devices whose read and write performance differ significantly.

➡ **Dynamic adjustment of update algorithms.** Parity RAID arrays would have to switch dynamically between full stripe (RAID Level 3) and partial stripe (RAID Level 5) update algorithms according to I/O load requirements. Limitation to a single update algorithm sharply diminishes an array's usefulness.

➡ **Elimination of the need to tune applications to achieve high sequential write performance.** Applications that write large sequential files are inherently suited to parallel access RAID update algorithms, even if they are not tuned to use them effectively. Parity RAID arrays would be more attractive for these applications if tuning were not required to exploit their inherent data transfer performance.

Write-back cache can be used to effect all three of these improvements, creating arrays whose read and write performance are both significantly higher than that of equivalent non-arrayed individual disks, regardless of I/O load characteristics.

Cache and I/O Performance

The concept of inserting a solid state cache memory into the I/O path to improve performance is well known. A *read cache* holds data in anticipation that it will soon be read, either because data at immediately preceding addresses has recently been read (*pre-fetch* cache) or because the data itself has recently been accessed (*most recently used* cache[55]). In either case, when an application requests cached data, the data can be delivered immediately, without *latency*, or delay, for disk seeking and rotation. Read requests that can be satisfied by accessing cached data complete faster, improving application responsiveness.

---

[55] The more familiar term is *least* recently used cache, which refers to the criterion used to decide which data in the cache should be discarded when cache space is required. If least recently used data is discarded, then clearly, most recently used data is retained.

Write cache can be used similarly to improve application responsiveness. An application write request causes data to be copied into the write cache, after which the application is notified that its request is complete, and can continue executing. The I/O system actually writes the data at some later time, ideally when thetarget disk(s) would otherwise be idle. Such a cache is called a *write-behind* cache, because actual writing of data occurs after, or *behind* the notification that it has been written. A write cache becomes a read cache as it is populated with data. Subsequent reads of recently written data can be satisfied directly from cache, up to the cache capacity.

A Complication With Write-Behind Cache

Write-behind cache introduces a complication, however, because unlike disk storage, solid-state cache memory is *volatile*, meaning that the integrity of its contents depends on a constant supply of electrical power. If a power failure occurs in a write-behind cache containing data waiting to be written to disks, that data is lost, even though applications may have been notified that it was safely stored.

Disk systems with volatile write-behind cache therefore do not behave exactly like disks. Applications can normally assume that once a disk system has signaled completion of a write, any subsequent read from the same address will return the data that was written, even if there have been system failures or power outages in the interim. If data held in a volatile write cache has not been written to disk prior to a failure, however, an inconsistency may develop:

➡ Since the application was notified that the write was complete, it may have taken subsequent action predicated on that assumption.

➡ Since cache contents are not preserved in the absence of electrical power, all rec-

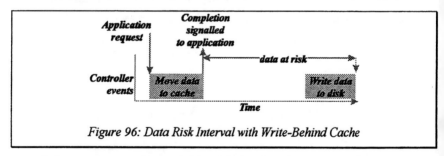

Figure 96: Data Risk Interval with Write-Behind Cache

ord of any updates pending at the time of failure may be lost.

Figure 96 illustrates this situation. As a practical example, consider a ticketing application which authorizes printing of a ticket after writing a debit record for the ticket's price to a disk. If a failure occurs while the debit record is still in a volatile write-behind cache, the customer may receive his ticket with nothing on record to cause his account to be billed.

Parity RAID arrays increase the risk of write-behind cache, since a single application write request results in multiple member disk writes. If these member disk writes utilize write-behind cache, the probability that a given I/O load will have unwritten user data or parity in cache when a failure occurs is higher for a parity RAID array than for an individual disk.

Moreover, the consequences of such a failure in a parity RAID array are potentially worse than just loss of data from an application active at the time of failure. If a power failure in a RAID array causes parity to become inconsistent with the user data it 'protects,' a subsequent device failure could lead to data being incorrectly regenerated.

Solving the Write-Behind Cache Problem

The situation described above essentially represents lower data integrity than is provided by a disk, which is contrary to the philosophy of RAID. Most RAID array systems therefore guard against the possibility of losing cached write data either by:

➡ not using write-behind cache, even if cache memory is present, or,

➡ implementing some mechanism to insulate the write cache from power failures and other service outages.

The latter mechanisms range from recommending or requiring that use of write cache be accompanied by installation of an uninterruptable power system (UPS) to equipping the disk system with sufficient emergency power to either flush its cache contents to disk or to retain cache contents for some period of time. Either of these techniques makes the cache *non-volatile*. A non-volatile write-behind cache is called a *write-back* cache because it allows cache contents to be written *back* to media after write completion is reported to the application without danger of data loss.

How Write-Back Cache Can Improve Parity RAID I/O Performance

Since it preserves unwritten data across service outages, write-back cache allows the use of alternative partial stripe update algorithms that can substantially increase parity RAID write performance. These algorithms can largely eliminate sensitivity to the read:write mix in an I/O load, making RAID data availability benefits available to most applications. The following sections describe how write-back cache can help overcome the three parity RAID array I/O performance deficiencies outlined above.

Reducing The Write Penalty

The most obvious parity RAID performance limitation is the partial stripe *write penalty*—the "extra" member I/O operations required when an application write request results in modification of part of a stripe.

"Extra" member I/O operations are required in this situation because both data and parity must be updated to satisfy an application's write request. To compute updated parity, access to *all* data in the stripe being modified is required:

➡ Data for blocks being modified is supplied by the application with its write request.

➡ Data from the strip's remaining blocks must be retrieved from the disks on which it is stored.

If fewer than half of the array's disks are to be updated, it is more efficient to retrieve the "old" parity (which was computed using data from all data blocks in the stripe), and "old" data from the block(s) to be modified, and compute the exclusive OR of the two to "back out" the old data's contribution to the parity, leaving the unmodified data's contribution. For application write requests requiring that half of an array's disks be updated, both algorithms have equal overhead. Figure 97 illustrates the sequence of steps to update a single block in a four-disk array. The algorithm that is optimal for modifying less than half of an array's disks is used.

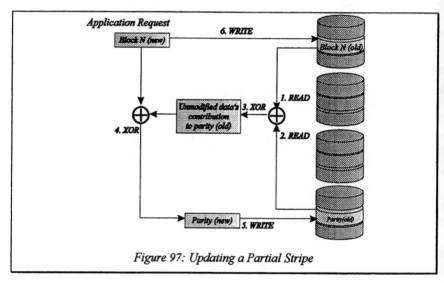

Figure 97: Updating a Partial Stripe

In Figure 97 the numbered steps represent the following operations:

1. Read existing contents of the block to be updated.

2. Read the corresponding parity block.

3. Compute the exclusive or of the two (steps 1. & 2.). The result is the exclusive or of the corresponding block contents from the two unmodified disks.

4. Compute the Exclusive OR of the result from Step 3. and the new data supplied by the application. The result is the updated parity.

5. Write updated parity (computed in Step 4.) to the parity disk.

6. Write the new data supplied by the application.

The first and second (read) steps retrieve data from different disks, and so can be executed concurrently, as can the fifth and sixth (write) steps. If the time to read or write a given number of blocks on a single disk is approximated by a constant *disk I/O time*, execution of an application write request to an array requires about two *disk I/O times*—one for the pair of member reads and one for the pair of member writes—plus the small amount of time required to compute the **Exclusive OR** functions.[56]

Except for transfer of the data specified in the application's write request to controller write-back cache, all of the operations required to execute an application write request can be performed after the application has been allowed to proceed. A parity RAID array with write-back cache can therefore significantly improve upon the write responsiveness of an independent disk. With the write penalty eliminated by using write-back cache, a parity RAID array can be treated as a disk with high I/O request execution capability (because multiple array members can satisfy separate application I/O requests concurrently) whose responsiveness to individual read and write requests is better than that of a single disk.

This conclusion cannot be extended to very heavy I/O loads. Even though the elapsed time for a single write request to a write-back cache-equipped parity RAID array is significantly shorter than that for an individual disk, the resource demands are not the same:

➡ More disk I/O resources are used (e.g., the two reads in the example above, where the application expects none).

➡ Eventually the write-back cache must be *flushed* of both user data and parity, using member disk I/O execution time. For moderate write loads, flushing can be done during intervals when no application I/O requests are outstanding. Heavy I/O loads, however, are likely not to have idle time in which to flush data without application impact.

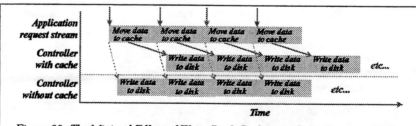

Figure 98: The Minimal Effect of Write-Back Cache on a Long Stream of Writes

Thus, a write-back cache-equipped parity RAID array must necessarily saturate at a lower write load level than an equivalent number of independent disks with a balanced I/O load.

---

[56] This example ignores the effect of I/O queues, and is therefore descriptive of a lightly-loaded system.

If a parity RAID array with write-back cache is given a steady stream of application write requests for long enough to fill its cache, the array's steady state performance becomes similar to that of an otherwise identical array *without* write-back cache. The reason is simple. If data for write requests constantly fills the cache, it must constantly be flushed to gain space for newly-arriving data. Once it fills for the first time, the cache merely delays the writing of data to disk, and write performance is bounded by the disks' collective ability to absorb data, just as it is when no cache is present.

This is not to say that write-back cache is of no value. The I/O load illustrated in Figure 98 is fortunately not common in applications (although it does occur). Far more frequently, application I/O loads contain

➡ idle periods, during which no I/O requests are made, and,

➡ periods during which I/O requests are predominantly reads.

Write-back cache flushing algorithms can take advantage of idle periods to make space available for more data as it is written by applications. For most applications, therefore, write-back cache improves responsiveness because write requests complete faster. The *Array Management Function* uses idle periods to "catch up" with the write load by flushing data and parity to disk.

Write-back cache minimizes the parity RAID write penalty in other ways as well. For applications that update certain disk blocks frequently, data from previous updates may still be in the cache when the next write request is made. This often occurs with database and file managers which update the root and nearby nodes of their index trees frequently. When this occurs in an array with write-back cache, cached data from the previous update is simply overwritten in the cache, completely eliminating a disk write (of user data), and, in RAID arrays, potentially a parity write.

An inherent property of parity RAID is the so-called *write hole*—the possibility of a false regeneration of data at a later time if an inopportune disk system failure while a partial stripe update is in progress results in either data or its corresponding parity being updated but not both. Most parity RAID arrays guard against this possibility by flagging some or all of their check data as unreliable during updates. If write-back cache is present, these *suspect parity* flags can be stored in it with virtually no overhead. If no write-back cache is present, these flags must usually be written to disk, further exacerbating the RAID write penalty.

> If the *Array Management Function* exploits them, the net effect of these possibilities is that a write-back cache can reduce the parity RAID write penalty to an insignificant level for all but the most write-intensive I/O loads.

Dynamic Adjustment of Update Algorithms

The second parity RAID performance limitation is the poor performance of both parallel access and independent access RAID update algorithms when either is used with I/O loads suited for the other. Ideally, a parity RAID array should be able to adjust between full stripe updates (RAID Level 3) and read-modify-write updates (RAID

Level 5) depending on the I/O load at the moment. Most arrays, in fact, do this. The inflexibility arises from the need to choose a fixed *stripe depth*, or number of consecutive virtual disk blocks mapped to consecutive member disk blocks (Figure 99) when the array is created. For maximum data transfer rate, a parity RAID array's stripe depth should be small enough so that all member disks participate equally in satisfying all application I/O requests. For example, in every stripe of a 5-member array, four members contain user data and one contains parity. If average application I/O request size is 64 Kbytes, then stripe depth should be 64 Kbytes/4=16 Kbytes, or 32 blocks.[57] This would allow each member disk to contribute 16 Kbytes to each I/O request, minimizing data transfer time.

Transaction applications, on the other hand, tend to make frequent requests for relatively small amounts of randomly located data. They require a larger stripe depth for optimal performance. A small request may be satisfied by accessing data on one disk, or it may have to be *split* because of data mapping, into two member disk accesses. Since two concurrently accessed disks that are not rotationally synchronized have a combined average rotational latency of 2/3 revolution, compared to 1/2 revolution for a single disk, a small request usually executes more rapidly when only one disk is accessed. For small requests, increased rotational latency and a more complex firmware path usually consume more time than is saved by parallel data transfer.

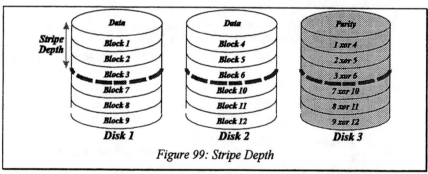

Figure 99: Stripe Depth

One rule-of-thumb is that 95% of the requests in an I/O load should be satisfied by a single member disk access for good transaction-intensive performance. For I/O loads that access data at a randomly distributed set of addresses, a probability of 95% that a data request will map to a single member disk means that the array's stripe depth must be 1.0÷0.05, or 20 times the average request size. For an average I/O request size of 4 Kbytes (8 blocks), this suggests a stripe depth of 160 blocks. A stripe depth this large in a 5-disk array would mean that only requests specifying 160x4=640 blocks (320 Kbytes with conventional 512-byte disk blocks) would be satisfied by full stripe write algorithms. Relatively few applications make such large requests, so such an array would seldom take advantage of full stripe write algorithms, even if it were programmed to use them when possible.

---

[57] Strictly speaking, use of full-stripe write algorithms would also require that application I/O request starting addresses be aligned with strip boundaries.

This example illustrates the natural conflict between *tuning* a parity RAID array (setting its stripe depth) for high data transfer rate and high I/O transaction rate. If a write-back cache is present, however, most of the member operations required by an application write request can be deferred, minimizing their effect on application responsiveness. For transaction I/O loads, this makes split I/O requests less of a factor, and therefore allows the use of smaller stripe depths. Smaller stripe depth increases the probability that full stripe write algorithms, with their higher data transfer performance can be used to satisfy large sequential I/O requests.

A write-back cache therefore allows an array to give both good transaction performance (high I/O request execution rate) and good data transfer performance (high data transfer rate), as long as:

- the array can be tuned (its stripe depth set) appropriately, and,

- applications requiring high data transfer rate make large I/O requests.

The latter constraint is precisely the third parity RAID performance limitation.

Reducing the Need To Tune
Applications To Use Parallel
Access Update Algorithms

The third parity RAID performance limitation is that applications tuned to take advantage of full-stripe parity RAID write performance are rare. Applications that transfer large files sequentially tend to use I/O requests that are too small for parity RAID full stripe write algorithms. While these applications could, in principle, be re-tuned to make full stripe write requests, there are two drawbacks:

➡ Application tuning is time-consuming, expensive, and error-prone. In some cases (e.g., application packages purchased from software vendors), it may not even be possible.

➡ An application tuned for a parity RAID array may not be suitable for other storage configurations (e.g., individual disks). Thus, one may be forced either to use RAID arrays for all instances of the application, or to maintain a differently tuned version of the application for each storage configuration. Neither of these alternatives is particularly attractive.

While smaller stripe depth tends to promote better full-stripe data transfer performance, there is a practical limit to how small it can be before firmware execution time and disk rotational latency interfere with getting useful work done. For full-stripe updates, a stripe depth of half a disk track is often regarded as a practical lower limit.[58] For a 5-disk parity RAID array with a member disk track capacity of 80 blocks, an application would have to make write requests specifying:

4 data disks x 40 blocks per half-track = 160 blocks (80 Kbytes)

---

[58] With *banded*, or zone-bit recorded disks, whose track capacity varies from inner to outer periphery, the conventional meaning of track capacity is generally replaced with an average track capacity.

in order for full-stripe update algorithms to be invoked. The only applications likely to do this are those whose I/O requirements are precisely-known at development time, and remain relatively constant throughout their lives. These applications can be tuned to make large I/O requests as they are designed. On the other hand, many applications have variable I/O loads, and still others read and write large files sequentially, but do so using small I/O requests. Into the former category fall multi-program application suites and systems in which storage is shared among several concurrent applications. Into the latter category fall many batch processing applications. Between them, these categories comprise the majority of data transfer-intensive applications.

Applications which use small I/O requests to write large sequential files do little or no full-stripe writing. In fact, they tend to emphasize the worst characteristics of parity RAID by requiring that read-modify-write algorithms be used repeatedly to write data across a single array stripe.

When a write-back cache is present, however, the data from these applications' small write requests can simply accumulate in the cache until enough is present for a full-stripe write. Figure 100 illustrates this.

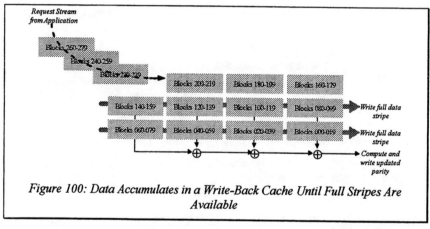

Figure 100: Data Accumulates in a Write-Back Cache Until Full Stripes Are Available

In Figure 100, data from the application's small sequential write requests accumulates in write-back cache until full stripes of data are available. The stripes of data may then be written without read-modify-write sequences. These writes have the properties that make parallel access parity RAID perform well for large sequential writes:

➡ Each member operation transfers a large amount of data.

➡ All members contribute to the execution of each request.

➡ Parity can be pre-computed, since all contributions to it are available in cache when the decision to write the stripe is made, and then written concurrently (or nearly so) with user data.

With a large write-back cache, this concept can be taken even further. If application data accumulates in cache until multiple adjacent strips for each member disk are

---

available, those adjacent strips can be consolidated into a single member write, saving rotational latency, and improving data transfer performance even further. Figure 101 illustrates this.

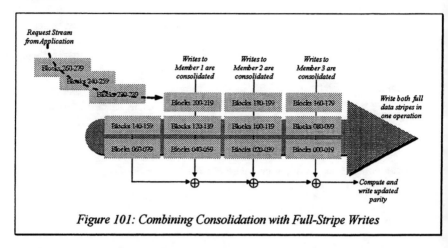

Figure 101: Combining Consolidation with Full-Stripe Writes

In Figure 101, as in Figure 100, data from the application's small sequential write requests accumulate in write-back cache until two full stripes of data are available. The difference is that in Figure 101, pairs of strips are consolidated. Parity is then computed for two or more stripes, and data and parity are both written using full-stripe write algorithms. Not only are individual member writes efficient (because multiple strips of data are transferred with each member operation), but full-stripe write algorithms can be used across the array's members for high data transfer performance.

With appropriate firmware for consolidating application I/O requests into full stripes, and even into multiple stripes, a write-back cache can obviate the need to tune data transfer-intensive applications to take advantage of a parity RAID array.

Conclusion

The inherent performance drawback of parity RAID technology, sensitivity to I/O load characteristics, can largely be overcome by adding write-back cache to an array, and adjusting update algorithms to take full advantage of it. The write penalty, inflexibility of update algorithms, and the need to tune applications to use the array effectively can all be eliminated as performance factors.

Parity RAID systems that incorporate write-back cache are readily available in the market. Write-back cache can be expected to become increasingly popular in parity RAID arrays as its potential benefits become clear to users and developers. When considering the purchase of a RAID array which includes cache, it is wise to examine the cache implementation closely to understand what features it implements and what benefits they will convey: The accompanying table lists some of the important attributes of cache in parity RAID arrays and summarizes their consequences.

FEATURE	CONSEQUENCE
Is caching of write data supported, or is the cache only used for reads?	Read caching can provide excellent performance for read requests, but without write caching, the inherent write performance of parity RAID technology governs array write performance.
Is the cache a *write-behind* or *write-back* cache?	A write-behind cache can provide excellent write performance, but in a parity RAID array, it puts data at risk unless other preventive measures (e.g., uninterruptable power supply) are taken.
For write-back caches, what mechanism is used to preserve data in the event of a system or power failure, and how long is the preservation period?	Data preservation mechanisms may either provide sufficient emergency power to flush the cache or a steady supply of power to preserve cache contents until system power can be restored.
What data preservation or recovery mechanisms are used at system startup?	If write cache contents are preserved across power failures, then controller startup firmware must recognize this and flush the cache before normal I/O operations can commence. If the data preservation strategy is flushing cache using emergency power, this is not necessary. In either case, the array must preserve certain array metadata, such as membership and member state, and verify them at startup.
Does the cache fully exploit the technology possibilities described in this chapter to maximize the array's performance potential?	Even if none of the RAID-specific techniques outlined in this chapter are implemented, basic write-back cache can substantially increase the utility of a parity RAID array. When these techniques are fully exploited, a parity RAID array can be the core of a truly high-performance, highly available on-line disk system.

Chapter 11: Dynamic Data Mapping[59]

Using Non-Algorithmic Data Mapping to Extend RAID's Flexibility

Discussions of RAID data mapping in preceding chapters have been predicated upon an assumption that data mapping, the method for determining the physical location of a block of data represented by a given virtual disk address, is *algorithmic*; that is, given a virtual disk address, an arithmetical formula can be applied to determine the member disk on which it is stored, and the block address on that member disk.

Recently, significant work has been done in the area of *tabular data mapping*, the use of a RAM table to represent part or all of the correspondence between physical data addresses on member disks and virtual disk data addresses. The name *AutoRAID*[60] is used by one vendor to describe such a mapping. Tabular data mapping makes the correspondence between virtual disk data addresses and the physical locations at which data is stored completely arbitrary and easy to change dynamically. This chapter describes tabular data mapping, and some of the performance and availability benefits that can accrue from its use in disk systems.

Dynamic Data Mapping Overview

Figure 102 (adapted from Figure 20, page 55) illustrates a form of dynamic data mapping.

---

[59] This chapter is adapted from material supplied by *RAID* Advisory Board member company Hewlett-Packard, whose contribution is gratefully acknowledged.

[60] AutoRAID is a trademark of Hewlett-Packard Corporation.

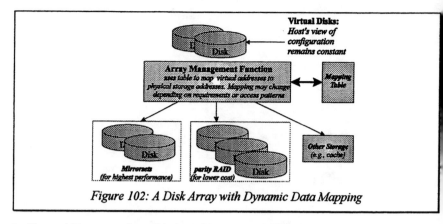

Figure 102: A Disk Array with Dynamic Data Mapping

In Figure 102, a mapping table in solid state memory contains the correspondence between virtual disk addresses and physical disk addresses. Since the mapping table can be changed rapidly and arbitrarily, any virtual disk address can be re-mapped to any physical disk location to meet changing requirements. As requirements change, the use of physical storage can be adjusted without altering the virtual disk image presented to the operating environment. This flexibility can be exploited in several ways:

➡ Disks of different capacities and performance can be used effectively (i.e., exploiting their capabilities fully) in a single disk array system.

➡ Frequently accessed data can be mapped to higher-performance types of storage (e.g., cache, or solid state or mirrored disks). As access frequency decreases, the *Array Management Function* can migrate data transparently to lower-cost storage.

➡ The parity RAID write penalty can be minimized by choosing optimal physical locations for application data and rearranging pointers so it is mapped correctly.

➡ Physical storage capacity can be added to an array, and mapped as new virtual disks (or as increased capacity for an existing virtual disk in operating environments that support disks of varying capacity) without requiring that existing application data be backed up and restored.

➡ Usable storage capacity, in the form of virtual disks, can be created and destroyed to meet application requirements. The physical space occupied by deleted virtual disks can be reallocated for other purposes, including, for example, shifting them between mirrored and parity RAID data protection, again without moving application data.

➡ Spare capacity can be distributed across multiple physical disks, improving rebuilding performance after a failure, since rebuilding speed is not limited by the performance potential of a single disk.

Using Disks of Different Capacities in an Array

Figure 103 illustrates a disk array system with five member disks of two different capacities. The disks' storage capacity is divided into p_extents (defined in Chapter 3, page 263), which in turn are organized as redundancy groups. Each member p_extent of a redundancy group exports a *ps_extent* of protected storage capacity. In Figure 103, redundancy group A, with two member p_extents, is mirrored, and exports 4 strips of storage. Redundancy group B is organized as an independent access parity RAID (RAID Level 5) array, and exports 24 strips of protected storage. Even though disks of different capacity are present, all available storage space in the system is util-

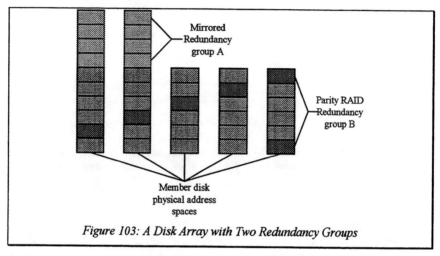

Figure 103: A Disk Array with Two Redundancy Groups

ized.

Dynamic Data Migration

Figure 104 illustrates the first few virtual disk addresses exported by the disk array system illustrated in Figure 103, along with the mapping table used to establish the correspondence between virtual addresses and physical storage located in the *ps_extents*. For each strip of storage capacity of the virtual disk address space, a strip in a *ps_extent* somewhere in the array is allocated.[61] *ps_extent* storage (i.e., physical storage available for user data) that is not part of a virtual disk address space is available either for additional virtual disk creation or for use as spare capacity.

---

61 In this context, the term *allocated* refers to *ps_extent* capacity to which virtual disk data addresses are mapped. From the operating environment's standpoint, this storage may be either allocated (i.e., in use as part of a file or database), or it may be free space on a virtual disk.

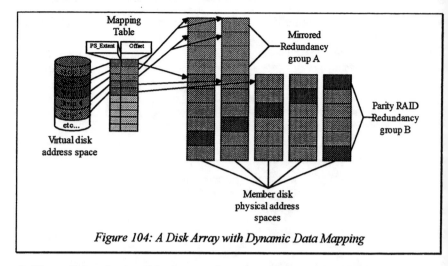

Figure 104: A Disk Array with Dynamic Data Mapping

In Figure 104, strips 2 and 3 are mapped to mirrored storage in redundancy group A, while strips 1, 4, and 5 are mapped to the parity RAID-protected storage in redundancy group B. Mapping table entries that point to strips in the mirrored storage may point to *both* mirrored array members, or more restrictive internal mapping techniques may be used. Since the mapping table contains *ps_extent* data addresses, the correspondence between virtual disk addresses and *ps_extent* addresses is completely arbitrary, and can be changed according to application or internal requirements. For example, if the array's *Array Management Function* were able to track access frequency for virtual disk addresses, and determine that virtual strip 1 is being accessed frequently, it could re-map virtual strip 1 to an unallocated strip in redundancy group A, which might be expected offer higher I/O performance. The *ps_extent* addresses in redundancy group B, previously occupied by virtual strip 1, would then be available for reallocation.

In Figure 105, the data mapped as virtual strip 1 is moved to redundancy group A. The *Array Management Function* moves the data transparently to applications. Once the data has been moved, the pointer in the mapping table is updated. Since mapping is through the table, the data can be moved to any free strip in a *ps_extent* with the desired characteristics (mirrored in the example). After the move, the strip in redundancy group B from which the data was moved can be re-allocated.

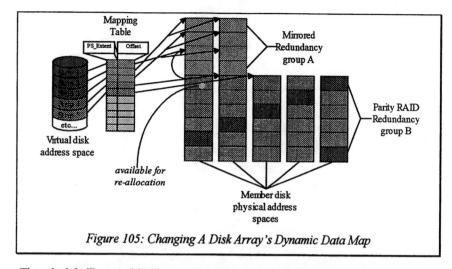

Figure 105: Changing A Disk Array's Dynamic Data Map

The principle illustrated in Figure 105 can be carried further, to the transparent movement of entire redundancy groups, to rearrange physical storage in response to changing data access patterns.

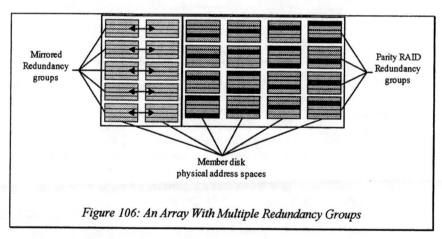

Figure 106: An Array With Multiple Redundancy Groups

In Figure 106, the leftmost two of the system's six disks have been organized as sets of mirrored redundancy groups, and the rightmost four as parity RAID redundancy groups. The parity RAID redundancy groups have been sized so that each *ps_extent* has the same capacity as a mirrored *p_extent*. For this example, the mirrored redundancy groups are assumed to be unallocated.

If the *Array Management Function* keeps a record of the access rate to each redundancy group, it might determine, for example, that the top-most parity RAID redundancy group is the busiest, and that its contents should be moved to unallocated mirrored redundancy groups to improve I/O performance. Figure 107 illustrates this move.

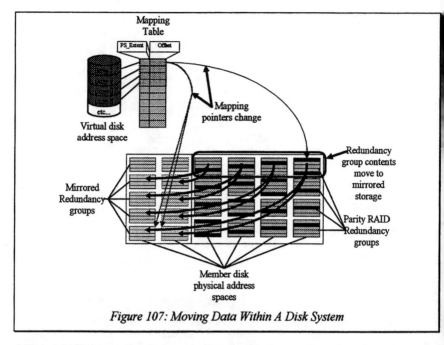

Figure 107: Moving Data Within A Disk System

Figure 107 illustrates the movement of *ps_extent* contents (user data) from the parity RAID array's redundancy group *ps_extents* to those of unallocated mirrored storage. The "move" actually requires copying data twice, which may be assisted by special hardware, or may require multiple member I/O operations. As data is moved, the disk system's mapping tables are updated so that correct data is delivered to applications at all times. When data has been moved, and the mapping tables updated, the capacity occupied by the parity RAID redundancy group is no longer allocated, and may be used for other purposes, including creation of additional mirrored redundancy groups. While this would imply a smaller usable storage capacity for the disk system, it could improve I/O performance by reducing the system-wide average write penalty of independent access parity RAID. Thus, with appropriate management access, the user could dynamically make a tradeoff between disk system capacity (cost) and I/O performance potential.

If such movements of data within a disk system are system administrator controlled, care must be taken that the member I/O implied by moving large amounts of data does not interfere with application I/O. Similarly, an automatic data movement policy must balance application I/O demands against internal data management I/O requirements.

Minimizing The Parity RAID Write Penalty

Writing partial stripes data to an independent access parity RAID array takes perceptibly longer and uses more resources than writing an equivalent amount of data to a disk. Chapter 10 (page 192) describes how write-back cache can be used to mitigate this performance penalty. A disk system equipped with dynamic data mapping can reduce the amount of cache required to take advantage of consolidation of cached writes to parity RAID arrays. Figure 108 (adapted from page 193) illustrates the consolidation of writes.

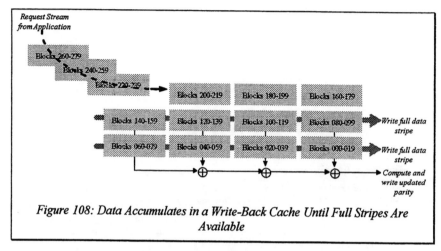

Figure 108: Data Accumulates in a Write-Back Cache Until Full Stripes Are Available

Figure 108 illustrates a stream of consecutive virtual disk blocks being written by an application to a parity RAID array. A disk system with write-back cache can allow these to accumulate in the cache until it has full stripes of application data, at which time, it can use parallel access RAID update algorithms, which do not require reading of "old" data from member disks, because the complete stripe is to be overwritten.

While this approach is efficient for applications that write large amounts of data sequentially, it is of no help to the more typical applications with transaction-like I/O profiles. These applications tend to write data to randomly assorted disk addresses, which would not tend to build up complete stripes in cache as illustrated in Figure 108.

If a disk system is capable of dynamic mapping, however, writes to non-sequential addresses can be written to a single stripe in a parity RAID redundancy group, and the mapping tables that relate virtual addresses to physical ones updated to reflect the actual location of data. Figure 109 illustrates consolidation of non-contiguous writes.

In Figure 109, the update stream arriving at the disk system is for non-sequential data. Since mapping is dynamic, however, the *Array Management Function* can choose an unallocated stripe in a parity RAID redundancy group, write the amount of data required to fill the stripe using full-stripe update algorithms, and then update the mapping pointers to reflect the actual data addresses. Most *Array Management Function* policies would dictate that this data eventually be re-consolidated so that adjacent virtual disk addresses tend to map to adjacent physical storage. This requires background member I/O activity, which can be carried out during otherwise idle periods.

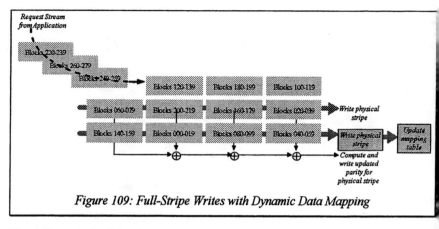

Figure 109: Full-Stripe Writes with Dynamic Data Mapping

The ability to write full stripes of data even when the I/O load is transaction-like improves parity RAID performance, and makes the technology applicable to a wider range of applications. The effect of dynamic mapping in these cases is similar to that of write-back cache, and, indeed, these two features operate well together. Dynamic mapping, however, tends to reduce the amount of cache required to deliver a given level of transaction performance, which in turn makes the disk system more economical.

Dynamic Expansion of Storage Capacity

When a new disk is introduced into an array with dynamic data mapping, the *Array Management Function* may rearrange one or more redundancy groups to include the new disk. The data in previously created redundancy groups that do not include the new disk is moved to new groups that do, thus including the new disk without user intervention. This tends to improve the I/O performance of already-existing virtual disks by distributing I/O load across more physical resources. The net gain in *ps_extent* space can be used to create new virtual disks, or it can be held as spare capacity. Figure 110 illustrates dynamic expansion of array capacity by the addition of a disk and rearrangement of data.

Figure 110 illustrates the sequence of strips' virtual addresses before and after a disk is added to the parity RAID redundancy group. The *Array Management Function* rearranges blocks of data and re-computes check data transparently to applications to accomplish this addition. The additional protected space is represented by the unnumbered stripe at the bottom of the diagram. This protected space is available for export to applications, most commonly as an additional virtual disk, since most operating

---

system environments cannot accommodate the concept of disks whose capacity changes.

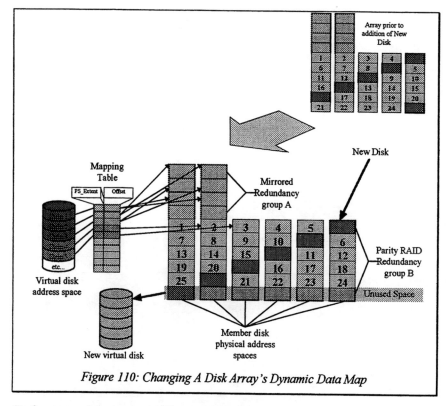

Figure 110: Changing A Disk Array's Dynamic Data Map

Performance of the array would presumably increase, with I/O load balanced across six physical disks rather than five. Care must be taken in performing this operation, since the member I/O operations required to rearrange data can interfere with application I/O performance. Since data rearrangement is not a time-critical operation, it is possible to give priority to application I/O over internal I/O operations.

The new capacity could also *not* become part of the parity RAID redundancy group, but could be used to form mirrored redundancy groups of its own. These could be exported as virtual disks, or they could be used within the array to improve I/O performance.

Distribution of Spare Capacity

When a disk failure occurs, data can be moved from redundancy groups that contain the failed disk to new groups that do not include the failed disk. Figure 111 illustrates the 6-disk array used in preceding examples with a failed disk. The failed disk includes a *p_extent* that had been a member of a mirrored array.

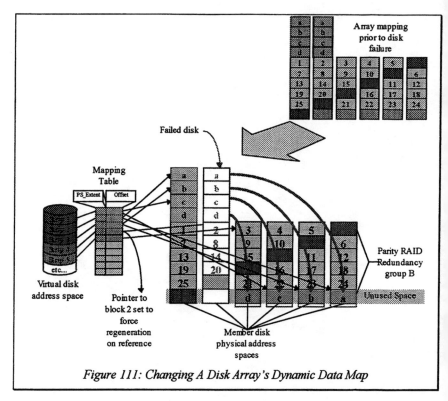

Figure 111: Changing A Disk Array's Dynamic Data Map

Figure 111 assumes that the disk system has a policy that declares the data stored in the mirrored array to be more important than the data stored in the parity RAID array. A consequence of this policy is that it is more important to restore the protected state of the mirrored array than that of the parity RAID array. For this reason, copies of the mirrored array's strips have been made in the previously unallocated space, and the pointers to the second copy of each mirrored array strip have been updated to point to the new data. Since the disk system does not have sufficient capacity to rebuild the parity RAID array's data, that array must run in reduced mode until additional capacity is made available.

Spare capacity may also be pre-allocated when an array is created. In Figure 112, a spare strip has been allocated adjacent to each parity strip. When a disk failure occurs, protection can be restored by regenerating the contents of each strip (parity or data) from the failed disk and writing the result in the spare strip for that stripe. Functionally, this is equivalent to allocating a spare disk to the array and rebuilding a failed disk's contents. From a performance standpoint, however, it distributes the write load of rebuilding across all of the array's disks for faster rebuilding. With dynamic mapping, moreover, when data is regenerated and stored in a spare strip, reads and writes can be satisfied using the array's algorithms for normal operation.

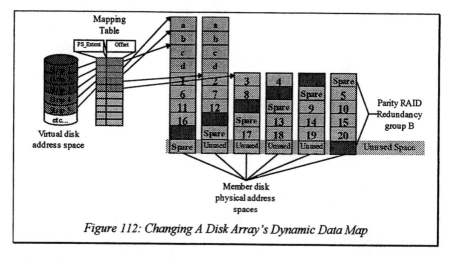

Figure 112: Changing A Disk Array's Dynamic Data Map

Either of these re-mappings would be subject to space limitations. rebuilding can only be done if the unallocated capacity of the remaining disks is sufficient to store all the virtual disks' data. If not, a new disk must be added to increase the physical capacity enough for rebuilding. Enabling the active hot spare feature causes enough virtual space to be reserved so that rebuilding will have space to complete even if the largest disk fails.

Distributed Spare Capacity

In a disk system with dynamic data mapping, it is relatively easy to distribute the spare capacity across multiple physical disks. This can be advantageous when a disk failure occurs, since rebuilding of the failed disk's data is not bound by the data transfer capability of a single disk, but can be distributed across all disks which contain spare capacity. Figure 113 illustrates this.

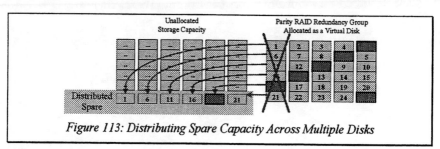

Figure 113: Distributing Spare Capacity Across Multiple Disks

Figure 113 illustrates a situation in which the left-most member disk of the allocated parity RAID array fails, in a disk system containing a relatively large amount of unallocated storage capacity. The disk system has implemented a policy of using unallocated capacity to restore data protection as rapidly as possible by rebuilding the failed member disk's contents onto storage on six different disks. Each strip's regeneration requires that four member disks be read and that one replacement disk be written. Since the member disks can be read continuously, strips of regenerated data or parity can be written to the replacement disk areas as they are ready, without waiting for writes of preceding information to be written, because each write is to a different disk. In this manner, rebuilding, and hence restoration of protected state, can be completed more rapidly than if it were throttled by a single target disk.

As strips are regenerated in this example, the disk system's map, which describes the correspondence of virtual disk data addresses to physical disks and data addresses on them is updated each time regeneration of a mapped unit of data is complete. When full protection has been restored, it is possible to further re-arrange data, for example, to consolidate it onto a single disk as it had been before the failure, but this is a background operation performed by the *Array Management Function*, which does not disturb the data's protected state.

Chapter 12: Distributed RAID Functions[62]

Distributing Primitive RAID Operations Across Disk System Components For Improved Update Performance

Separation of Primitive RAID Operations

The primitive operations that comprise a write operation to a parity RAID array can be implemented using different resources of a disk system. This has already been illustrated in the case of independent access RAID, in which the member reads and writes required to execute an application update are necessarily executed by different disks. This principle can be taken further, however. For example, the Exclusive OR computations required to maintain check data consistency may be performed by member disks rather than by a controller-resident *Array Management Function*. This can reduce the load on an array controller's processing resources, as well as reducing the amount of member data that must be transferred within the disk system to perform a partial stripe update.

Conventional Parity RAID Array Updates

For an application write request to an independent access parity RAID array, the parity blocks protecting all modified data blocks must be updated to reflect new data block contents. In a conventional array, the *Array Management Function*, sometimes

---

62 This chapter is adapted from material supplied by *RAID* Advisory Board member company EMC Corporation, whose contribution is gratefully acknowledged.

assisted by special-purpose hardware, computes and writes updated parity for each modified data block. Figure 114, repeated for convenience from page 131, illustrates the primitive functions required to execute an application write request that modifies data on one array member:

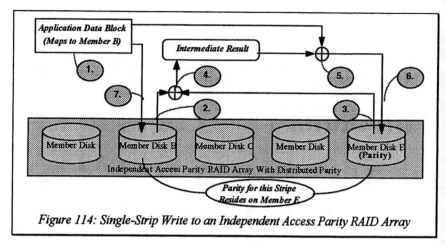

Figure 114: Single-Strip Write to an Independent Access Parity RAID Array

Each circled number in Figure 114 represents a primitive operation required to execute the application request. The *Array Management Function* performs or directs the following actions:

1. *acquires* data from the host,

2. *reads* the contents of the target blocks and holds them internally.

3. *reads* the contents of the corresponding blocks from the parity disk (i.e., the parity blocks which protect the target data blocks) into an internal buffer.

4. *removes* the target blocks' contribution to the parity by computing the Exclusive OR of the two.

5. *computes* the new parity as the Exclusive OR of the result from the previous step and the new data to be written.

6. *writes* the updated parity back to the parity disk.

7. *writes* the application's data to the proper block locations on the target member disk.

Steps 1 and 2 can be performed concurrently, as can steps 5 and 6, provided that they use separate resources. Step 3 can be concurrent with steps 1 and 2 if a hardware assist is present, or it may have to follow them, if the Exclusive OR computation is performed in firmware. Step 5 relies on the result of step 4, which in turn relies on the results of steps 1, 2, and 3, step 5 cannot begin until steps 1, 2, 3, and 4 are complete.

The key performance determining factors in this sequence of events are:

➡ An amount of data equal to that specified in the application request must move four times within the disk system (Steps 1, 2, 5, and 6.)

➡ Since the member writes depend on the results of the member reads, an "average" application write takes twice as long as an average member I/O operation, even if all possible primitive operations are performed in parallel.

Disks capable of computing the $\texttt{Exclusive OR}$ function may be used to improve this situation somewhat. In a parity RAID array such as that represented in Figure 114, the check data for a stripe, denoted $P(1\text{-}4)_{old}$ in the example, is computed as:

$$P(1\text{-}4)_{old} = Strip1_{old} \oplus Strip2 \oplus Strip3 \oplus Strip4.$$

where the symbol $\oplus$ denotes the $\texttt{Exclusive OR}$ function.

The conventional array represented in Figure 114 reads $Strip1_{old}$ in Step 1, and $P(1\text{-}4)_{old}$ in Step 2, and computes the $\texttt{Exclusive OR}$ of the two:

$$P(1\text{-}4)_{old} \oplus Strip1_{old} = Strip1_{old} \oplus Strip1_{old} \oplus Strip2 \oplus Strip3 \oplus Strip4,$$

$$P(1\text{-}4)_{old} \oplus Strip1_{old} = (Strip1_{old} \oplus Strip1_{old}) \oplus Strip2 \oplus Strip3 \oplus Strip4,$$

since the $\texttt{Exclusive OR}$ of a bit pattern with itself is zero. Therefore,

$$P(1\text{-}4)_{old} \oplus Strip1_{old} = Strip2 \oplus Strip3 \oplus Strip4,$$

results in the $\texttt{Exclusive OR}$ of the data strips unaffected by the application update. This partial sum, whose computation is designated as Step 3 in Figure 114 is required in the computation of new check data.

$$P(1\text{-}4)_{new} = Strip1_{new} \oplus Strip2 \oplus Strip3 \oplus Strip4,$$

This computation is designated as Step 4 in Figure 114. The writing of $P(1\text{-}4)_{new}$ and $Strip1_{new}$ are designated as steps 5 and 6 respectively. An alternative way of computing $P(1\text{-}4)_{new}$, however is:

$$P(1\text{-}4)_{new} = Strip1_{new} \oplus P(1\text{-}4)_{old} \oplus Strip1_{old},$$

An Alternative Parity RAID Update Technique

Since the results of a series of $\texttt{Exclusive OR}$ computations are independent of the order in which the computations are performed, this is equivalent to:

$$P(1\text{-}4)_{new} = (Strip1_{new} \oplus Strip1_{old}) \oplus P(1\text{-}4)_{old}.$$

Arrays that use disks capable of computing the $\texttt{Exclusive OR}$ function take advantage of this fact. Such disks usually implement two special commands:

➡ $\texttt{Exclusive OR}$ $READ$, which reads data from designated disk addresses, computes its $\texttt{Exclusive OR}$ with an equal amount of data written to it by the host, optionally writes the host-supplied data to the disk, and returns the difference to the host.

➡ *Exclusive OR WRITE*, which reads data from designated disk addresses, computes its *Exclusive OR* with an equal amount of data written to it by the host, and writes the result to the disk.

Figure 115 illustrates how these operations can be used to improve the performance of a partial stripe update to an independent access parity RAID array.

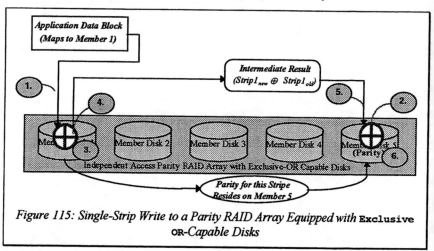

Figure 115: Single-Strip Write to a Parity RAID Array Equipped with Exclusive OR-*Capable Disks*

The numbered circles in Figure 115 represent the following actions:

1. The *Array Management Function* Exclusive OR *reads* the target disk, supplying the new data from the application and its target addresses.

2. The *Array Management Function* Exclusive OR *writes* to the parity disk, specifying the same block addresses as those to which the data to be updated maps. This causes the check data disk to read $P(1-4)_{old}$ and hold it in an internal buffer, awaiting the difference data for Exclusive OR computation.

3. Member disk 1 *computes* the difference data, $(Strip1_{new} \oplus Strip1_{old})$, using data read from the target disk addresses and data supplied to it by the *Array Management Function*. When this computation is complete, the new data, $Strip1_{new}$, can be written to member disk 1.

4. The difference data, $(Strip1_{new} \oplus Strip1_{old})$, is sent to the controller, completing the Exclusive OR *read*. The controller sends this difference data to the check data disk (member disk 5).

5. Member disk 5 *computes* the new parity $P(1-4)_{new}$ using $P(1-4)_{old}$ read from the disk and $(Strip1_{new} \oplus Strip1_{old})$ sent to it by the controller.

6. Member disk 5 *writes* $P(1-4)_{new}$ to the check data disk, completing the Exclusive OR *write*. At this point the controller can signal completion of the application's write request.

This implementation improves I/O performance in at least three ways:

➡ Data moves on controller-to-device channels three times (Steps 1, 4, and 5), as compared to four such data movements (Steps 1, 2, 5, and 6) in the conventional example of Figure 114.

➡ The controller performs only two member I/O setups (one *Exclusive OR read* and one *Exclusive OR write*), as compared to four in the conventional case.

➡ The two *Exclusive OR* computations are performed by different resources, whether hardware-assisted or firmware executed. This introduces additional parallelism into the array.

Reduced Mode Operations

When a disk failure occurs in a parity RAID array, the array is said to be *reduced*, or *operating in reduced mode*. If the virtual disk addresses of data requested by an application map to surviving array members, the data is delivered as if the array were intact. If any of the addresses maps to the failed member, the *Array Management Function regenerates* the data by reading corresponding blocks from all surviving members and computing the *Exclusive OR* of their contents. Figure 116 illustrates the operations required to execute an application request to read data from a single strip on failed member disk D.

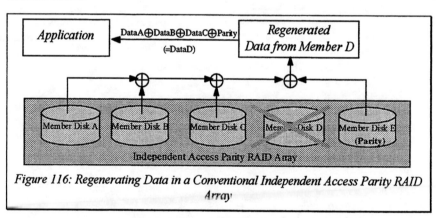

Figure 116: Regenerating Data in a Conventional Independent Access Parity RAID Array

In essence, a read request that maps to the failed member in an *n*-member parity RAID array requires *n-1* member reads and *n-2 Exclusive OR* computations to regenerate the data. If *Exclusive OR*-capable disks are present, this process can be optimized somewhat by spreading the *Exclusive OR* compute load across member disks, as illustrated in Figure 117.

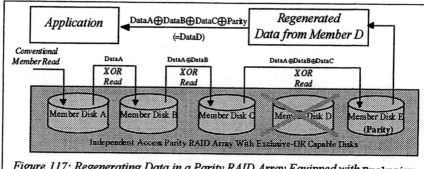

Figure 117: Regenerating Data in a Parity RAID Array Equipped with Exclusive OR-Capable Disks

In Figure 117, the *Array Management Function* begins to respond to an application read request that maps to failed member disk 4 by making a conventional member read request to the same block addresses on member disk 1. The result of this read request is used as the input data to an **Exclusive OR** *read* request to member disk 2, with the *write-to-media* portion of the operation inhibited. That result, in turn is used as the input data to an **Exclusive OR** *read* request to member disk 3, with the *write-to-media* portion of the operation inhibited. Finally, that result is used as the input data to an **Exclusive OR** *read* request to the member disk containing the stripe's parity. The data returned by the final **Exclusive OR** *read* request is the regenerated data from the failed member disk, and is returned to the application.

Figure 118 depicts the steps in a single-strip a write operation to the failed disk in an array equipped with **Exclusive OR**-capable disks. Data supplied by the application is used as input to an **Exclusive OR** *read* operation to corresponding block addresses on the array's first member disk. The write-to-media part of the **Exclusive OR** *read* operation is inhibited. The result of the first operation is used as input to the second,

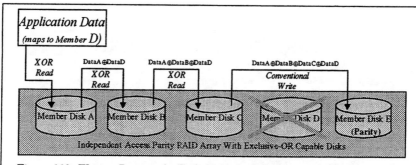

Figure 118: Writing Data to the Failed Member of a Parity RAID Equipped with Exclusive OR-Capable Disks

and so on, until the parity disk is the only member (besides the failed one) not yet affected. At this point, the partial result is the new parity, as it should appear if all array members were functioning. This new parity is written to the parity disk using a conventional write command, following which, the application can be notified that its request has been completed.

Figure 119 illustrates writing to a surviving disk in a reduced array equipped with **Exclusive OR**-capable disks. It is functionally identical to a write in normal mode.

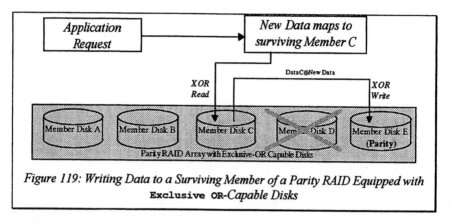

Figure 119: Writing Data to a Surviving Member of a Parity RAID Equipped with **Exclusive OR**-*Capable Disks*

Further Optimizations

As a further optimization, some implementations gradually turn parity into data in an array with a failed member disk. They do this by:

➡ *not* inhibiting the *write-to-media* portion of the **Exclusive OR read** operation directed at the parity disk in the regeneration sequence described in Figure 117, and,

➡ writing the application-supplied data directly to the corresponding block addresses of the parity disk instead of going through the sequence of steps depicted in Figure 118

➡ regenerating failed member data for addresses corresponding to application writes that map to any surviving members, and writing the regenerated data to corresponding addresses on the parity disk.

This strategy eliminates all but the first regeneration of any data referenced after the member disk failure, leading to better performance while in reduced mode. This improved reduced mode performance comes at the expense of additional metadata storage (the array must keep track of which parity blocks are actually storing check data, and which are storing regenerated data from the failed disk).

This optimization also makes rebuilding data to a replacement disk slightly more complex, since blocks that have been accessed while the array was in reduced mode must be read from the check data locations and copied to the replacement disk, followed by a re-computation of parity for the corresponding block addresses on the parity disk. This contrasts with the conventional rebuilding mechanism of regenerating every block for the replacement disk using the mechanism described in Figure 116.

Chapter 13: RAID and Functional Redundancy

Using RAID Data Protection as the Kernel of Failure-Tolerant Disk Systems

RAID, defined in Chapter 1 (page 12) as a combination of data protection and data mapping in a disk array, protects against data loss due to failure of one or more disks in an array, or the paths by which they are accessed. Perhaps more importantly, in most cases RAID also protects against loss of data *availability* in the event of the same types of failures. In other words, a RAID array can continue to respond to application read and write requests by delivering and storing data, even if one or more (depending on the data protection mechanism used) of its disks are unavailable.

RAID and Disk System Availability

A disk system consists of several different types of functional components, however, and the failure of some of these can affect data availability adversely, and indeed, data integrity as well. In order for a disk system to be completely failure tolerant, rather than simply tolerant of disk failures, it must protect against data and I/O service loss due to the failure of one of these other functional components as well.

Figure 120 illustrates some major disk system functional components whose failure can affect data availability.

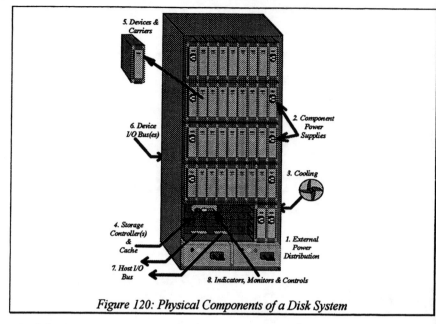

Figure 120: Physical Components of a Disk System

The following components are illustrated in Figure 120:

➡ **Power distribution system.** These components receive externally supplied electrical power, *condition* it (in some cases) and distribute within the disk system's enclosure.

➡ **Component power supplies.** These components convert electrical power from the power distribution system to appropriate voltage levels and current forms, condition it to required tolerances, and distribute it to active components (electrically powered) within the disk system.

➡ **Cooling system.** These components help dissipate the heat generated by the disk system's active electrical components.

➡ **Storage controllers and cache.** These components provide device fanout, as well as (in some cases) advanced functions such as RAID.

➡ **Storage devices and carriers.** Storage devices store data and deliver it on demand. Their failure rates (MTBF) may affect data availability, as may their ability to be hot-swapped or not.

➡ **Device channels.** Device channels move commands and data between devices and storage controllers. Device channels can affect data availability by failing themselves, as well as by being, for example, the single path to two disks of a parity RAID array.

➡ **Host I/O buses.** Host I/O buses move data and commands between one or more host computers and a disk system. Their failure may affect availability by blocking the path between applications and the disk system.

➡ **Indicators, monitors and controls.** These components may affect data availability insofar as they warn system managers of conditions requiring attention. These conditions may lead to data loss if additional failures occur before they have been remedied, so effective indicators can reduce the period of time during which applications are exposed to data loss due to a second failure.

Failure Tolerance

A system's *failure tolerance* is its ability to continue to perform its function in the presence of some set of functional component failures. For disk systems, failure tolerance is usually defined as a system's ability to survive the failure of a single component of a given type and continue to store and deliver data. There are two aspects to failure tolerance:

➡ The ability of a system to *recognize* and *react* to failures (usually by placing a functionally equivalent component into service, or by shifting the role of the failed component to one or more other components already in use).

➡ The ability of a system to *recover* from a failure to a degree that makes it able to survive a second failure of the same type.

For example, a parity RAID array is able to react to the failure of a member disk by using the data regeneration algorithms described in Chapter 5 to recreate the failed disk's data. The failed disk's role is shifted to the surviving disks by their participation in regeneration. When the failed disk's contents are rebuilt (including any updates that occurred during the outage period) to a replacement disk is complete, the system has recovered, and is again able to survive a disk failure.

Disk System Component Roles in Failure Tolerance

Power Distribution System

A disk system's power distribution system receives power from an external source and distributes it to active components within the system. The power distribution system usually *conditions* externally supplied power, and may also convert it, or it may pass it through at the levels supplied by the external source.

For failure tolerance, protection against failure of the power distribution system itself, as well as against interruption of externally supplied power must be provided. Power distribution system failure tolerance is typically achieved through redundancy, or complete replication of the power distribution system. In such a configuration, each power distribution system must be capable of supplying all of the disk system's needs. The outputs of the two redundant power distribution systems are electrically connected. Figure 121 illustrates redundant power distribution systems.

To protect against disk system failure due to interruption of externally supplied power, one of two techniques is typically used:

➡ Two redundant power distribution systems are connected to separate external power grids. (This is a site responsibility rather than a property of the disk system.) In principle, these power grids are widely separated electrically, so that simultaneous failure of both is unlikely.

➡ One of two redundant power distribution systems is connected to an *uninterruptable power supply* (UPS), either in the form of batteries and a charging system or in the form of a generator.

In either case, redundant power distribution systems must be designed so that neither removal or restoration of an external power source nor removal or installation of a power distribution system causes a disruptive surge or drop in the distribution system's output.

Component Power Supplies

Component power supplies receive the output of the power distribution system and distribute it to designated subsets of disk system active components. In most cases, component power supplies perform the conversion to the low-voltage direct current required by storage devices and other active components. For reduced cost, improved availability, and packaging convenience, a single component power supply usually powers only a small subset of a disk system's components, for example, those housed in a single rack or shelf.

Component power supply failure tolerance is usually achieved through redundancy. Two or more component power supplies' outputs are connected together and to a set of active components. The supplies' net output is sufficient to power the attached components if one of them is inoperative. Figure 121 illustrates this.

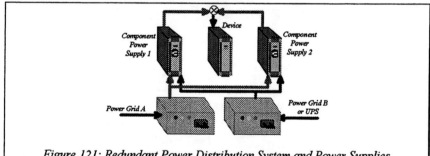

Figure 121: Redundant Power Distribution System and Power Supplies

In Figure 121, component power supplies 1 and 2 both provide DC power to the same devices. Either is capable of powering all of the devices to which they are connected, so the failure of one leaves that set of devices fully operational, although unprotected against further component power supply failures.

Like the power distribution system, redundant power supplies must be designed so that power surges that occur when one of them fails or is replaced are contained, and do not interrupt operation or cause damage to the devices.

Cooling System

A disk system's cooling system dissipates the heat generated by its active components during operation. Disk system cooling is almost always provided by fans or blowers that force air across active components and exhaust it into the environment. (This implies that the environment itself must be cooled for stable long-term operation.)

Like component power supplies, a single cooling device typically cools a small subset of a disk system's components. Often, fans mounted in or near a single rack are designed to cool the active components mounted in that rack.

Also like power supplies, cooling fans are usually made failure tolerant by replication. Two or more fans are mounted so as to cool a certain set of components. The fans capacity is such that they provide adequate cooling for these components, even if one of them in inoperative.

Failure tolerant cooling systems must have separately powered fans so that failure of a power supply, which might in itself be tolerated, does not result in loss of cooling.

Storage Controller

Perhaps the most complex element of a disk system in terms of failure tolerance is the storage controller. While some controllers contain redundant internal components, a more common design approach is to design the disk system to accommodate two redundant controllers connected to the same devices. In such configurations, one controller is able to take over control of all devices in the event that the other fails. Figure 122 illustrates redundant storage controllers.

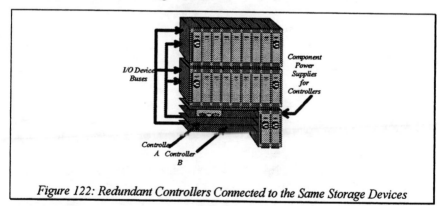

Figure 122: Redundant Controllers Connected to the Same Storage Devices

In Figure 122, both controller A and controller B are connected to the same storage devices. Disk system designs differ in how redundant controllers operate under normal circumstances (when all components are functioning properly).

In *dual active* controller designs, both controllers operate concurrently. Each device is managed by one of the controllers. If one of the controllers fails, the other assumes control of the failed controller's devices in addition to its own.

In *active-passive* designs, all devices are managed by an active controller; the passive controller takes over if the active one fails.

In both dual active and active-passive designs, the controllers must constantly exchange signals so that a failure can be recognized. Moreover, the two controllers must share sufficient configuration information for one to take control of the other's devices (e.g., RAID array membership). Finally, there must be a mechanism for shifting I/O load from the failed controller to the surviving one. At a minimum, all I/O outstanding at the time of failure must fail in such a way that the host recognizes the nature of the failure and takes appropriate compensating action.

Redundant controllers require support from their host computers, at least in the form of robust I/O driver software. If two redundant controllers are connected to the same host bus, one can masquerade as the other in the event of a failure, responding to the same virtual device addresses at the same host bus address. If the controllers are connected to different host I/O buses, however, or if they can only respond to fixed host I/O bus addresses, then more extensive host involvement is required. In the latter case, the host must redirect I/O requests to virtual device addresses on the failed controller to the surviving one. Figure 123 illustrates this.

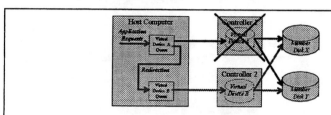

Figure 123: Redirection of An I/O Stream to the Surviving Controller of a Redundant Pair

In Figure 123, disks X and Y are connected to both controllers 1 and 2, which are connected to their host computer on different host I/O buses, or at different host I/O bus addresses. The two disks are organized as a RAID array. When all components are functioning, controller 1 manages the two disks, and presents them to the host as virtual device A.

If controller 1 fails, controller 2 takes over management of the two disks, and, since its host bus address is different, presents the RAID array as virtual device B. The host must cooperate with the controllers at least to the extent that it can recognize that virtual device B represents the same storage as virtual device A, and can redirect the I/O request stream for either to the other.

Redundant storage controllers have both electrical power and extensive logical connections, both to host and device channels, and to each other. For this reason, many controllers do not support hot swapping. For those that do, replacement of a failed controller while the surviving one is executing a host I/O load is possible. Part of controller hot swapping is the communication of the device configuration to the new controller at the time of replacement, and the reassignment of devices in dual active configurations to their original control sites. This fail-back operation requires host cooperation as well. In some implementations, it is necessary to quiesce the devices to be failed back.

Cache

As described in Chapter 10, disk system cache, usually implemented as part of the controller, or controlled by it, is primarily a performance enhancement device. When write-back cache is used, however, the possibility of two failure modes that can affect data integrity arises:

➡ A controller can fail with unwritten application data in its write-back cache.

➡ A write-back cache can itself fail with unwritten application data in it.

For the former case, it must be possible for the surviving controller to recognize that there was, in fact, unwritten data in the cache, and to extract it and write it to the appropriate disks. For disk systems that use a write-back cache to store *metadata* about RAID array state, the metadata must be retrieved as well, and appropriate actions taken. A controller may gain access to a partner controller's cache if the cache is implemented as a memory shared between the two controllers, however, this design approach makes it difficult to guarantee that a controller can fail without adversely affecting its partner. Other implementations include separate cache memories for each controller, with a secondary port for each controller to gain access to the other's cache.

Protection against failure of a write-back cache itself is most often achieved by replication of the entire cache memory in the domain of a separate component power supply. In such implementations, it is necessary not only to replicate the cache memory itself, but also both controllers' access paths to it. Moreover, since large amounts of data move into and out of a cache, redundant data movement engines should be provided, so that writing multiple copies of data into the cache does not adversely affect performance.

Devices and Carriers

A disk system's devices affect its failure tolerance primarily by being organized into RAID arrays as described in Chapter 4 and Chapter 5. An additional property of devices that can have a significant effect on data availability, however, is their ability to be hot-swapped (or the lack of it). Like storage controllers, devices have both power and logic connections to the disk system (the device channel). For a device to be hot-swappable, its device channel connection must allow removal or insertion without disturbing other bus activity. Some implementations require that a device channel be brought to an idle state (i.e., that all bus activity cease momentarily) before a device is removed or added. This is usually accomplished by a command to the controller. Other device channel connection designs are sufficiently robust that devices can be inserted and removed while the bus is active. In most of these, a momentary disturbance may be visible to the controller, which is able to recover. Hot swapping can be simplified through the use of point-to-point device channels, although this is seldom done in modern controllers for cost reasons.

In many failure-tolerant disk systems, the electrical and logic interface between devices and I/O buses is simplified through the use of device *carriers*, which partially or completely enclose individual devices and are designed for easy insertion into and removal from the disk system enclosure. In addition to providing robust power and logic connections, device carriers have other benefits. They offer a degree of mechanical protection, and may block RFI emissions, helping to meet regulatory requirements. They may also help channel air appropriately past the device, improving cooling for greater MTBF.

Device Channels

Device channels may contribute to disk system failure tolerance both by providing failure tolerant connections between controller and devices and by being failure tolerant in their own right. A device channel consists of a physical connection (usually a multi-conductor cable) between two or more nodes, and logic *port* at each of the nodes that sends and receives signals on the connection. Device channels may be *point-to-point*, connecting a controller to one device, or they may be *multi-point*, or *party-line* buses that connect multiple controllers to multiple devices, and have a *protocol*, or set of rules for communication, observed by all connected nodes. The SCSI-2 bus that is by far the most prevalent device channel for disk systems is a multi-point bus, with versions capable of supporting eight and 16 ports available.

A single-port device connects to one device channel; a multi-port device can connect to two or more device channels. Multiple ports connected to different I/O buses allow a device to continue operating when one of the buses fails. A single-port device cannot operate if the bus to which it is connected becomes inoperative, and so the failure of the bus to which a single-port device is connected is tantamount to failure of the device. Devices that connect to SCSI-2 buses normally support a single port.

I/O creates a natural master-slave relationship between controller and device. The controller issues I/O commands which the device executes. The device retrieves and sends data, or receives and stores it only in response to controller commands.[63] Multi-point buses may support a single *master*, or issuer of commands (the controller), or they may support multiple masters. Buses that support multiple masters require protocols by which a device can communicate with a specific master. A bus that supports multiple masters allows the devices attached to it to continue operating when a controller fails. SCSI-2 supports multiple masters, using a feature called *dual initiator* support.

In practice, the most common device channel configuration in failure-tolerant disk systems is:

➡ single-port devices to minimize device cost.

➡ multiple device channels to allow configuration of RAID arrays that can tolerate a bus failure as well as a device failure.

---

[63] Under certain circumstances, such as conditions requiring attention, devices may initiate communication with their masters. The principal relationship, however, is that of the controller as master and the device as slave, and I/O bus protocols are designed to optimize that usage.

➡ multiple (usually two) controllers attached to the same I/O bus. Figure 124 illustrates this configuration.

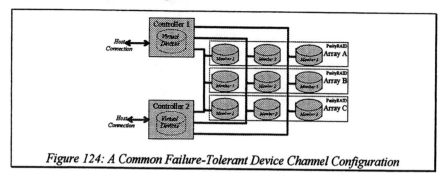

Figure 124: A Common Failure-Tolerant Device Channel Configuration

In Figure 124 each of the device channels is a multi-point bus that attaches to two masters (controllers). Disk arrays (collections of disks under common management) are configured *across* I/O buses. No more than the number of disks whose simultaneous failure can be tolerated by the RAID algorithms (one in the case illustrated in Figure 124) is attached to a single bus. This configuration can survive a variety of failures:

➡ Failure of a disk is tolerated by using the array's other member disks to perform parity RAID regeneration according to rules outlined in Chapter 5.

➡ Failure of a device channel is equivalent to failure of one member in each of the disk system's three arrays. All three arrays are reduced, but all can continue to deliver data by regenerating it from surviving members.

➡ Failure of a controller causes control of all arrays to be assumed by the partner controller (assuming that both controllers are connected to the same host(s)).

Device channels are normally intimately embedded in disk system packaging, and disk systems in which an I/O bus itself can be hot swapped are not common. Physical connection failure is relatively unusual, however. More commonly, an "I/O bus failure" is actually a failure of a device or controller port attached to the bus, and swapping that component cures the bus failure. In many cases, devices and controllers are designed to be hot-swappable or warm-swappable.

Host I/O Bus(es)

The host I/O bus is the disk system's connection to one or more host computers. In many respects, its role in providing overall system failure tolerance is similar to the role of the device channel in providing disk system failure tolerance. Host I/O buses tend, therefore, to have many features in common with device channels. One very popular host I/O bus is a high performance variant of the SCSI-2 bus used as a device interconnect.

Most host I/O buses are multi-point buses, with one or more host computers as masters driving one or more slave storage controllers. As with device channels, the slave controllers predominantly respond to commands from the masters, but are also capable of signaling conditions requiring attention by originating bus transactions of their own.

Failures related to host I/O buses include failure of the bus itself (interruption of the physical connection or failure of the bus control logic in one or more ports), and failure of a controller or host. Some host I/O buses are designed to be failure tolerant; others achieve failure tolerance through redundant configuration.

Each host computer or storage controller port attached to a host I/O bus has an *address* on that bus to distinguish it from other ports. A controller responds to commands sent to its host I/O bus address and ignores others. (Typically, the body of the command contains the address of the specific device at which the command is targeted.)

Figure 125 illustrates two redundant host bus configurations.

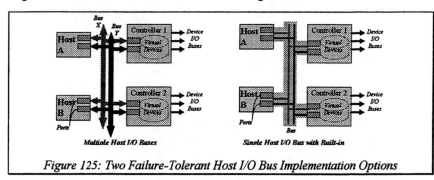

Figure 125: Two Failure-Tolerant Host I/O Bus Implementation Options

The left side of Figure 125 depicts a failure tolerant computer system configured using two non-redundant host I/O buses. Each host and controller has a single port to each host I/O bus. The failure of a host I/O bus (interruption of the physical connection or failure of a port in a way that renders the bus inoperable) causes I/O traffic to be re-routed to the other bus. This causes controller addresses to change (the controller's address on both buses may be the same, but from the host's point of view, the controller is addressed using a different bus, making it a "different" controller.) There must be sufficient cooperation from the host operating environment to recognize that devices addressed on the backup bus are actually the ones addressed at the same addresses on the primary bus before the failure, and not merely different devices configured with the same addresses.

The right side of Figure 125 depicts a failure tolerant configuration achieved through the use of a single failure-tolerant host I/O bus. From a failure tolerance standpoint, this configuration is the same as that depicted on the left side of Figure 125. Even though the host I/O bus may be packaged and presented as a single component, for it to be failure-tolerant, it must contain two (or more) independent electrical paths, and two independent ports at each node. In some implementations, the single failure tolerant bus configuration may allow I/O load balancing across the two paths on its bus. This is practical when the two ports are designed to be presented to hosts and controllers as a single interface. It is not usually possible in the dual bus configuration depicted on the left side of Figure 125, because it is difficult for host operating software to perform this level of coordination.

Failure tolerance may also be achieved using controllers that offer only a single host I/O bus connection. Figure 126 depicts this configuration.

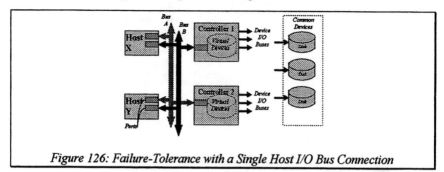

Figure 126: Failure-Tolerance with a Single Host I/O Bus Connection

In Figure 126, each controller has only a single host I/O port, and can therefore connect only to a single host I/O bus. In this configuration, failure of a controller causes its I/O traffic to be re-routed through the other controller, which has the effect of presenting it to the host on the other I/O bus. In this sense, failure of a controller is identical to failure of the I/O bus to which it is connected. This configuration requires cooperation from the host operating environment to recognize that devices presented through the other controller on a different I/O bus are actually the same ones that were presented by a different controller on a different host I/O bus before the failure.

Disk System Indicators, Monitors, and Controls

As the importance of failure tolerance in disk systems has increased, the importance of knowing that a fault exists has also increased. For the most part, disk systems can be designed to recognize and react to faults without human intervention. RAID arrays can be reduced, and data regenerated, automatic spares can be used for rebuilding, and I/O traffic can be re-re-routed to bypass failed buses or controllers. Recovery from the reduced states, however, and restoration of failure tolerance is more difficult to automate. Replacement of a failed device or controller module usually requires human intervention.

Thus, it is vital for even a self-healing failure tolerant disk system to make a responsible authority aware that a fault has occurred, and to provide adequate information for the fault to be remedied. This need goes somewhat counter to the trend in recent years to eliminate visible symbols of computer system operation, such as activity lights.

Providing information about disk system fault conditions may take several forms, and system capabilities tend to be tailored to the markets for which the systems are targeted. At the lowest level are local, immediate indications of failure, such as warning lights and audible alarms. Many systems are designed with a highly visible system-wide fault indicator that is used to indicate that there is an attention-worthy fault somewhere within the system. These tend to be integrated with per-device fault indicators specific to disks, controllers, power supplies, and cooling devices.

Some disk systems also make fault information available to operators, either through a serial interface between the disk system and a terminal that can be monitored by a computer operator, or by using the host I/O bus itself to send messages to the operating environment. The latter approach, while simpler to comprehend, requires support from the host operating environment, and also requires that the host I/O bus be functional. In some implementations, the latter capability is integrated with the host's error logging mechanisms, providing a detailed, durable record of disk system events that can be examined and analyzed after the fact. Information provided in this way can sometimes be integrated with a multi-host system management facility, so that multiple disk systems connected to multiple host computers can be monitored from a single management station.

A third level of fault indication is remote fault indication, in which information about disk system faults is sent to a management location over a local or wide area network. The most popular facility for this is the *Simple Network Management Protocol* (SNMP). Originally designed for network management, SNMP is finding wide application in a variety of system management areas, including disk system management.

As the target site for fault indication becomes further from the site of the fault, it becomes increasingly important not only to receive information about faults at a remote site, but also to control the disk system in which the fault occurred. Fault indication is usually embedded in a more general purpose management protocol (such as SNMP) which allows a remotely located system manager to take action in response to fault or other events. Obviously, remote action is limited to logical operations (e.g., making a disk eligible to be a spare for a RAID array); human presence is still necessary to perform physical actions such as disk swapping. What remote fault notification and control *can* do, however, is allow emergency action to be taken to maintain or restore service, thus "buying time" to get a repair person to a remote site and effect a permanent repair.

Part 4: Appendixes

Appendix 1: The *RAID* Advisory Board

Description of the *RAID* Advisory Board

The *RAID* Advisory Board is an association of suppliers and consumers of RAID-related products and other organizations with an interest in RAID technology. The goal of the *RAID* Advisory Board is to foster an orderly development of RAID and related disk array technology and introduction of RAID-related products into the marketplace.

Member organizations pay a fee to belong to the *RAID* Advisory Board, as well as devoting the time and travel cost required by their individual representatives' participation.

RAID Advisory Board Charter

The *RAID* Advisory Board has adopted the following activities as its charter:

➡ promotion of RAID and related technologies throughout the industry and user community,

➡ stimulation and coordination of RAID-related standardization efforts,

➡ resource-sharing among members, and,

➡ influencing of disk and related hardware suppliers to provide products suitable for RAID applications.

The following paragraphs elaborate these activities.

Promotion of RAID Technology

The fundamental purpose of the *RAID* Advisory Board is the promotion of RAID technology. It is the Board's belief that the benefits of this technology are so great that

RAID in some form will become pervasive in computer disk systems by the late-1990s. The Board's efforts are aimed at smoothing the broad-based introduction of RAID technology by:

➡ conducting educational events for both system integrators and end users,

➡ providing vendors of RAID-related products with the opportunity to exhibit their products at *RAID* Advisory Board-sponsored events,

➡ issuing press releases covering key RAID technology and application developments,

➡ promoting the submission of RAID-related material to trade and technical journals,

➡ publication of RAID-related educational material (e.g., this book), and,

➡ publication of RAID functional and performance test specifications and RAID Advisory Board certified test reports.

The RAID Advisory Board sponsors two types of educational events:

➡ forums, targeted primarily at integrators who use RAID technology in computer system products which they in turn sell to end users.

➡ seminars, targeted primarily at end users of RAID technology, and,

RAID Advisory Board seminars approach RAID technology and applications from the end user's point of view. They tend to include technology and product surveys, and relate the use of RAID to application benefits.

RAID Advisory Board forums, on the other hand, deal with current technical issues and areas of research. that are typically of greater interest to system integrators and RAID suppliers themselves.

Standardization Efforts

The *RAID* Advisory Board believes strongly that the storage industry and user community alike will benefit greatly from the standardization of RAID technology in several dimensions. To this end, the Board has formulated several standardization objectives:

➡ **Terminology.** The *RAID* Advisory Board's objective is to standardize RAID-related terminology (through this book and its other educational vehicles), primarily to allow prospective purchasers of RAID-related products to make rapid, objective and accurate comparisons.

➡ **Functional Testing.** The *RAID* Advisory Board's objective is to promote a standardized program of functional tests that verify that RAID products subjected to them perform a basic set of RAID-related functions correctly. The *RAID* Advisory Board intends to carry this effort to the extent of becoming a certifying agency for RAID products.

➡ **Performance Testing.** The *RAID* Advisory Board's objective is to promote standardized reporting of disk array performance toward the end of providing data that will allow objective and meaningful performance comparisons of RAID products.

➠ Standards Extensions. The *RAID* Advisory Board's objective is to cooperate with the appropriate standards bodies in developing standards to deal with the emerging disk array technologies. For example, the RAID Advisory Board is cooperating with the ANSI X3T10 Committee to extend SCSI-3 protocols to support the configuration of complex disk arrays. Other efforts center around the specification of disks and enclosures that are particularly suitable for disk arrays.

Resource Sharing among Members

The *RAID* Advisory Board actively encourages members to share certain resources such as test suites and market forecasts, toward the end of minimizing unproductive reinvention and allowing members to concentrate their resources on providing true added value.

Influencing Hardware Suppliers

The *RAID* Advisory Board's objective is to promote the development of hardware components, particularly disks, that are optimized for RAID applications. As its first step, the Board expects to develop a common set of RAID requirements for SCSI-attached disks, and then to persuade the major disk manufacturers to include them in products.

RAID Advisory Board Membership

The *RAID* Advisory Board membership includes both producers and consumers of RAID products, as well as interested members from the academic and business communities. For an up-to-date listing, consult the publication *RABInfo*, which is issued periodically by the RAID Advisory Board.

Becoming a Member of the *RAID* Advisory Board

Membership in the *RAID* Advisory Board is open to all organizations interested in participating in activities which contribute to the goals of the Board as outlined in this and related *RAID* Advisory Board publications, and who wish to share in the many tangible and intangible benefits that accrue from membership. Organizations interested in *RAID* Advisory Board membership are invited to contact the Chairman, Joe Molina at:

> The RAID Advisory Board
> Affiliated with Technology Forums
> 13 Marie Lane
> St. Peter, MN 56082-9423
> 507 931-0967 FAX 507 931-0976 MCI Mail 470-6032

for further information.

RAID Advisory Board Trademark Programs

As part of its effort to promote standardization of RAID-related technology across the industry, the *RAID* Advisory Board has established a series of trademarks whose use it grants to vendors of RAID-related products and/or services when these vendors meet certain RAID Advisory Board criteria. The trademarks have the form

Descriptive Legend

where the "Descriptive Legend" characterizes the organization or product to which the trademark applies. In general, these trademarks may apply either to organizations (e.g., test agents for any of the RAID Advisory Board's certification testing programs) or to products (e.g., arrays that have met RAID Advisory Board criteria for a given RAID level). The trademarks, the criteria by which license to use them is granted, and the rules under which they may be displayed are described in the publication *RABInfo*, available from the RAID Advisory Board; contact Joe Molina, Chairman of the RAID Advisory Board, at the address listed on page 233.

Appendix 2: RAID Reference List

This appendix contains a list of RAID-related publications to which the reader can refer for further information about RAID technology and products. The list is also the reference for bibliographic references in the text.

[Ouchi78] N. K. Ouchi: "System for Recovering Data Stored in Failed Memory Unit", US Patent Number 4,092,732, May 30, 1978

[Lawlor81] F. D. Lawlor: "Efficient Mass Storage Parity Recovery Mechanism", IBM Technical Disclosure Bulletin 24,2, July 1981

[Kim85] M. Y. Kim: "Parallel Operation of Magnetic Disk Storage Devices: Synchronized Disk Interleaving", Proceedings of the Fourth International Workshop on Data-Base Machines, 1985

[Kim85] M. Y. Kim and A. Patel: "Error-Correcting Codes for Interleaved Disks with Minimum Redundancy", IBM Research Report RC 11185, May 1985

[Salem86] K. Salem and H. Garcia-Molina: "Disk Striping", Proceedings of the second International Conference on data Engineering, 1986

[Kim86] M. Y. Kim: "Synchronized Disk Interleaving", IEEE Transactions on Computers, November 1986

[Park86] A. Park and K. Balasubramanian: "Providing Fault Tolerance in Parallel Secondary Storage Systems", Technical report CS-TR-057-86, Princeton University, November 1986

[Kim87] M. Y. Kim and A. N. Tantawi: "Asynchronous Disk Interleaving", IBM Research Report RC 12497, January 1987

[Ng87] S. Ng: "Design Alternatives for Disk Duplexing", IBM Research Report RJ 5481, January 30, 1987

[Clark88] B. E. Clark, et al: "Parity Spreading to Enhance Storage Access", US Patent 4,761,785, August 1988

[Garcia-Molina88] H. Garcia-Molina and K. Salem: "The Impact of Disk Striping on Reliability", IEEE Data Base Engineering Bulletin, March 1988

[Hartness88] C. B. Hartness: "Data Error Correction System", US Patent Number 4,775,978, October 4, 1988

[Kurzweil88] F. Kurzweil: "Small Disk Arrays -- The Emerging Approach to High Performance", CompCon, Spring, 1988

[Ng88] S. W. Ng, D. Lang, and R. D. Sellinger: "Trade-offs Between devices and Paths in Achieving Disk Interleaving", Proceedings of the 15th Annual International Symposium on Computer Architecture, June 1988

[Patterson88] Patterson, David A., Garth A. Gibson, Randy H. Katz, "A Case for Redundant Arrays of Inexpensive Disks (RAID)," Proceedings of the 1988 ACM SIGMOD Conference on Management of Data, Chicago IL, June 1988, pp 109-116.

[Schultze88] M. E. Schultze: "Considerations in the Design of a RAID Prototype", Technical Report UCB/CSD 88/448, UC Berkeley, August 1988

[Vasudeva88] A. Vasudeva: "A Case for Disk Array Storage System", Proceedings of Reliability Conference, Santa Clara, CA, 1988

[CTR89a] IBIS Systems, "Is A Disk Array A Cost-Effective Option?," Computer Technology Review, May, 1989, p. 23.

[CTR89b] ENDL Consulting, "RAID Arrays Making A Slow Start," Computer Technology Review, September, 1989, p. 22.

[Copeland89] G. Copeland and T. Keller: "A Comparison of High-Availability Median recovery Techniques", ACM SIGMOD Conference, 1989

[Crockett89] T. W. Crockett: "File Concepts for Parallel I/O", ACM, 1989

[Gibson89] G. A. Gibson: "Performance and Reliability in Redundant arrays of Inexpensive Disks", CompCon, February 1989

[Gibson89a] G. A. Gibson, L. Hellerstein, R. M. Karp, R. H. Katz and D. A. Pattereson: "Failure Correction Techniques for Large Disk Arrays", Proceedings of the 3rd International Conference on Architectural Support for Programming Languages and Operating Systems, 1989

[Gibson89b] Gibson, Garth A., Lisa Hellerstein, Richard M. Karp, Randy H. Katz, David A. Patterson, "Coding Techniques for Handling Failures in Large Disk Arrays," Third International Conference on Architectural Support for Programming Languages and Operating Systems (ASPLOS III), Boston MA, April 1989, pp. 123-132.

[Katz89] Katz, R. H., G. A. Gibson, D. A. Patterson, "Disk System Architectures for High Performance Computing," Proceedings of the IEEE, 77, 12, December 89, pp. 1842-1858.

[Katz89a] Katz, Randy H., John K. Ousterhout, David A. Patterson, Peter M. Chen, Ann L. Chervenak, Rich Drewes, Garth A. Gibson, Ed K. Lee, Ken C. Lutz, Ethan L. Miller, Mendel Rosenblum, "A Project on High Performance I/O Subsystems", ACM Computer Architecture News, 17, 5, Invited paper, September 1989, pp 24-31.

[Meador89] W. E. Meador: "Disk Array Systems", CompCon, February 1989

[Ng89] S. Ng: "Pitfalls in Designing Disk Arrays", CompCon February 1989

[Schulze89] M. Schulze, G. Gibson, R. Katz and D. Patterson: "How Reliable is a RAID?", CompCon, February 1989

[Olson89] T. M. Olson: "Disk Array Performance in a Random IO Environment", Computer Architecture News, September 1989

[Patterson89] D. A. Patterson, G. Gibson and R. H. Katz: "Introduction to Redundant Arrays of Inexpensive Disks (RAID)", CompCon, February 1989

[Reddy89] A. L. N. Reddy and P. Banerjee: "An Evaluation of Multiple-Disk I/O Systems", IEEE Transactions on Computers, December 1989

[Brady90] J. Brady: "Organization of XOR Hardware in Disk Arrrays", IBM Invention Disclosure SA90-91-004, January 1990

[Brady90a] Brady, et al: "Method and Means for Accessing DASD Arrays with Tuned data Transfer Rate and Concurrency", European patent application EU: 91304503.5, May 24, 1990

[Chen90a] Chen, Peter M., Garth A. Gibson, Randy H. Katz, David A. Patterson, "An Evaluation of Redundant Arrays of Disks Using an Amdahl 5890," Proc. of the 1990 ACM SIGMETRICS Conference on Measurement and Modeling of Computer Systems, Boulder CO, May 1990.

[Chen90b] Chen, Peter M., David A. Patterson, "Maximizing Performance in a Striped Disk Array," Proceedings of the 1990 ACM SIGARCH 17th Annual International Symposium of Computer Architecture, Seattle WA, May 1990.

[Chervenak90] A. L. Chervenak: "Performance Measurements of the First RAID Prototype", Technical Report UCB/CSD 90/674, UC Berkeley, May 1990

[CTR90a] Ciprico, Inc., "Redundant Disk arrays Enhance Data Safety To Support Network Servers," Computer Technology Review, Winter, 1990, p. 20.

[Dunphy90] R. H. Dunphy, Jr., et al: " Disk Drive Memory", US Patent 4,914,656, April 1990

[Gray90] J. Gray, B. Horst and M. Walker: "Parity Striping of Disk Arrays: Low-Cost Reliable Storage With Acceptable Throughput", Proceedings of the 16th International Conference on Very Large Data Bases, August 1990

[Lee90] E. K. Lee: "Software and Performance Issues in the Implementation of a RAID Prototype", Technical Report UCB/CSD 90/573, UC Berkeley, May 1990

[Muntz90] R. R. Muntz and J. C. S. Lui: "Performance Analysis of Disk Arrays under Failure", Proceedings of the 16th International Conference on very Large Data Bases, August 1990

[Ohrenstein90] E. Ohrenstein: "Supercomputers Seek High Throughput and Expandable Storage", Computer Technology Review, Spring 1990

[Stonebreaker90] M. Stonebreaker and G. A. Schloss: "Distributed RAID -- a New Multiple Copy Algorithm", Proceedoings of the Sixth International conference on Data Engineering, February 1990

[Beal91] D. G. Beal, et al: "Data Storage System for Providing Redundant Copies of Data in Different Disk Drives", International Patent Application, Publication Number WO 91/20034, December 26, 1991

[Belsan91] S. J. Belsan, et al: "Deleted Data File Space Release Mechanism for a Dynamically Mapped Virtual Data Storage Subsystem", International Patent Application, Publication Number WO 91/20025, December 26, 1991

[Bond91] M. F. Bond, B. E. Clark and R. S. McRoberts: "Method and Apparatus for Recovering Parity Protected Data", European Patent Application, Publication Number 0 462 917 A2, May 22, 1991

[Burkhard91] W. A. Burkhard, K. C. Claffy, and T. J. E. Schwarz: "Performance of Balanced Disk Array Schemes", Digest of Papers, Eleventh IEEE Symposium on Mass Storage Systems, October 1991

[Cabrera91] L-F. Cabrera and D. D. E. Long: "SWIFT: Using Distributed Disk Striping to Provide High I/O Data Rates", Computing Systems, Fall 1991

[Chen91] C. H. Chen: "Reliability of Some Redundant Systems", IBM Technical Report TR-L41-C-1, 1991

[Chen91a] C. H. Chen: "Performance Models for Disk Arrays", IBM Technical report TR-L41-C-3, 1991

[Chen91b] C-H. Chen: "M/G/1 Models of Disk Arrays with Small Data Transfer Size", IBM May 1991

[Chen91a] P. M. Chen and D. A. Patterson: "Maximizing Performance in a Striped Array", CMG Transactions, Fall 1991

[Chervenak91] Chervenak, Ann L., Randy H. Katz, "Performance of a RAID Prototype," 1991 ACM SIGMETRICS Conference on Measurement and Modeling of Computer Systems, San Diego CA, May 1991.

[Chervanak91a] A. L. Chervanak and R. H. Katz: "Performance of a Disk Array Prototype", CMG Transactions, Fall 1991

[CTR91a] Micropolis Corp., "Drive Crash Terror Boosts RAID Market," Computer Technology Review, February, 1991, p. 12.

[CTR91b] Staff, "Arrays More For Bandwidth Then Capacity," Computer Technology Review, May, 1991, p. 20.

[CTR91c] Storage Concepts, "Is RAID The Disk Strategy For The Masses?," Computer Technology Review, May, 1991, p. 23.

[CTR91d] NCR Corp., "Disk Arrays Diving Into The Computer Mainstream," Computer Technology Review, October, 1991, p. 12.

[CTR91e] DigiData, "RAID Slow Getting Off The Ground," Computer Technology Review, Winter, 1991, p. 44.

[DataQuest91] DataQuest Disk Array Forecast, January 1991

[Gibson91] G. A. Gibson: "Redundant Disk Arrays: Reliable Parallel Secondary Storage", UC Berkeley Technical Report UCB/CSD 90/613, March 1991

[Goldstein91] S. Goldstein: "Array Storage Devices: Teaching Old DASD New Tricks", CMG Transactions, Fall 1991

[Kim91] M. Y. Kim and A. N. Tantawi: "Asynchronous Disk Interleaving: Approximating' Access Delays", IEEE Transactions on Computers, July 1991

[Lee91] E. Lee: "Hardware Overview of RAID-II", UC Bereley RAID Retreat, Lake Tahoe, January 1991

[Lee91a] Lee, Edward K., Randy H. Katz, "Performance Consequences of Parity Placement in Disk Arrays," Fourth International Conference on Architectural Support for Programming Languages and Operating Systems (ASPLOS IV), Palo Alto CA, April 1991.

[Manka91] P. S. Manka: "Direct Access Storage Device with Independently Stored Parity", US Patent number 5,072,378, December 10, 1991

[Mattson91] R. L. Mattson, et al: "Method for Balancing the Frequency of DASD Array accesses When Operating in Degraded Mode", European Patent Application, Publication Number 0 469 924 A2, August 2, 1991

[Menon91] J. Menon and J. Kasson: "Methods for Improved Update Performance of Disk Arrays", Proceedings of the Twenty-Fifth Hawaii International Conference on System Sciences, 1991 (see also IBM Research Report RJ 6928, July 1989)

[Menon91a] J. Menon and D. Mattson: "Performance of Disk Arrays in Transaction Processing Environments", CMG Transactions, Fall 1991

[Merchant91a] A. Merchant and P. S. Yu: "Modeling and Comparisons of Striping Strategies in Data Replication Architectures", IBM Research Report RC 16960, 1991

[Milligan91] C. A. Milligan and J. M. Graziano: "Logical track Write scheduling System for a Parallel Disk Drive Array Data Storage Subsystem", International Patent Application, Publication Number WO 91/16711, October 31, 1991

[Mourad91] A. N. Mourad, W. K. Fuchs, and D. G. Saab: "Performance Evaluation of Redundant Disk Array Support for Transaction recovery", Coordinated science Laboratory, University of Illinois, Urbana, Nov. 11, 1991

[NCR91] NCR Corporation, "NCR Disk Arrays: Solutions For Your Business Environment" NCR publication, copyright 1991

[NCR91a] NCR Corporation, "What Are Disk Arrays" NCR publication, copyright 1990, 1991

[Osterhout91] J. Osterhout and F. Douglis: "Beating the I/O Bottleneck: A Case for Log-Structured File Systems", CMG Transactions, Fall 1991

[Reddy91] A. L. N. Reddy: "Reads and Writes: When I/O's aren't quite the same", IBM Research Report RJ 8033, March 1991

[Reddy91a] A. L. N. Reddy: "Reads and Writes: When I/O's Aren't Quite the Same", Proceedings of the Twenty-Fifth Hawaii International Conference on System Sciences, 1991

[Reddy91b] A. L. N. Reddy and P. Banerjee: "Gracefully Degradable Disk Arrays", Digest of Papers, Twenty-First International Symposium on Fault Tolerant Computing, June 1991

[Rosenblum91] M. Rosenblum and J. K. Osterhaut: "The LFS Storage Manager", CMG Transactions, Fall 1991

[Rosenblum91a] M. Rosenblum and J. Osterhout: "The Design and Implementation of a Log Structured File System", Proceedings of the Thirteenth ACM Symposium on Operating System Principles, October 1991

[Weikum91] G. Weikum, P. Zabback and P. Scheuermann: "Dynamic File Allocation in Disk Arrays", Proceedings of the 1991 ACM SIGMOD, May 1991

[Adaptec92] Adaptec Corporation: "Selecting An Array Interface", Computer Technology Review, March, 1992, p. 27

[Bhide92] A. Bhide and D. Dias: "RAID Architectures for OLTP", IBM Research Report RC 17879, March 24, 1992

[Gibson92] Garth A. Gibson: "Redundant Disk Arrays/Reliable, Parallel Secondary Storage", MIT Press, 1992

[Chandy92] J. Chandy and A. L. N. Reddy: "Failure Evaluation of Disk Array Organizations", IBM Research Report RC 8706, March 30, 1992

[Chantal92] Chantal, A Division of BusLogic, "Why Disk Arrays" Chantal Systems publication, copyright 1992

[CTR92a] Storage Concepts, "RAID5 Is Less Than Expected," Computer Technology Review, March, 1992, p. 12.

[CTR92b] Staff, "RAID Breaks Out Of Level-5 Straightjacket," Computer Technology Review, March, 1992, p. 1.

[CTR92c] Staff, "RAID Becoming The People's Choice," Computer Technology Review, August, 1992, p. 36.

[CTR92c] Staff, "RAID Board To Play The Number Game," Computer Technology Review, November, 1992, p. 41.

[Dynatek92] Dynatek Corporation, "Implementing RAID in Cross-Platform Environments," Computer Technology Review, Winter, 1992, p. 43.

[HIDATA92] HI-Data Corporation, "One RAID Solution Does Not Fit All," Computer Technology Review, November, 1992, p. 37.

[Interphase92] Interphase Corporation, "Planning for Disk Array Integration," Computer Technology Review, November, 1992, p. 38.

[Legacy92] Legacy Storage Systems, "Back To Basics—A Disk Array Technology Primer," Computer Technology Review, October, 1992, p. 42.

[Lo92] R. W-M. Lo and N. S. Matloff: "A Probabilistic Limit on the Virtual Size of Replicated Disk Systems", IEEE Transactions on Knowledge and Data Engineering, February 1992

[Menon92] J. Menon and R. Mattson: "Distributed Sparing in Disk Arrays", CompCon, February 1992

[Menon92a] J. Menon and D. Mattson: "Comparison of Sparing Alternative for Disk Arrays", Proceedings of the International Symposium on Computer Architecture, May 1992

[Merchant92] A. Merchant and P. S. Yu: "Design and Modeling of Clustered RAID", IBM Research Report RC 17572, January 15, 1992

[Bellcore93] Bellcore Applied Research Area, "Profile of RAID—An Emerging Robust On-Line Storage Technology" Bell Communications Research publication, copyright 1992

[CTR93a] Staff, "No Cop-Outs on Backup With RAID," Computer Technology Review, February, 1993, p. 1.

[CTR93b] Staff, "Is SCSI Out of Sync With RAID," Computer Technology Review, March, 1993, p. 1.

[CTR93c] Staff, "Controllers Basic to RAID Success," Computer Technology Review, May, 1993, p. 35.

[CTR93d] Staff, "Arrays: Hardware or Software RAID," Computer Technology Review, July, 1993, p. 26.

[CTR93e] Staff, "How to Select Betwen RAID and Solid State," Computer Technology Review, September, 1993, p. 41.

[CTR93f] Staff, "RAID Fights Fog for Channel," Computer Technology Review, October, 1993, p. 1.

[CTR93g] Staff, "RAID6 Adding Another Level of Confusion," Computer Technology Review, November, 1993, p. 1.

[Form93] Formation, "Choosing Hardware/Software RAID," Computer Technology Review, July, 1993, p. 39.

[Gibson93] G. Gibson and D. Patterson, "Designing Disk Arrays for High Data Reliability," Journal of Parallel and Distributed Computing, January, 1993, pp. 4-27.

[NCR93a] NCR Corporation, "Can Fault Resilience Protect RAIDs?," Computer Technology Review, February, 1993, p. 28.

[NCR93b] NCR Corporation, "Can Fault Resilience Protect RAIDs?," Computer Technology Review, March, 1993, p. 40.

[Quantum93] Quantum Corporation, "SCSI Array Features Can Cost Integrators," Computer Technology Review, July, 1993, p. 14.

[TFL93] Technology Forums, Ltd., "Is RAID Five Levels of Confusion?," Computer Technology Review, February, 1993, p. 37.

[CTR94a] Staff, "RAID Has To Get Its Numbers Straight—And Fast," Computer Technology Review, January, 1994, p. 1.

[CTR94b] Staff, "Certification Coming," Computer Technology Review, January, 1994, p. 1.

[StorDim94] Storage Dimensions, "Which RAID Meets the Application?", Computer Technology Review, February, 1994, p. 37.

Appendix 3: Glossary of *RAID* Advisory Board Terminology

Purpose Of This Glossary

In pursuing its mission to promote understanding of storage systems, and of RAID disk array systems in particular, the RAID Advisory Board has determined that communication between vendors and users is greatly facilitated if certain widely-used terms are used consistently. This glossary is the defining document for all such terms that have been deemed by the RAID Advisory Board to require formal definition. Other RAID Advisory Board publications are expected to use these terms as they are defined in this Glossary.

It is the philosophy of the RAID Advisory Board to be descriptive of what is being done in the industry and the market, rather than prescriptive of what ought to be done. To that end, this Glossary is updated periodically, and new definitions may be added or existing ones modified as deemed necessary by the RAID Advisory Board.

Terms in this Glossary are defined *as they are to be understood when encountered in RAID Advisory Board publications and statements*. The reader is cautioned that other organizations and publications may apply alternative definitions and connotations to these terms, or may use alternative terms to denote similar concepts.

Conventions Used In This Glossary

Certain terms commonly used in the context of storage systems are often abbreviated by the omission of a noun. For example, hot spare disks are typically referred to simply as *hot spares*. When such terms are defined in this Glossary, the often-omitted noun is included in parentheses, for example, **hot spare (disk)**.

The RAID Advisory Board has worked closely with the ANSI X3T10 *RAID Study Group* in defining many of the disk system-related terms, particularly those having to do with RAID data mapping. Several terms that appear frequently in RAID Advisory Board publications are the product of this joint work. These are identified in this Glossary by the phrase (An ANSI X3T10 term) in their definitions. In all cases, relevant ANSI documents contain the ruling definition.

Computer-related industries are acronym-rich, and many acronyms, among which RAID is notable, assume the status of words over time. For this reason, acronyms defined in this glossary are written without periods and alphabetized as if they were words. For example, **RU**, meaning replaceable unit, appears as if it were the two letter word *ru*.

Many storage system-related terms incorporate the acronym "I/O," meaning "input/output." Terms beginning with I/O, such as I/O adapter, I/O driver, etc., have been alphabetized as if they began with the letters *io*.

Computer-related industries are also rich in synonyms. In many instances, there are two or more terms in widespread use to denote the same concept. In most such cases, the *RAID* Advisory Board has adopted a preferred term, which is the one defined in this glossary. Synonyms are identified as such, and the user of the glossary is referred to the preferred term, where the definition is located.

The Glossary of *RAID* Advisory Board Terminology

Common storage system-related terms and the definitions applied to them in RAID Advisory Board publications

 A

active component
A storage system component that requires electrical power to operate. In a typical storage system, active components may include power supplies, disks and other storage devices, fans, and controllers. By contrast, the enclosure housing would not be considered an active component.

active-active (controllers)
Synonym for dual active controllers (q.v.)

active-passive (components)
Synonym for hot standby. (q.v.)

adapter
Synonym for I/O adapter (q.v.)

adaptive array
A disk array whose *Array Management Software* is capable of changing data address mapping dynamically (i.e., while the array is operating) to meet changing data protection requirements or access patterns.

aggregation
The combination of multiple similar and related objects or operations into a single one. Used as a synonym for consolidation (q.v.) in the context of combining member disk data streams into an *aggregate* data stream for an array, as well as combining

two or more I/O requests for adjacently located data into a single request to minimize request processing overhead and rotational latency.

American National Standards Institute   A standards organization whose working committees are responsible for many of the computer system-related standards in the United States. Often abbreviated ANSI. The ANSI working committee most closely aligned with the RAID Advisory Board's activities is called X3T10, and is principally responsible for the SCSI (q.v.) family of I/O interface standards.

ANSI   American National Standards Institute (q.v.)

array   A storage array (q.v.), i.e., a disk array (q.v.) or tape array (q.v.).

Array Management Function   The body of software that provides common control and management for one or more disk or tape arrays (q.v.). *Array Management Function* presents the arrays of disks or tapes it controls to its operating environment as one or more virtual disks or tapes (q.v.). *Array Management Function* may execute in a disk controller or intelligent host bus adapter, or in a host computer. When it executes in a disk controller or adapter, *Array Management Function* is often referred to as *firmware*.

asynchronous operations Operations which bear no relationship to each other in time. Asynchronous operations may overlap in time. The concept of asynchronous I/O operations is central to the use of independent access arrays in throughput-intensive applications.

application I/O request, application read request, application write request
I/O requests made by a disk system's external clients, as distinguished from member I/O requests made by *Array Management Function*. RAID Advisory Board publications do not generally distinguish between I/O requests made by the operating environment (e.g., for paging, swapping, and file system directory lookups, etc.) and those made by user applications.

ASIC   Application-specific integrated circuit.

asynchronous I/O requests I/O requests which bear no relationship to each other in time. Asynchronous I/O requests may overlap in time. Independent access disk arrays can execute asynchronous I/O requests which overlap in time and address data that maps to dif-

---

ferent member disks concurrently. Parallel access disk arrays cannot.

atomic operation An indivisible operation that occurs either in its entirety or not at all. The concept of atomic operations is important to RAID technology when discussing the effects of a component failure on user data. Certain operations, for example the writing of a single block to a virtual disk, should be atomic when performed by a RAID array, even if a failure occurs while they are being performed. If a component failure occurs in a RAID array while an atomic operation is being performed, the array's behavior after recovery is permitted to reflect either completion of the operation, failure to execute it at all, or an indication that the data involved is unrecoverable, but must not reflect partial execution of the operation.

auto-swap Abbreviation for automatic swap (q.v.) *cf.* **cold swap, hot swap, warm swap**

automatic failover Synonym for failover (q.v)

automatic swap The functional substitution of a replacement unit (RU—q.v.) in a disk system for a defective one, where the substitution is performed by the disk system itself while it continues to perform its normal function (possibly at a reduced rate of performance). Automatic swaps are functional rather than physical substitutions, and do not require human intervention *cf.* **cold swap, hot swap, warm swap**

automatic switchover Synonym for failover (q.v)

B

backing store Non-volatile memory. The term *backing store* is often used in connection with cache, which is a (usually) volatile random access memory used to speed up I/O operations. Data held in a volatile cache must be replicated in a non-volatile backing store so that it can survive a system crash or power failure.

Berkeley RAID Levels A family of disk array data protection and mapping techniques described by Garth Gibson, Randy Katz, and David Patterson in papers written while they were performing research into I/O systems at the University of California at Berkeley

[**Patterson88, Katz89b**]. There are six Berkeley RAID Levels, usually referred to by the names RAID Level 1, etc., through RAID Level 6.

blind mating
The ability of pairs of components which must connect electrically to be connected without the electrical terminals of the connection being visible. Blind mating is usually accomplished by mechanical guides (e.g., slots and rails) on the components to be connected.

block
Short for disk block (q.v.).

boot, booting
bootstrapping (q.v.)

bootstrapping
The loading of operating system code from a disk or other storage device into a computer's memory. Bootstrapping is so-called because it typically occurs in steps, starting with a very simple program to read a sequence of blocks from a fixed location on a pre-determined disk into a fixed memory location. The data thus read is the code for the next stage of bootstrapping; it typically causes an operating system to be read into memory, which then begins to execute.

C

channel
Any path used for the transfer of data and control information between storage devices and a storage controller or I/O adapter. A channel consists of cables, connectors, and all associated drivers, receivers, transducers, and other electronics required to make it function. The term *channel* has several meanings in other branches of computer technology. The definition given here is specific to the purposes of RAID Advisory Board publications.

chunk
A synonym for strip (q.v.).

chunk size
A synonym for stripe depth and strip size. (q.v.).

CKD (architecture)
Count-key-data disk architecture (q.v.)

cold swap
The substitution of a replacement unit (RU—q.v.) in a storage system for a defective one, where power must be removed from the storage system in order to perform the substitution. A cold

swap is a physical substitution as well as a functional one. *cf.*
automatic swap, hot swap, warm swap

complex array

A disk array whose *Array Management Function* protects and maps data according to more complex algorithms than those of the Berkeley RAID Levels (q.v.). The most common complex arrays are multi-level disk arrays (q.v.), which perform more than one level of data address mapping, and adaptive arrays (q.v.), which are capable of changing data address mapping dynamically.

conditioning

Synonym for power conditioning (q.v.)

consolidation

The process of accumulating the data for a number of sequential write requests in a cache, and performing a smaller number of larger write requests to achieve more efficient device utilization.

controller-based array

A disk array whose *Array Management Function* executes in the disk system's controller or host I/O bus adapter. The member disks of a controller-based array are necessarily part of the same disk system. *cf.* **host-based array**.

copyback

The replacement of a properly functioning array member by another disk, including copying of the member's contents to the replacing disk. Copyback, which is most often used to create or restore a particular physical configuration for an array (e.g., a particular arrangement of array members on disk channels), is accomplished without reduction (q.v.) of the array.

count-key-data

A disk data organization model in which the disk is assumed to consist of a fixed number of tracks, each having a maximum data capacity. Multiple records of varying length may be written on each track of a count-key-data disk, and the usable capacity of each track depends on the number of records written to it. Count-key-data architecture, also known as CKD architecture, derives its name from the record format, which consists of a field containing the number of bytes of data, an optional key field by which particular records can be easily recognized, and the data itself. *cf.* **fixed-block architecture**

CRU

Abbreviation for customer replaceable unit (q.v.)

customer replaceable unit

A unit, or component of a system that is designed to be replaced by "customers;" i.e., individuals who may not be trained as computer system service personnel. *cf.* **field-replaceable unit**

D

data availability   Expressed as *Mean Time to (Loss of) Data Availability (MTDA*—q.v.). The length of expected continuous span of time over which applications can access correct data stored by a population of identical disk systems in a timely manner.

data reliability   Expressed as *Mean Time to Data Loss (MTDL*—q.v.). The length of the expected continuous span of time over which data stored by a population of identical disk systems can be correctly retrieved.

data segment   The amount of contiguously addressed storage space on an array's virtual disk that is mapped to contiguously addressed storage space on a single member disk in a disk array. The size of a data segment is constant for a p_extent (q.v.), but may vary among the p_extents comprising a virtual disk.

data transfer capacity   The maximum amount of data per unit time that can be moved through a channel or I/O bus. For disk system I/O, data transfer capacity is usually expressed in Mbytes/second (millions of bytes per second, where 1 million = 10^6). *cf.* **throughput, data transfer capacity**

data transfer-intensive (application)   A characterization of applications. A data transfer-intensive application is an I/O intensive (q.v.) application which makes large I/O requests (q.v.). Data transfer-intensive applications' I/O requests are usually sequential (q.v.).

data transfer rate   The amount of data per unit time moved through a channel or I/O bus in the course of execution of an I/O load. For disk system I/O, data transfer capacity is usually expressed in Mbytes/second (millions of bytes per second, where 1 million = 10^6). *cf.* **data transfer capacity**

data stripe depth   User data extent stripe depth (q.v.).

device   A storage device (q.v.).

device fanout   The ability of a storage controller to connect one or more host computers to multiple storage devices over a single I/O bus address. Device fanout allows computer systems to connect to substantially more storage devices than could be connected directly.

disk

A non-volatile, randomly addressable, re-writable data storage device. This definition includes both rotating magnetic and optical disks and *solid-state disks*, or non-volatile electronic storage elements. It does not include specialized devices such as *write-once-read-many (WORM)* optical disks, nor does it include so-called *RAM disks* implemented using software to control a dedicated portion of a host computer's volatile random access memory.

disk array

A collection of disks from one or more commonly accessible disk systems, combined with an *Array Management Function* (q.v.). The *Array Management Function* controls the disks' operation and presents their storage capacity to hosts as one or more virtual disks.[64] The ANSI X3T10 committee refers to the *Array Management Function* as a *storage array conversion layer* (SACL). The committee does not have an equivalent of the term *disk array* in the sense in which it is used by the *RAID* Advisory Board.

disk block

The unit in which data is stored and retrieved on a fixed-block architecture (q.v.) disk. Disk blocks are of fixed usable size (with the most common being 512 bytes), and are numbered consecutively. Disk blocks are also the unit of data protection; whatever mechanism a disk employs to protect against data errors protects blocks of data. *cf.* **sector**

disk striping

A disk array data mapping technique in which fixed-size sequences of virtual disk data addresses are mapped to sequences of member disk addresses in a regular rotating pattern. Disk striping is commonly called RAID Level 0 because of its similarity to common RAID data mapping techniques. Disk striping includes no data protection, however.

disk system

A storage system (q.v.) capable of supporting only disks. The ANSI X3T10 SCSI-3 Controller Command Standard refers to a disk system that uses SCSI-3 as its host attachment as a *SCSI Disk Array* (SDA).[65]

---

[64] The *Array Management Function* is often referred to as *firmware* or *microcode* when it executes in a disk controller rather than a host computer.

[65] At the time of writing, the ANSI X3T10 committee is creating a standard governing SCSI-attached disk arrays (Project 1047D, ANSI Draft X3.276-1996). In the course of creating this standard, terminology similar to that defined by the *RAID* Advisory Board has been developed. Differences between the ANSI and *RAID* Advisory Board terms for similar concepts are noted in the text.

double buffering An application or data manager technique often used to maximize data transfer rate by constantly keeping two I/O requests for adjacently addressed data outstanding. A software component begins a double-buffered I/O stream by making two I/O requests in rapid sequence. Thereafter, each time an I/O request completes, another is immediately made. If a disk system can process requests fast enough, double buffering allows data to be transferred at a disk or disk array's full-volume transfer rate (q.v.).

driver, driver software An I/O driver (q.v.).

dual active (components) A pair of components, such as storage controllers in a failure tolerant storage system that share a task or set of tasks when both are functioning normally. When one component in a dual-active pair fails, the other takes on the entire load. Most often used to describe controllers. Dual active controllers are connected to the same set of devices, and provide a combination of higher I/O performance and greater failure tolerance than a single controller. Dual active components are also called *active-active* components.

E

electronic storage element A solid state disk (q.v.).

embedded storage controller An intelligent storage controller that mounts in a host computer's housing and attaches directly to a host's memory bus with no intervening I/O adapter (q.v.) or I/O bus. Embedded storage controllers differ from I/O adapters in that they provide functions beyond bus protocol conversion (e.g., RAID).

extent A set of consecutively addressed member disk blocks that is part of a single virtual disk-to-member disk mapping. A single member disk may have multiple extents of (possibly) different sizes, and may have multiple (possibly) non-adjacent extents that are part of the same virtual disk-to-member disk mapping. Extents are sometimes called *logical disks* (q.v.).

F

failback

The restoration of a failed system component's share of a load to a replacement component. For example, when a failed controller in a redundant configuration is replaced, the devices that were originally controlled by the failed controller are usually *failed back* to the replacement controller to restore the I/O balance, and to restore failure tolerance. Similarly, when a defective fan or power supply is replaced, its load, previously borne by a redundant component can be *failed back* to the replacement part.

failed over

A mode of operation for failure tolerant systems in which a component has failed and its function has been assumed by a redundant component. A system operating in failed over mode is not failure tolerant, since failure of the redundant component may render the system unable to function.

failover

The automatic substitution (q.v.) of a functionally equivalent system component for a failed one. The term failover is most often applied to intelligent controllers connected to the same storage devices and host computers. If one of the controllers fails, failover occurs, and the survivor takes over its I/O load.

failure tolerance

The ability of a system to continue to perform its function (possibly at reduced performance), even when one of its components has failed,. Failure tolerance is often implemented by including in a system redundant (q.v.) instances of components whose failure would render the system incapable of performing its function, and with the capability to swap these redundant components into service automatically in the event of a failure.

fanout

Synonym for device fanout (q.v.)

fault tolerance

Synonym for failure tolerance (q.v.)

FBA

Fixed-block architecture (q.v.)

field replaceable unit

A unit, or component of a system that is designed to be replaced "in the field;" i.e., without returning the system to a factory or repair depot. Field replaceable units may either be customer-replaceable, or their replacement may require trained service personnel. *cf.* **customer-replaceable unit**

fixed-block architecture A model of disks in which storage space is organized as linear, dense address spaces of blocks of a fixed size. Abbreviated FBA. FBA is the disk model on which SCSI (q.v.) is predicated. *cf.* **count-key-data**.

formatting The preparation of a disk for use by writing required information in all of its blocks.

FRU Abbreviation for field replaceable unit (q.v.)

full-volume data transfer rate The average rate at which a single disk transfers a large amount of data (more than one cylinder). The full-volume data transfer rate accounts for any delays (e.g., due to inter-sector gaps, inter-track switching time and seeks between adjacent cylinders) that may occur during the course of a large data transfer.

G

Gbyte Shorthand for 1,000,000,000 (10^9) bytes. Pronounced *gigabyte*. RAID Advisory Board publications use the 10^9 convention commonly found in I/O-related literature rather than the 1,073,741,824 (2^{30}) convention sometimes used in describing computer system random access memory.

H

high availability The ability of a system to perform its function continuously (without interruption) for a significantly longer period of time than the reliabilities of its individual components would suggest. High availability is most often achieved through failure tolerance (q.v.). High availability is not an easily quantifiable term. Both the bounds of a system that is called highly available and the degree to which its availability is extraordinary must be clearly understood on a case-by-case basis.

host A host computer (q.v.)

host adapter An I/O adapter (q.v.)

host-based array	A disk array whose *Array Management Function* executes in host computer(s) rather than in a disk system. The member disks of a host-based array may be part of different disk systems. *cf.* **controller-based array**.
host bus	A host I/O bus (q.v.)
host bus adapter	An I/O adapter (q.v.) that connects a host I/O bus (q.v.) to the host's memory system.
host computer	Any computer system to which disks are attached and accessible for data storage and I/O. Mainframes, servers, workstations and personal computers, as well as multiprocessors and computer complexes such as clusters and sysplexes are all referred to as host computers in RAID Advisory Board publications.
host I/O bus	An I/O bus (q.v.) used to connect a host computer to storage systems or storage devices.
hot disk	A disk whose capacity to execute I/O requests is saturated by an I/O load.
hot file	A frequently accessed file. Hot files are generally the root cause of hot disks (q.v.), although this is not always the case. A hot disk can also be caused by operating environment I/O, such as paging or swapping.
hot spare (disk)	A disk being used as a hot standby component (q.v.)
hot standby (component)	A redundant component in a failure tolerant storage system that has power applied and is ready to operate, but which does not perform its task as long as the primary component for which it is standing by is functioning properly. Hot standby components are used to increase storage system availability by allowing systems to continue to function in the presence of a failed component. When the term hot standby designates a disk, it specifically means a disk that is spinning and ready to be written to, for example, as part of a rebuilding (q.v.) operation.
hot swap	The substitution of a replacement unit (RU—q.v.) in a storage system for a defective unit, where the substitution can be performed while the system is performing its normal function. Hot swaps are manual operations typically performed by humans— *cf.* **automatic swap, cold swap, warm swap**.

I

Independent access array   A disk array whose data mapping is such that different member disks can execute multiple application I/O requests concurrently. *cf.* **parallel access array**

inherent cost   The cost of a system expressed in terms of the number and type of components it contains. The concept of inherent cost allows technology-based comparisons of disk system alternatives by expressing cost in terms of number of disks, ports, modules, fans, power supplies, cabinets, etc. Because it is inexpensively reproducible, software is generally assumed to have negligible inherent cost.

I/O adapter   A hardware device that converts between the timing and protocol of a host's memory bus and that of an I/O bus. In the context of storage systems, I/O adapters may be contrasted with **embedded storage controllers** (q.v.) , which perform timing and protocol conversion functions as well as others such as device fan-out, cache, and RAID.

I/O bus   Any path used for the transfer of data and control information between I/O adapters and storage controllers or storage devices. An I/O bus consists of cables, connectors, and all associated drivers, receivers, transducers, and other electronics required to make it function. *cf.* **channel**

I/O bottleneck   Any resource in the I/O path (e.g., a device driver, an I/O adapter, an I/O bus, an intelligent controller, or a disk) whose performance limits the performance of a storage system or I/O system as a whole.

I/O driver   A host computer software component (usually part of an operating system) whose function is to control the operation of peripheral controllers or adapters attached to the host computer. I/O drivers communicate between applications and I/O devices, and in some cases may participate in data transfer, although this is rare with disk drivers, since most disk adapters and controllers contain hardware that performs data transfers.

I/O-intensive   A characterization of applications. An I/O-intensive application is one whose performance depends strongly on the performance of the I/O system that provides its I/O services.

I/O load	A sequence of I/O requests made to an I/O system. The requests that comprise an I/O load include both user I/O and host overhead I/O, such as swapping, paging, and file system activity.
I/O load balancing	Load balancing (q.v.)
I/O system	A collective term for all of a computer system's or integrated computing environment's storage systems.

K

Kbyte	One kilobyte, or 1,024 (2^{10}) bytes of data. RAID Advisory Board publications use the software convention (2^{10}) for Kbytes and the data transmission conventions for Mbytes (10^6) and Gbytes (10^9). This is due primarily to the contexts in which the terms are normally used.

L

large read request	
large write request	
large I/O request	An I/O request that specifies the transfer of a large amount of data. 'Large' obviously depends on the context, but typically refers to requests for 64 Kbytes or more of *cf.* **small I/O request**
latency	(1.) A synonym for I/O request execution time, the time between the making of an I/O request and completion of the request's execution. (2.) Short for rotational latency, the time between the completion of a seek and the instant of arrival of the first block of data to be transferred at the disk's read/write head.
latent fault	The failure of a redundant component that is not used during normal operation in a failure tolerant storage system. Latent faults may prevent the redundant component from operating when it is required (e.g., because of failure of the component it backs up), and therefore, defeat failure tolerance. Well-designed

failure tolerant systems perform periodic testing and compensate for significant latent faults.

load balancing

The adjustment of system and/or application components and data so that application I/O demands are spread as evenly as possible across an I/O system's physical resources. I/O load balancing may be done manually (by a human) or automatically (by some means that does not require human intervention). *cf.* **I/O load optimization, load sharing**

load optimization

The division of an I/O load or task in such a way that the performance of the task is optimal by some objective metric. When participating components are of equal performance, load optimization is most often achieved by load balancing (q.v.). If, however, the performance of individual components differs markedly, then load optimization may be achieved by directing a disproportionate share of the load to higher-performing components. *cf.* **load balancing, load sharing**

load sharing

The division of an I/O load or task among several storage system components, without any attempt to equalize each component's share of the work. Each affected component bears a percentage of a shared load. When a storage system is load sharing, it is possible for some of the sharing components to be operating at full capacity, to the point of actually limiting performance, while others are underutilized. *cf.* **I/O load balancing, load optimization**

logical disk

A set of consecutively addressed member disk blocks that is part of a single virtual disk-to-member disk mapping. Logical disks are used in some array implementations as constituents of logical volumes or partitions (q.v.). Logical disks are normally not visible to the host environment, except when the array containing them is being configured. *cf.* **extent**

logical volume

A virtual disk made up of logical disks (q.v.). Also called a *virtual disk*, *volume set*, or *partition*.

M

mapping

Conversion between two data addressing spaces. Most commonly used in RAID Advisory Board publications to refer to conversion between member disk physical block addresses and

---

block addresses of the virtual disks presented to the operating environment by *Array Management Function*.

mandatory test A test that must be successfully executed as a condition of obtaining RAID Advisory Board verification of the applicable test report.

mapping boundary A virtual disk block address of some significance to a disk array's mapping algorithms. The first and last blocks of a user data space strip or check data strip are mapping boundaries.

Mbyte Shorthand for 1,000,000 (10^6) bytes. Pronounced *megabyte*. RAID Advisory Board publications use the 10^6 convention commonly found in data transfer-related literature rather than the 1,048,576 (2^{20}) convention common in computer system random access memory and software literature.

member (disk) A disk that is in use as a member of a disk array. A disk may be a member of an array at times and used independently at other times.

metadata Data that describes data. In disk arrays, metadata consists of items such as array membership, member extent sizes and locations, descriptions of logical disks and partitions, and array state information.

minimum strip size The least common denominator of the member strip sizes of a disk array. The RAID Advisory Board specification of disk array data mapping requires all array member strip sizes to be multiples of the minimum strip size.

mirroring A form of RAID in which the *Array Management Function* maintains two or more identical copies of data on separate disks. Also known as RAID Level 1 and disk shadowing.

mirrors, mirrored disks The disks of a mirrored array (q.v.).

mirrored array Common term for a disk array that implements RAID Level 1, or mirroring (q.v.) to protecting data against loss due to disk or channel failure.

monitor (program) A program that executes in an operating environment (q.v.) and keeps track of system resource utilization. Monitors typically record CPU utilization, I/O request rates, data transfer rates, RAM utilization, and similar statistics. A monitor program, which may be an integral part of an operating system, a separate software product, or a part of a related component, such as a database management system, is a necessary prerequisite to manual I/O load balancing.

MTBF An abbreviation for *Mean Time Between Failures*, the average time from start of use to failure in a large population of identical systems, components, or devices.

MTDA An abbreviation for *Mean Time until (Loss of) Data Availability*; the average time from startup until a component failure causes a loss of timely user data accessibility in a large population of disk arrays. Loss of availability does not imply loss of data; for many classes of failures, (e.g., failure of non-redundant intelligent storage controllers, data remains intact, and can again be accessed after the failed component is replaced.

MTDL An abbreviation for *Mean Time until Data Loss*; the average time from startup until a component failure causes a permanent loss of user data in a large population of disk arrays. The concept is similar to that of physical MTBF used to describe physical device characteristics, but takes into account the possibility that RAID redundancy can protect against data loss due to single component failures.

multi-level disk array A disk array with two levels of data mapping. The virtual disks created by one mapping level become the members of the second level. The most frequently encountered multi-level disk arrays use mirroring at the first level, and stripe data across the resulting mirrored arrays at the second level.

multi-threaded Having multiple concurrent or pseudo-concurrent execution sequences. Used to described processes in computer systems. Multi-threaded processes are one means by which I/O request-intensive applications can make maximum use of disk arrays to increase I/O performance.

N

normal operation A state of a system in which all components are functioning properly, no extraordinary actions (e.g., reconstruction) are being performed, environmental conditions are within operational range, and the system is able to perform its function.

O

open access device   A storage device designed so that its media can be readily removed and inserted. Tapes, CDROMs, and optical disks are open access devices.

open interconnect   A standard interconnect (q.v.).

operating environment   The hosting environment within which a storage system operates. The operating environment includes the computer(s) to which the storage system is attached, I/O buses and adapters, host operating system instances, and any required software. For host-based disk arrays (q.v.), the operating environment includes I/O driver software for the array and possibly also for the member disks, but does not include *Array Management Function*, which is more properly regarded as part of the array itself.

optional feature   A disk system feature that is not required to in order to obtain RAID Advisory Board verification of a RAID Advisory Board test report. If a disk system submitted to the RAID Advisory Board includes an optional feature, and the petitioner wishes the optional feature to be mentioned in the test report, then the corresponding optional test (q.v.) must be completed successfully.

optional test   A test of an optional feature (q.v.).

P

p_extent   (An ANSI X3T10 term) Physical extent (q.v.)

p_extent block number   (An ANSI X3T10 term) A conceptual position assigned to a block within a p_extent (q.v.). p_extent block numbers are used only to develop higher-level constructs in the ANSI X3T10 SCC disk array model, and not for data mapping purposes.

p_extent spare   (An ANSI X3T10 term) A p_extent (q.v.) reserved for the purpose of substituting for a failed p_extent that is part of a redundancy group. A p_extent spare is not considered to be part of

---

any redundancy group, but may be *associated* with any redundancy group(s) for which it is eligible to be a spare. *cf.* **spare**

parallel access array A disk array in which the data access model assumes that all member disks operate in unison, and that all member disks participate in the execution of every application I/O request. A parallel access array is inherently capable of executing one I/O request at any instant. True parallel access arrays require physical disk synchronization; much more commonly, arrays approximate true parallel access behavior. *cf.* **independent access array**

parity RAID A collective term used to refer to Berkeley RAID Levels (q.v.) 3, 4, and 5.

parity RAID array A RAID array (q.v.) whose data protection mechanism is one of Berkeley RAID Levels (q.v.) 3, 4, or 5.

partition A virtual disk (q.v.). The term partition is most often used when a redundancy group (q.v.) is presented as more than one virtual disk. Also used in complex arrays with dynamic mapping to denote a collection of redundancy groups that provides storage for a subset of an array's virtual disks.

partitioning The presentation of the full usable storage capacity of a disk or array of disks to an operating environment in the form of several virtual disks whose aggregate capacity approximates that of the underlying disk or array. Partitioning is usually performed by storage controllers, but may also be done by a host computer system. (Partitioning is common in MS-DOS and UNIX environments.) Partitioning is useful with hosts which cannot support the full capacity of a large disk or array in one device. It can also be useful administratively, for example, to create administrative boundaries in large quanta of storage.

petitioner An individual or organization who has made a written request that the RAID Advisory Board grant a license to use one of its trademarks for the prescribed purpose.

physical disk A disk. Often used to emphasize a contrast with virtual disks (q.v.).

physical extent (An ANSI X3T10 term) A number of consecutively addressed physical blocks on an array member disk. Physical extents are created by *Array Management Function* as building blocks

---

from which redundancy groups and volume sets are created. Commonly called p_extent.

policy processor In an intelligent storage controller, adapter, or device, the processor that schedules the controller's overall activities. In some intelligent controllers, the policy processor is augmented by additional processors, state machines, or other activity sequencers that perform lower-level functions within an overall policy.

port (1.) An I/O adapter (q.v.) used to connect an intelligent storage controller to storage devices. (2.) A synonym for channel (q.v.).

power conditioning The regulation of power supplied to a system so that acceptable ranges of voltage and frequency are maintained. Power conditioning is sometimes done by a storage system, but may also be an environmental requirement.

proprietary interconnect An I/O interconnect (either a host interconnect or a device interconnect) whose transmission characteristics and protocols are the intellectual property of a single vendor, and which require the permission of that vendor to be implemented in the products of other vendors.

protected space, protected space extent (An ANSI X3T10 term) The storage space available for application data in a p_extent (q.v.) that is part of a redundancy group. Also called *ps_extent*.

protocol A set of rules for using a signaling channel so that information conveyed on the channel can be correctly interpreted by all parties to the communication. Protocols include such aspects of communication as data item ordering, message formats, message and response sequencing rules, block data transmission conventions, and so forth.

ps_extent (An ANSI X3T10 term) Protected space extent (q.v.)

R

RAID (1.) An acronym for *Redundant Array of Independent Disks,* a family of techniques for managing multiple disks to provide desirable cost, data availability, and performance characteristics to host environments. (2.) A Redundant Array of Independent Disks (q.v.).

RAID Advisory Board	An organization of suppliers and users of storage systems and related products whose goal is to foster the understanding of storage system technology among users, and to promote all aspects of storage technology in the market.
RAID Array	A Redundant Array of Independent Disks (q.v.).
RAID-related product	Any computer system storage product that implements RAID technology as described in RAID Advisory Board publications in some significant way. RAID-related products may include disk controllers, disk systems, disks, software, and test equipment.
RAMdisk	A quantity of host system RAM managed by software and presented to applications as a high-performance disk. RAMdisks generally emulate disk I/O functional characteristics, but unless they are augmented by special hardware to make their contents non-volatile, they lack one of the key capabilities of actual disks, and are not generally considered disks by the RAID Advisory Board. *cf.* **solid state disk**
random I/O, random I/O load, random reads, random writes	An I/O load whose consecutively issued read and/or write requests do not specify adjacently located data. Random I/O is characteristic of I/O request-intensive applications. *cf.* **sequential I/O**
rank	(1.) A set of physical disk positions in an enclosure, usually denoting the disks that are or can be members of a single array (q.v.). (2.) The set of corresponding target identifiers on all of a controller's device channels. Like the preceding definition, the disks identified as a rank by this definition usually are or can be members of a single array. (3.) Synonym for a stripe in a redundancy group. Because of the diversity of meanings attached to this term by developers of disk systems, the RAID Advisory Board generally discourages its use.
rebuilding	The regeneration (q.v.) and writing onto one or more replacement disks of all of the data from a failed disk in a RAID Level 1, 3, 4, 5, or 6 array. Rebuilding can occur while applications are accessing data on the array's virtual disks.
reconstruction	Synonym for rebuilding (q.v.).
reduced mode	A mode of RAID array operation in which not all of the array's member disks are functioning, but the array as a whole is functioning properly (responding to application read and write requests made to its virtual disks).

reduction	The removal of a member disk from a RAID array, placing the array in reduced mode (q.v.). Reduction most often occurs because of member disk failure, however, some RAID implementations allow reduction for system management purposes.

reduction The removal of a member disk from a RAID array, placing the array in reduced mode (q.v.). Reduction most often occurs because of member disk failure, however, some RAID implementations allow reduction for system management purposes.

redundancy The inclusion of extra components of a given type in a system (beyond those required by the system to carry out its function).

redundancy group (An ANSI X3T10 term) A collection of p_extents organized by an *Array Management Function* for the purpose of providing data protection. Within one redundancy group, a single type of data protection is used. All of the user data storage capacity in a redundancy group is protected by check data stored within the group, and no user data capacity external to a redundancy group is protected by check data within it.

redundancy group stripe (An ANSI X3T10 term) The correspondingly numbered consecutive sequences of p_extent blocks in each of the member p_extents of a redundancy group. The blocks in a redundancy group stripe are either part of the protected space or reserved for check data.

redundancy group stripe depth (An ANSI X3T10 term) The number of consecutively numbered blocks in one p_extent of a redundancy group stripe. The RAID Advisory Board definition requires redundancy group stripe depth to be constant for an entire redundancy group.

redundant (components) Components of a system that have the capability to substitute for each other when necessary, as, for example, when one of the components fails, so that the system can continue to perform its function. In storage systems, power distribution units, power supplies, cooling devices, and controllers are often configured to be redundant. The members of a mirror set are redundant. A parity RAID array's members are redundant, since surviving members may collectively replace the function of a failed disk.

redundant (configuration, system) A system or configuration of a system in which failure tolerance is achieved by the presence of redundant instances of all components that are critical to the system's operation.

Redundant Array of Independent Disks A disk array (q.v.) in which part of the physical storage capacity is used to store redundant information about user data stored on the remainder of the storage capacity. The redundant information enables regeneration (q.v.) of user data in the event that one of the array's member disks (q.v.) or the access path to it fails.

regeneration

Recreation of user data stored on a failed member disk of a RAID Level 1, 3, 4, 5, or 6 array using check data and user data from surviving members. Regeneration is used to recover data when a member disk fails. It may also be used to recover data when an unrecoverable media error is encountered on a member disk. Data regeneration in a RAID Level 1 array consists of delivering an alternate copy of the data. Data regeneration in a RAID Level 3, 4, or 5 array consists of executing the array's parity computation algorithm on the appropriate user and check data. Data regeneration in a RAID Level 6 array consists of choosing the more convenient of two parity algorithms, rebuilding the data, and adjusting the alternate parity value as required.

replacement disk

A disk available for use as or used to replace a failed member disk in a RAID array.

replacement unit

A component or collection of components in a storage system which are always replaced (*swapped*—q.v.) as a unit when any part of the collection fails. Abbreviated RU. Replacement units may be field replaceable (q.v.), or they may require that the system of which they are part be returned to a factory or repair depot for replacement. Field replaceable units may be customer replaceable (q.v.), or their replacement may require trained service personnel.

Typical replacement units in a disk system include disks, controller logic boards, power supplies, cooling devices, and cables.

Replacement units may be cold, warm, or hot, swapped (q.v.).

representative configuration A system configuration selected by a petitioner for submission to a RAID Advisory Board verification test process. A representative configuration should represent a balance between popularity (i.e., the configuration most frequently sold or installed by the petitioning vendor) and completeness (i.e., exercising the major system features implied by the license that the petitioner is seeking).

request-intensive (application) A characterization of applications. Also known as *throughput-intensive* (q.v.). A request-intensive application is an I/O-intensive application whose I/O load consists primarily of large numbers of I/O requests for relatively small amounts of data. Request-intensive applications are typically characterized by random I/O loads (q.v.).

rotational latency   The interval between the end of a disk seek and the time at which the starting block address specified in the I/O request passes the disk head. Rotational latency is difficult to calculate exactly, but the assumption that on the average, requests have to wait for half of a disk revolution time of rotational latency works well in practice. Half of a disk revolution time is therefore defined to be *average rotational latency.*

RU   Abbreviation for replaceable unit (q.v.) *cf.* **CRU, FRU**

S

saturated disk   A disk whose instantaneous I/O load is as great as or greater than its capability to satisfy the requests comprising the load. Mathematically, a saturated disk's I/O queue eventually becomes indefinitely long. In practice, however, user reaction or other system factors generally reduce the rate of new request arrival for a saturated disk.

script   A list of primitive I/O bus operations intended to be executed in sequence. Often used with respect to channels (q.v.), which may have the capability of processing scripts autonomously.

SCSI   Small Computer Storage Interface (q.v.).

sector   The unit in which data is physically stored and protected against errors on a fixed-block architecture (q.v.) disk. A sector typically consists of a synchronization pattern, a header field containing the block's address, data, a checksum or error correcting code, and a trailer. Adjacent sectors are often separated by information used to assist in track centering. Most often, each sector holds a block (q.v.) of data. *cf.* **disk block**

sequential I/O, sequential I/O load, sequential reads, sequential writes
An I/O load consisting of consecutively issued read or write requests to adjacently located data. Sequential I/O is characteristic of data transfer-intensive applications (q.v.). *cf.* **random I/O**

---

single (component) configuration A configuration in which the referenced component is not redundant. *cf.* **Redundant (component)**

Small Computer Storage Interface (SCSI) A collection of ANSI standards and proposed standards which define I/O buses primarily intended for connecting storage systems or devices to hosts through I/O bus adapters. Originally intended primarily for use with small (desktop and desk-side workstation) computers, SCSI has been extended to serve most computing needs, and is arguably the most widely implemented I/O interconnect in use today.

small read request
small write request
small I/O request An I/O, read, or write request that specifies the transfer of a relatively small amount of data. 'Small' usually depends on the context, but most often refers to 8 Kbytes or fewer. *cf.* **large I/O request**

solid state disk A disk (q.v.) whose storage capability is provided by solid-state random access memory rather than magnetic or optical media. A solid state disk generally offers very high access performance compared to that of rotating magnetic disks, because it eliminates mechanical seek and rotation time. It may also offer very high data transfer capacity. Cost per byte of storage, however, is typically quite high, and volumetric density is lower. The RAID Advisory Board definition requires that a solid state disk include some mechanism such as battery backup or magnetic backing store that allows it to be treated by its operating environment as non-volatile storage. *cf.* **RAMdisk**

spare (disk, p_extent) A disk or p_extent reserved for the purpose of substituting for a like entity in case of failure of that entity. *cf.* **p_extent spare**

spiral data transfer rate The full-volume data transfer rate (q.v.) of a disk.

split I/O request An I/O request made to a virtual disk whose data mapping is such that the request must be satisfied by executing two or more member I/O requests to different member disks.

standard interconnect An I/O interconnect (either a host interconnect or a device interconnect) whose specifications are readily available to the public, and which can therefore easily be implemented in a vendor's products.

---

storage array	A collection of disks or tapes from one or more commonly accessible storage systems, combined with a body of *Array Management Function* (q.v.).
storage device	A collective term for disks, tape transports, and other mechanisms capable of non-volatile data storage.
storage system	A system consisting of one or more storage controllers (q.v.) or I/O bus adapters connected to storage devices such as CDROMs, tape transports, removable media loaders and robots, that provides I/O services to one or more host computers.
strip	A number of consecutively addressed blocks in a single extent (q.v.). The ANSI X3T10 SCC disk array architecture requires that all strips in an extent contain the same number of blocks. A disk array's *Array Management Function* uses strips to map virtual disk block addresses to member disk block addresses. Also known as stripe element.
strip size	The number of blocks in a strip (q.v.). The ANSI X3T10 SCC disk array architecture requires that all strips in an extent be of the same size. Also known as chunk size and stripe depth.
stripe	The set of strips (q.v.) in corresponding locations of each of a disk array's p_extents. The strips in a stripe are associated with each other in a way (e.g., relative p_extent block addresses) that allows membership in the stripe to be uniquely and unambiguously determined by an array's *Array Management Function*. The *Array Management Function* uses stripes to map virtual disk block addresses to member p_extent block addresses.
stripe depth	Synonym for strip size (q.v.). The number of blocks in a strip. Also, the number of consecutively addressed virtual disk blocks mapped to consecutively addressed blocks on a single member of a disk array. In the ANSI X3T10 SCC disk array model, stripe depth is constant for a p_extent (q.v.), but may vary among the p_extents comprising a virtual disk.
stripe element	A synonym for strip (q.v.).
stripe size	The number of blocks in a stripe (q.v.). Stripe size in a parity RAID array is the product of stripe depth and one less than the number of disks in the array.

striped array, striped disk array   A collection of disks comprising an array which implements the RAID Level 0 or disk striping (q.v.) mapping technique.

stripeset   A striped array (q.v.).

striping   Short for disk striping (q.v.); also known as RAID Level 0. A mapping technique in which fixed-size consecutive ranges of virtual disk data addresses are mapped to successive array members in a cyclic pattern.

swap, swapping   The installation of a replacement unit in place of a defective unit in a system. *Units* are any parts of a system which may either field replaceable (FRUs) by a vendor service representative or consumer replaceable (CRUs).

A physical swap operation may be cold, warm, or hot, (q.v.), depending on the state in which the disk system must be in order to perform it. A functional swap operation may be an auto-swap (q.v.) or it may require human intervention.

switch-back   Synonym for failback (q.v.)

switch-over   Synonym for failover (q.v.)

switched over (system)   Synonym for failed over (q.v.)

synchronous operations   Operations which have a fixed time relationship to each other. Most commonly used to denote I/O operations which occur in time sequence, i.e., a successor operation does not occur until its predecessor is complete.

system disk   The disk on which a system's operating software is stored. The system disk is usually the disk from which the operating system is *bootstrapped* (initially loaded into memory). The system disk frequently contains the system's swap and/or page files. It may also contain libraries of common software shared among several applications.

system under test   In a RAID Advisory Board test procedure, the disk system being tested. In all RAID Advisory Board test and other examination procedures, the petitioner (q.v.) must clearly define the system under test, and distinguish it from the test system (q.v.).

T

tape array　　　　　　A collection of tapes from one or more commonly accessible storage systems, combined with a body of *Array Management Function* (q.v.).

test system　　　　　In a RAID Advisory Board test procedure, the collection of equipment used to perform a test. In all RAID Advisory Board test procedures, the petitioner (q.v.) must clearly define the test system, and distinguish it from the system under test (q.v.).

throughput　　　　　The number of I/O requests satisfied per unit time. Expressed in I/O requests/second, where a *request* is an application request to a storage system to perform a read or write operation.

throughput-intensive (application)　　　A request-intensive application (q.v.).

U

usable capacity　　　The storage capacity in a disk array that is made available for storing user data. Usable capacity is generally the sum of the physical capacities of the array's member disks minus the capacity required for check data (q.v.) and metadata (q.v.).

user data extent　　　(An ANSI X3T10 term) A collection of consecutively numbered ps_extent blocks. In RAID arrays, collections of user data extents comprise the *volume sets*, or *virtual disks*, presented to the operating environment.

user data extent stripe depth　　　(An ANSI X3T10 term) The number of consecutive ps_extent blocks in a single user data extent that are mapped to consecutive volume set block addresses. Each user data extent in a volume set may have a unique user data extent stripe depth, which may differ from the redundancy group stripe depth of the ps_extent in which it resides.

V

virtual device   A device presented to an operating environment by *Array Management Function*. From an application standpoint, a virtual device is equivalent to a physical one. In some implementations (e.g., host based arrays), virtual devices may differ from physical ones from the operating system point of view (e.g., booting may not be possible).

virtual disk   Synonym for volume set (q.v.).

virtual tape   A virtual device (q.v.) with the characteristics of a tape (q.v.).

volume set   (An ANSI X3T10 term) A collection of user data extents (q.v.) presented to an operating environment as a range of consecutive logical block addresses. A volume set is the disk array object most closely resembling a disk when viewed by the operating environment.

**W**

warm spare (disk)   A spare disk in a storage system to which power is applied, and which is not spinning, but which is otherwise usable as a hot spare (q.v.)

warm swap   The substitution of a replacement unit (RU—q.v.) in a disk system for a defective one, where in order to perform the substitution, the system must be stopped (caused to cease performing its function), but power need not be removed. Warm swaps are manual (performed by humans—*cf.* **auto-swap, cold swap, hot-swap.**

write hole   A potential data corruption problem for parity RAID arrays resulting from an array failure while application I/O is outstanding, followed by an unrelated member disk failure (some time after the array has been returned to service). Data corruption can occur if member data and parity become inconsistent due to the array failure, resulting in a false regeneration when data from the failed member disk is subsequently requested by an application.

write-through cache A caching technique in which the completion of a write request is not signaled until data is safely stored on non-volatile media. Write performance with a write-through cache is approximately that of a non-cached system, but if the data written is also held in cache, subsequent read performance may be dramatically improved.

write-back cache A caching technique in which the completion of a write request is signaled as soon as the data is in cache, and actual writing to non-volatile media occurs at a later time. Write-back cache includes an inherent risk that an application will take some action predicated on the write completion signal, and a system failure before the data is written to non-volatile media will cause media contents to be inconsistent with that subsequent action. For this reason, good write-back cache implementations include mechanisms to preserve cache contents across system failures (including power failures) and to flush the cache at system restart time. *cf.* **write-through cache**

write penalty Low apparent application write performance to independent access RAID arrays' virtual disks. The write penalty is inherent in independent access RAID data protection techniques, which require multiple member I/O requests for each application write request, and ranges from minimal (mirrored arrays) to substantial (RAID Levels 5 and 6). Many RAID array designs include features such as write-back cache specifically to minimize the write penalty.

Appendix 4:

RAB, RAID and EDAP - Unscrambling The Acronyms

A paper describing the *RAB's* position on RAID Levels and the *RAB's* Classification Program

Joe Molina
Chairman

September • 1997

RAB, RAID and EDAP - Unscrambling The Acronyms

Introduction

After briefly describing the *RAID* Advisory Board's *(RAB)* history and achievements, this paper proceeds to state the author's views on the evolution of the RAID (Redundant Arrays of Independent Disks) market, to cite the *RAB's* initial and current position on RAID Levels, and lastly to describe the *RAB's* Storage System Classification Program - a program designed to assist end-users in the procurement of storage systems, which in today's market, offer a rich selection of Extended Data Availability and Protection (EDAP) attributes.

Definitions

Since the words for which the acronym letters stand do not provide sufficient meaning, definitions of both acronyms are necessary at this point:

- **RAID:** A storage system with RAID capability can protect its data and provide on-line, immediate access to its data, despite a single (some RAID storage systems can withstand two concurrent disk failures) disk failure. RAID capability also provides for the on-line reconstruction of the contents of a failed disk to a replacement disk.
- **EDAP:** A storage system with EDAP capability can protect its data and provide on-line, immediate access to its data, despite failure occurrence within the storage system, within attached units or within its environment. The location, type and quantity of failure occurrences determine the degree of EDAP capability attributed to the storage system, with RAID capability being the lowest level of EDAP capability.

About The *RAB*

Formed in August of 1992, and open to all, the *RAB* consists of over 50 member companies whose goal it is to assist users make more informed storage procurement decisions. The *RAB's* goal is achieved by means of three key programs: (1) Education, (2) Standardization and (3) Classification and Test.

In the area of education, the *RAB* has published many books and articles and sponsored annual conferences and seminars. Prominent among its publications are the *RAIDbook* and the Storage System Enclosure Handbook.

In the area of standards, the *RAB,* working closely with the American National Standards Institute (ANSI) for the past three years, has developed the SCSI Controller Commands and SCSI-3 Enclosure Services Command Set standards.

In the Classification and Test area, the *RAB* has developed Functional and Performance specifications and established the RAB RAID Level Conformance Program and the *RAB* Storage System Classification Program. Over 20 *RAB* members are currently licensed to display the RAB Logo and legends indicating that the products identified by the logos have met certain criteria established by the *RAB*

Activities are underway in the areas of storage management, clustering, et al which will yield additional achievements in the areas of education, standardization and classification and test.

RAID Market Evolution

Designers who developed the ability of a storage system to protect its data and to provide on-line, immediate access to its data in the event of a failure first focused their attention on where the data resides - on disk. This focus led first to Mirrored disk systems in the seventies and later to storage systems incorporating Parity RAID in the late eighties. Parity RAID systems were an attractive alternative to Mirrored systems because of lower cost. But these early Parity RAID systems tended to have less performance than Mirrored systems.

Sales of Parity RAID systems did not flourish until the performance lost from Parity RAID was regained. This effort, which resulted in extensive use of cache memory, disks used as non-volatile cache, parallel processing, and other techniques ushered in a period of high growth for RAID.

Successful Parity RAID implementations coupled with increasing disk reliability shifted the focus of concern for data availability and protection from disks to other storage system components. Failure of a controller, power supply, device channel, etc. could impact data availability and protection just as effectively as loss of a disk without RAID. This shifting focus initiated the advent of storage systems which could withstand the failure of any one of its field replaceable units (FRU) by continuing to supply reliable, on-line data immediately to application I/O requests.

For some applications, storage systems providing EDAP with a tolerance of any one FRU failure are unsuitable. For these applications, storage systems with even higher levels of EDAP continue to make their debut in the storage market.

The storage market now offers products which provide a wide range of EDAP capability. The *RAB* has responded by defining the criteria by which the degree to which a storage system exhibits EDAP may be accurately determined and labeled.

The RAB also suggests that, since the acronym RAID pertains only to EDAP for disks via Mirroring and Parity RAID, and that the market has gone beyond RAID, the acronym EDAP be adopted as a more comprehensive term that can apply to the entire storage system, the channels and hosts to which it is attached and its environment.

RAID Levels Outlive Their Usefulness
In addition to being historically significant, an outpouring of articles on RAID and RAID Levels, after the first Berkeley Paper in 1988,

helped sell RAID. Unfortunately, the positive affect of the RAID publicity was offset by the inference implied by the RAID Level numerical sequence that a higher numbered RAID Level was better than a lower numbered one. This inference was also exploited by some RAID vendors with product names such as RAID 10, 53, etc.

To offset this confusion and exploitation, the *RAB* established the RAID Level Conformance program about three years ago. The basis of the program were the descriptions of the RAID Levels, which after review and approval by the *RAB,* were included in the *RAB's* official publication entitled The *RAID*book - a Storage System Technology Handbook. The RAID Levels included in the *RAID*book were limited to those covered in the Berkeley Papers. Additionally, no attempt was made to depart from the RAID Level descriptions found in the Berkeley Papers. This approach, namely to recapitulate rather than to re-invent, was taken to preserve the Berkeley Papers as an important historical reference point and to recognize that RAID Levels 0-6 basically define all known data mapping and protection schemes for disk.

The published RAID Level descriptions in the *RAB's RAID*book became the basis for analyzing RAID vendors' products to determine which RAID Levels the products supported. Successful completion of this process ended with licensing vendors to display *RAB* Conformance Logos with legends which stated the RAID Levels supported by the logo-identified products. End-users could be certain, for example, that a product identified with a RAID Level 5 Conformance Logo supported the *RAB's* description of RAID Level 5 as published in the *RAB's RAID*book.

The *RAB's* Conformance Logo program has been replaced with the RAB's Storage System Classification Program. The *RAB* believes that the information provided by classifying a storage system in accordance with the degree to which it exhibits EDAP attributes is more useful to end- users involved in procuring storage systems than knowing which RAID Levels a product supports. RAID Levels basically describe how data and redundant data are mapped across the disks of an array; information which is less important than an understanding of just how much EDAP is provided by a storage system.

RAID - What To Remember

In the late eighties, Patterson, Gibson and Katz of the University of California at Berkeley identified various Extended Data Availability and Protection techniques for disk as RAID Levels 1-6. This taxonomy describes how data and redundant data are mapped across the multiple disks of an array to provide EDAP in the event of a disk failure.

Two types of RAID provide EDAP for disks: Mirroring and Parity RAID. Mirroring predated Parity RAID and was identified in the Berkeley Papers as RAID Level 1. Its disadvantage is that, unlike Parity RAID, Mirroring requires 100% redundancy. Its advantages, unlike Parity RAID, are that read performance is improved, the impact on write performance is generally modest and a higher percentage of disks in a Mirrored redundancy group may fail simultaneously as compared to a Parity RAID redundancy group.

Parity RAID is identified in the Berkeley Papers as RAID Levels 3, 4, 5 and 6. In these cases, overhead (redundant data in the form of Parity) as compared to Mirroring (redundant data in the form of a complete copy) is significantly reduced to a range of 10% to 33%. Again, in all cases, there are varying degrees of performance degradation intrinsically associated with Parity RAID. The differences between RAID Levels 3-6 pertain to the manner in which data and redundant data are mapped to the disks comprising the RAID array. These differences are of concern to RAID designers, but are generally of little interest and importance to end-users.

One exception to this rule is RAID Level 6. Unlike RAID Levels 3-5 which provide EDAP in the event of a failure of one disk, RAID Level 6 provides EDAP when two disks fail at the same time or when a second disk fails during the reconstruction period resulting from the first disk failure.

To complete the RAID Level review, three additional points need to be made: (1) RAID Level 0 is Striping which is incorporated in Parity RAID and often in Mirroring. It does not, by itself, contribute to EDAP. (2) RAID Level 2 requires the use of non-standard disk drives and is therefore not commercially viable. (3) Unlike the other Parity RAID Levels whose disks operate independently, RAID Level 3 describes an array wherein the disks operate in parallel. RAID Level 3 therefore lends itself to high bandwidth applications, as opposed to RAID Levels 4, 5 and 6 which are more suitable for high transaction rate applications. It should be noted that this is an array characteristic independent of whether the array supports some form of EDAP.

More About EDAP

A storage system with some degree of EDAP capability may be in any one of three states: (1) A normal or protected state during which the EDAP capability is not being employed to counteract a failure; (2) A reduced or vulnerable state during which the EDAP capability is in use to counteract the first failure (and possibly a second failure depending upon the type of EDAP capability) and not available to counteract the next failure; and, (3) A down state during which data can not be stored or retrieved.

During its normal or protected state, a storage system with EDAP capability provides on-line access to reliable data at its peak performance as opposed to reduced performance during the vulnerable state. The performance loss is due to the fact that the EDAP capability being invoked at the time of a failure requires that tasks such as the regeneration of data from a failed disk and the reconstruction of a replacement disk be executed. The execution of such tasks places additional burdens on the available processing power, thus impacting the overall I/O performance. Good EDAP design must mitigate this impact by providing for a level of performance during a storage system's vulnerable state which is sufficient for successful execution of all applications.

In addition to maintaining immediate on-line access to reliable data in the event of a failure, EDAP can also minimize the period of time during which a storage system is in a reduced or vulnerable state by supporting on-line sparing of disks in order that reconstruction can begin immediately upon a disk failure as opposed to waiting for manual replacement of the failed disk.

EDAP can also minimize the period in which a storage system is in a down state by providing for hot swapping of all FRUs. Failed FRUs may then be replaced (hot swapped) without removing power and putting the system in a down state.

EDAP and Backup

Data stored on disk is "backed up" by periodically copying it, or by concurrently recording disk transactions, to some form of removable media (typically tape) which is then stored off site. In the event of the loss of the data stored on disk, the removable media containing the backup data can be used to restore the storage system.

Regardless of the level of EDAP supported by a storage system, backup is still a requirement. No amount of EDAP can protect a storage system from human error - the greatest single cause of lost or corrupted data. Bad data will be as well-protected by EDAP as good data.

Additionally, storage systems which are not disaster tolerant can only be restored with backup data stored off site if a disaster strikes the system.

EDAP Classification

RAB Storage System Classification goes beyond RAID, as RAID is EDAP for disks only. The degree to which a storage system may exhibit EDAP properties varies from none to full support for all EDAP criteria established by the *RAB.* Certain storage system EDAP criteria have been established by the *RAB* as the minimum requirement for categorizing a storage system as one which exhibits EDAP properties;

these are:

- Reliable on-line data is available immediately in the event of the failure of one disk. This capability is referred to as regeneration.
- The contents of a failed disk are reconstructed on-line and recorded on a replacement disk while maintaining acceptable application I/O performance. This capability is referred to as reconstruction.
- Data is protected in the event of the failure of any Field Replaceable Unit (FRU) in the storage system, I/O channel(s) and attached host(s). (Storage system cache failure is an exception.)
- Consistency between the data and its related redundant data is maintained.
- An indication of storage system failure is provided to the user.

Regeneration and reconstruction, the first two capabilities listed above, are provided by RAID technology, either in the form of Mirroring (RAID Level 1) or Parity RAID (RAID Levels 3, 4 and 5).

Storage systems meeting the above minimum EDAP criteria are classified by the *RAB* as "Failure Resistant".

A storage system may exhibit other EDAP properties beyond those which the *RAB* has established as a minimum for classification as "Failure Resistant". For the next highest *RAB* classification, "Failure Tolerant", the storage system must meet the EDAP criteria listed above for "Failure Resistant" plus:

- Data is protected in the event of power failure or overheating.
- Storage system failure monitoring is upgraded from an indication (see above) to a warning.
- Disk Hot Swapping is supported by the storage system.
- Reliable, on-line data is available immediately in the event of the failure of any one storage system Field Replaceable Unit, including device channels, controllers, cache, and power

supply.

For the highest classification "Disaster Tolerant," all EDAP criteria listed above for "Failure Tolerant" must be met plus:

- The capability to attach to multiple I/O channels and multiple external primary power sources is supported.
- All FRUs are hot swappable.
- Reliable, on-line data is available immediately in the event of the failure of any one zone of a multi-zoned storage system which provides for physical separation of the zones.
- Disk hot sparing is supported.

In the interest of brevity, only the three major EDAP classifications have been defined. There are actually seven classifications, with four of the seven being variations of the three major classifications. These four use plus signs added to the three major classifications. For example, "Disaster Tolerant +" includes the criteria that the zones must be separated by at least ten kilometers. See Pages 287-292 for a description of all seven EDAP classifications.

Conclusion

The ability of a storage system to protect its data and to provide on-line, immediate access to its data in the event of a disk failure (provided by RAID technology) has become a base-line requirement for almost all storage systems. EDAP requirements now extend beyond RAID and impact the entire storage system, the channels and hosts to which it is attached and the environment. Users must be able to easily select a storage system which meets the EDAP requirements imposed upon it by the users' applications. Buying more EDAP than is required by the user's applications is a waste of money. Not buying enough could mean disastrous loss of data. The *RAB's* EDAP Classification Criteria and the classifications defined by the criteria are a highly effective tool for matching application and storage system EDAP requirements and capabilities, respectively. RAID Levels, which provide little help in this matching process, remain important to designers and to the history of RAID.

About The Author

Joe Molina is Chairman of the *RAB* and has 40 years of experience in the computer industry. For further information about the *RAB*, please visit the following web site: http://www.raid- advisory.com.

RAID Advisory Board (RAB) Summary of Classification Criteria for Disk Systems Providing Extraordinary Data Availability and Protection

Failure Resistant Disk System (FRDS)
- Protection against data loss and loss of access to data due to disk failure
- Reconstruction of failed disk contents to a replacement disk
- Protection against data loss due to a "write hole"
- Protection against data loss due to host and host I/O bus failures
- Protection against data loss due to component failure
- FRU monitoring and failure indication

Failure Resistant Disk System Plus (FRDS+)
- Protection against data loss and loss of access to data due to disk failure
- Reconstruction of failed disk contents to a replacement disk
- Protection against data loss due to a "write hole"
- Protection against data loss due to host and host I/O bus failures
- Protection against data loss due to component failure
- FRU monitoring and failure indication
- Disk hot swap
- Protection against data loss due to cache component failure
- Protection against data loss due to external power failure
- Protection against data loss due to a temperature-out-of-operating-range condition
- Component and environmental failure warning

Failure Tolerant Disk System (FTDS)

- Protection against data loss and loss of access to data due to disk failure
- Reconstruction of failed disk contents to a replacement disk
- Protection against data loss due to a "write hole"
- Protection against data loss due to host and host I/O bus failures
- Protection against data loss due to component failure
- FRU monitoring and failure indication
- Disk hot swap
- Protection against data loss due to cache component failure
- Protection against data loss due to external power failure
- Protection against data loss due to a temperature-out-of-operating-range condition
- Component and environmental failure warning
- Protection against loss of access to data due to device channel failure
- Protection against loss of access to data due to controller failure
- Protection against loss of data access due to cache component failure
- Protection against loss of data access to data due to power supply failure

Failure Tolerant Disk System Plus (FTDS+)

- Protection against data loss and loss of access to data due to disk failure
- Reconstruction of failed disk contents to a replacement disk
- Protection against data loss due to a "write hole"
- Protection against data loss due to host and host I/O bus failures
- Protection against data loss due to component failure
- FRU monitoring and failure indication
- Disk hot swap
- Protection against data loss due to cache component failure

- Protection against data loss due to external power failure
- Protection against data loss due to a temperature-out-of-operating-range condition
- Component and environmental failure warning
- Protection against loss of access to data due to device channel failure
- Protection against loss of access to data due to controller failure
- Protection against loss of data access due to cache component failure
- Protection against loss of data access to data due to power supply failure
- Protection against loss of access to data due to host and host I/O bus failures
- Protection against loss of access to data due to external power failure
- Protection against loss of data access due to FRU replacement
- Disk hot spare

Failure Tolerant Disk System Plus Plus (FTDS++)

- Protection against data loss and loss of access to data due to disk failure
- Reconstruction of failed disk contents to a replacement disk
- Protection against data loss due to a "write hole"
- Protection against data loss due to host and host I/O bus failures
- Protection against data loss due to component failure
- FRU monitoring and failure indication
- Disk hot swap
- Protection against data loss due to cache component failure
- Protection against data loss due to external power failure
- Protection against data loss due to a temperature-out-of-operating-range condition
- Component and environmental failure warning

- Protection against loss of access to data due to device channel failure
- Protection against loss of access to data due to controller failure
- Protection against loss of data access due to cache component failure
- Protection against loss of data access to data due to power supply failure
- Protection against loss of access to data due to host and host I/O bus failures
- Protection against loss of access to data due to external power failure
- Protection against loss of data access due to FRU replacement
- Disk hot spare
- Protection against data loss and loss of access to data due to multiple disk failures in an FTDS+

Disaster Tolerant Disk System (DTDS)
- Protection against data loss and loss of access to data due to disk failure
- Reconstruction of failed disk contents to a replacement disk
- Protection against data loss due to a "write hole"
- Protection against data loss due to host and host I/O bus failures
- Protection against data loss due to component failure
- FRU monitoring and failure indication
- Disk hot swap
- Protection against data loss due to cache component failure
- Protection against data loss due to external power failure
- Protection against data loss due to a temperature-out-of-operating-range condition
- Component and environmental failure warning
- Protection against loss of access to data due to device channel failure

- Protection against loss of access to data due to controller failure
- Protection against loss of data access due to cache component failure
- Protection against loss of data access to data due to power supply failure
- Protection against loss of access to data due to host and host I/O bus failures
- Protection against loss of access to data due to external power failure
- Protection against loss of data access due to FRU replacement
- Protection against loss of data access due to zone failure

Disaster Tolerant Disk System Plus (DTDS+)

- Protection against data loss and loss of access to data due to disk failure
- Reconstruction of failed disk contents to a replacement disk
- Protection against data loss due to a "write hole"
- Protection against data loss due to host and host I/O bus failures
- Protection against data loss due to component failure
- FRU monitoring and failure indication
- Disk hot swap
- Protection against data loss due to cache component failure
- Protection against data loss due to external power failure
- Protection against data loss due to a temperature-out-of-operating-range condition
- Component and environmental failure warning
- Protection against loss of access to data due to device channel failure
- Protection against loss of access to data due to controller failure
- Protection against loss of data access due to cache component failure

- Protection against loss of data access to data due to power supply failure
- Protection against loss of access to data due to host and host I/O bus failures
- Protection against loss of access to data due to external power failure
- Protection against loss of data access due to FRU replacement
- Disk hot spare
- Protection against loss of data access due to zone failure
- Long distance protection against loss of data access due to zone failure

Other *RAB* Publications
- Storage System Enclosure Handbook - $20.00
- RAID Ready SCSI Drive Profile - $75.00
- Storage System Classification Report (2) - $95.00
- SCSI Functional Test Specification (Three parts) - $640.00
- Performance Test Specification - $290.00
- Fibre Channel Functional Test - $125.00
- SCSI Controller Commands (SCC) Standard (Available from ANSI)
- SCSI Enclosure Services (SES) Standard (Available from ANSI)

Notes: The above publications are available to *RAB* Members at a 50% discount. Prices shown are for non-members, and do not include postage.

To order any of the above publications, or to have an order form faxed to you, please call the *RAB* at:

RAID Advisory Board, Inc.
48 John Drive • North Grafton, MA 01536
Tel: 508-839-0654 • Fax: 508-839-4923
Email: tforumsltd@aol.com • www.raid-advisory.com

Index

ANSI X3T10 (Committee), 8, 10, 24, 26, 34, 43, 59, 60, 63, 64, 65, 66, 68, 70, 71, 72, 73, 75, 76, 77, 84, 88, 249, 262

Array Management Function, xv, xvi, 8, 9, 10, 12, 20, 34, 35, 36, 37, 38, 39, 41, 42, 43, 45, 50, 57, 60, 63, 64, 65, 66, 67, 68, 69, 71, 89, 90, 93, 94, 98, 99, 100, 101, 102, 103, 110, 114, 115, 117, 118, 123, 125, 126, 127, 128, 129, 133, 140, 141, 142, 143, 156, 157, 158, 159, 160, 165, 166, 167, 168, 169, 170, 173, 174, 175, 176, 177, 185, 195, 196, 197, 198, 206, 214, 216, 217, 219, 220, 224, 225, 226, 228, 229, 230, 264, 267, 269, 273, 277, 279, 281, 283, 287, 289, 290

automatic-swap, 52, 53, 118, 157, 158, 159, 160

cache, xvii, 18, 37, 100, 120, 132, 133, 144, 145, 157, 158, 159, 161, 190, 191, 192, 197, 201, 203, 206, 209, 210, 211, 214, 219, 234, 239

dual-copy, 191

flush, 203, 205, 206, 212, 291

mirrored, 191

read, 135, 153, 191, 201, 202

write, 191, 202, 203

write-back, xix, 39, 115, 132, 133, 135, 144, 148, 151, 152, 191, 201, 203, 205, 206, 208, 209, 210, 212, 219, 220, 239

write-behind, 191, 202, 203, 212

cache,, 201

check data, xv, xvi, xvii, xix, 12, 15, 16, 17, 42, 47, 49, 59, 63, 70, 71, 72, 73, 74, 75, 76, 77, 79, 80, 83, 84, 85, 86, 98, 107, 108, 110, 113, 123, 148, 150, 159, 160, 193, 197, 205, 206, 221, 225, 227, 228, 229, 232

cold-swap, 52, 157, 158, 159, 160

cost, xiii, xvi, xviii, 3, 4, 5, 9, 11, 13, 16, 17, 19, 22, 23, 24, 30, 31, 39, 47, 91, 105, 107, 109, 145, 150, 170, 177, 183, 200, 201, 214, 218, 236, 240, 241, 247

inherent, xviii, 15, 22, 38, 96, 100, 104, 109, 113, 166, 173, 174, 176

data availability, xiii, xv, xvi, xviii, 5, 6, 10, 11, 12, 13, 16, 17, 18, 19, 23, 24, 31, 37, 38, 41, 43, 48, 49, 50, 51, 52, 81, 87, 91, 109, 118, 129, 143, 145, 148, 163, 166, 167, 168, 171, 174, 177, 185, 193, 201, 203, 212, 213, 233, 234, 235, 236, 239

disk system, failure tolerant, xiii, 17, 18, 51, 163, 233, 240, 241, 244 disk, member, xviii, xix, 9, 10, 11, 12, 13, 14, 15, 19, 20, 21, 35, 36, 37, 38, 39, 40, 41, 42, 43, 45, 46, 47, 48, 49, 51, 53, 57, 58, 59, 60, 61, 62, 63, 64, 65, 66, 67, 68, 69, 70, 71, 74, 75, 79, 83, 84, 87, 88, 89, 90, 91, 93, 94, 96, 97, 98, 99, 100, 101, 102, 103, 104, 105, 107, 108, 109, 110, 111, 112, 113, 114, 115, 116, 117, 118, 119, 120, 121, 123, 124, 125, 126, 127, 128, 129, 131, 133, 134, 135, 137, 138, 139, 140, 141, 142, 143, 145, 148, 149, 151, 155, 156, 157, 158, 159, 160, 166, 167, 168, 169, 171, 174, 175, 176, 185, 186, 187, 188, 193, 195, 197, 205, 207, 208, 210, 213, 215, 216, 219, 222, 224, 225, 226, 229, 230, 231, 232, 235, 241

disk, virtual, xv, 8, 9, 10, 11, 12, 13, 14, 15, 17, 34, 35, 40, 41, 42, 43, 44, 45, 46, 47, 57, 58, 59, 60, 61, 62, 63, 64, 65, 66, 67, 68, 69, 70, 71, 76, 77, 78, 80, 81, 82, 83, 84, 86, 88, 89, 90, 91, 94, 96, 97, 98, 99, 101, 107, 110, 112, 113, 114, 115, 120, 121, 122, 123, 124, 125, 126, 127, 128, 131, 132, 133, 134, 135, 136, 139, 140, 141, 144, 145, 149, 151, 156, 157, 159, 160, 165, 167, 170, 171, 174, 175, 180, 185, 195, 207, 213, 214, 215, 216, 219, 220, 221, 223, 224, 229

exclusive OR, 108, 110, 111, 112, 117, 118, 124, 126, 127, 129, 130, 131, 141, 142, 143, 149, 150, 175, 205, 225, 226, 227, 228, 229, 230, 231, 232

failover, 51

failure tolerance, 18, 28, 50, 51, 105, 152, 163, 189, 190, 193, 235, 236, 237, 239, 240, 241, 242, 243

hot-swap, xvi, 18, 52, 53, 118, 143, 234, 238, 239, 240, 241

I/O load, 7, 13, 30, 34, 47, 49, 51, 64, 78, 80, 113, 131, 134, 136, 145, 168, 175, 193, 198, 200, 201, 203, 205, 206, 207, 209, 211, 238, 239

balance, 32, 33, 69, 82, 84, 94, 98, 99, 135, 144, 151, 167, 169, 174, 176, 187, 206, 220, 221, 243

balance, automatic, 33

balance, manual, 33

data transfer-intensive, 46, 47, 176, 200

I/O request-intensive, 32, 47, 145, 170, 176

instantaneous, 21

large-file, 134, 189, 191, 193

read-mostly, 15, 131, 134, 146, 151, 200

rebuilding, 175

transaction, 31, 43, 46, 187, 188, 189, 191, 199, 200, 208, 220

I/O performance, 5, 6, 7, 11, 12, 13, 15, 16, 17, 18, 23, 24, 31, 32, 39, 41, 43, 50, 64, 78, 79, 82, 86, 87, 88, 91, 92, 94, 95, 96, 104, 109, 119, 131, 132, 135, 136, 145, 163, 165, 166, 169, 171, 175, 176, 177, 182, 183, 187, 188, 189, 190, 193, 195, 196, 197, 200, 201, 203, 216, 218, 220, 221, 229

mirrored array, xviii, 12, 13, 20, 24, 39, 49, 50, 51, 61, 74, 91, 96, 98, 99, 100, 101, 102, 103, 104, 105, 113, 157, 165, 166, 167, 168, 169, 170, 171, 192, 195, 216, 222

mirroring, xv, xvii, xviii, 10, 11, 12, 13, 14, 15, 16, 17, 20, 22, 23, 24, 36, 39, 49, 51, 59, 72, 87, 96, 109

Molina, Joe, xv, xx, 249, 250

RAB, xiii

RAID Advisory Board, xiii, xv

RAID Level, xv, xix

RAID Level 0, xviii, 16, 17, 39, 49, 68, 88, 155, 166

RAID Level 1, xviii, 14, 17, 20, 39, 96, 156, 166

RAID Level 2, xviii, 17, 20, 47, 107

RAID Level 3, xviii, 15, 17, 20, 37, 39, 86, 107, 108, 113, 121, 157, 166, 175, 200, 201, 207

RAID Level 4, xix, 17, 20, 21, 37, 39, 76, 108, 113, 123, 137, 148, 158

RAID Level 5, xix, 15, 17, 20, 21, 37, 39, 74, 85, 108, 113, 123, 131, 134, 137, 145, 148, 160, 166, 198, 200, 201, 207, 215

RAID Level 6, xix, 14, 16, 17, 49, 72, 148, 149, 150, 151, 152

RAID Level Conformance, 19, 155

RAID Levels, Berkeley, 13, 14, 15, 16, 17, 18, 21, 47, 86, 155

RAIDbook, xiii

RAID-related product, xiii, 14, 18, 247, 248, 250

rebuilding, xvi, xvii, xviii, xix, 49, 82, 83, 101, 102, 104, 118, 143, 156, 158, 159, 160, 168, 174, 175, 215, 222, 223, 224, 232, 243

regeneration, xvi, xvii, xviii, xix, 14, 47, 108, 117, 129, 142, 151, 152, 206, 224, 232, 235, 241

responsiveness, 8, 39, 102, 104, 133, 152, 169, 175, 182, 183, 184, 186, 189, 190, 191, 193, 202, 205, 206, 208

throughput, 182, 190

I/O request, 92, 183, 184

transaction, 188, 189, 191

warm-swap, 52